baking
&
desserts

baking
&
desserts

Bath · New York · Singapore · Hong Kong · Cologne · Delhi · Melbourne

This edition published by Parragon in 2009

Parragon Publishing
Queen Street House
4 Queen Street
Bath BA1 1HE, UK

ISBN: 978-1-4075-4707-7

Printed in Indonesia

Notes for the Reader
This book uses both metric and imperial measurements. Follow the same units of measurement throughout; do not mix metric and imperial. All spoon measurements are level: teaspoons are assumed to be 5 ml, and tablespoons are assumed to be 15 ml. Unless otherwise stated, milk is assumed to be full fat, eggs and individual vegetables are medium and pepper is freshly ground black pepper.

The times given are an approximate guide only. Preparation times differ according to the techniques used by different people and the cooking times may also vary from those given. Optional ingredients, variations or serving suggestions have not been included in the calculations.

Recipes using raw or very lightly cooked eggs should be avoided by infants, the elderly, pregnant women, convalescents and anyone suffering from an illness. Pregnant and breastfeeding women are advised to avoid eating peanuts and peanut products. Sufferers from nut allergies should be aware that some of the ready-made ingredients used in the recipes in this book may contain nuts. Always check the packaging before use.

contents

introduction

Whether rhythmically rolling out pastry, vigorously kneading bread dough, inhaling the spicy aroma of a fruitcake in the oven, or neatly arranging lines of cookies on a wire rack, baking is an intensely sensuous and satisfying type of cooking. While preparing family meals day after day can sometimes feel like a chore, baking is always fun and appeals to the creative instincts of cooks. Home-baked cakes and cookies, tarts and pies, breads and savory snacks are always greeted with enthusiasm too.

Home-baked goods are surprisingly easy to make. After all, helping mom by spooning cake batter into paper cases or stamping out shapes of cookie dough is, for many children, their first experience of cooking. Rustling up a batch of muffins or whisking up a sponge cake takes very little time and making more elaborate, special occasion gâteaux, tortes, cheesecakes, and other desserts

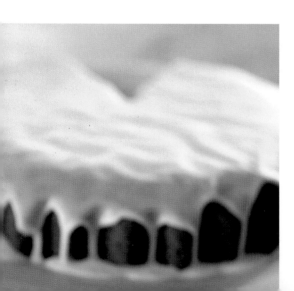

is so rewarding that any extra effort involved seems negligible. Some, although not all breads require plenty of time to rise before baking, but you can leave them alone to get on with it, so this is hardly a problem.

It's probably more important with baking than with any other kind of cooking to use the specified ingredients, measure them accurately, and follow the recipe carefully. Different flours, for example, vary in their characteristics and if you use the wrong one, the results are likely to be disappointing. However, if you have run out of self-rising flour, you can make a satisfactory, but not perfect substitute by sifting $2\frac{1}{2}$ teaspoons baking powder with $2\frac{1}{4}$ cups all-purpose flour. Similarly, don't substitute soft tub margarine if the recipe specifies butter or block margarine, because the texture of the mixture will become much wetter.

The proportions of the ingredients are critical and if you use too much fat or flour or too many eggs when making cakes, they will fail to rise and be dull and stodgy. Paradoxically, too much rising agent will cause a cake to sink when you remove it from the oven. Measure both dry ingredients and liquids carefully in a measuring cup. Use a set of proper measuring spoons for

small quantities. When measuring dry ingredients, such as baking powder or dried yeast, scoop up a heaping spoonful, then level it off with the blade of a knife. Don't measure directly over the mixing bowl because accidental spillage can result in disaster.

Following the recipes is very straightforward. Don't skip any instructions, such as sifting the flour and rising agent together, preheating the oven to the correct temperature, or lining the pan. Do be careful not to overheat liquids when baking with yeast because this will kill it and the bread will not rise. Also bear in mind that the rising time may vary depending on external factors, such as the temperature. Always let stand long enough to reach the required stage, such as doubled in size. It is important, too, to use the right size

pan, otherwise cakes and loaves may crack or collapse. Set the oven timer for the baking time specified and resist the temptation to open the door during cooking.

All this is really just common sense, but there are a few "tricks of the trade" that are worth knowing. If the recipe requires eggs, remove them from the refrigerator 30 minutes or so before you want to use them so that they can come to room temperature. Adding cold eggs to a creamed mixture is likely to result in their curdling. It's also better to add them gradually. Remember that adding liquid to a dry mixture containing baking powder or baking soda activates the rising agent immediately, so don't leave the mixture standing around. You can speed up the rising process, sometimes called proving, for yeast doughs in the microwave. Put the kneaded dough into a clean nonmetallic bowl, cover with plastic wrap, and heat on high for 10 seconds. Leave the dough in a warm place or in the microwave for about 20 minutes, by which time it will have doubled in size. If not, heat on high for another 10 seconds, then let rise for another 10 minutes. Finally, when testing cakes to see if they are cooked, warm a skewer before inserting it into the cake. If it comes out clean, the cake is ready.

cakes

Home-baked cakes are always a special treat, whether a quick and easy layer cake simply dusted with sugar or an impressive gâteau elaborately decorated with melt-in-your-mouth frosting and chocolate curls. The choice is immense and there are delicious confections for all tastes and dozens of occasions. There are cakes for kids, perfect partners for morning coffee or afternoon tea, luscious dinner party desserts, wonderful home-baked gifts, great any-time-of-day snacks, and mouthwatering centerpieces for celebrations and special occasions. Even those watching their weight can enjoy an occasional moment of self-indulgence with a fat-free whisked sponge. Recipes feature cakes flavored with coffee, bittersweet chocolate, semisweet chocolate, white chocolate, nuts, fresh fruit, dried fruit, candied fruit, spices, seeds, honey, and liqueurs. They may be plain, frosted, dredged with sugar or unsweetened cocoa powder, drenched with syrup, smothered with chocolate, or lavishly coated with cream.

The great thing is that they are not difficult to make, although some will take more time than others. Many are based on the technique of creaming, that is beating fat, usually butter, and sugar together until light and fluffy. This is most easily done with an electric mixer, but be careful not to overmix

or the cake will end up with uneven air pockets and look like Swiss cheese when it's sliced. Fold in the flour gradually using a metal spoon or rubber spatula in a gentle figure-eight movement to avoid knocking out the air. Nothing could be simpler—you might say, it's a cakewalk.

coffee & walnut cake

ingredients

SERVES 8

3/4 cup butter, plus extra
    for greasing
3/4 cup light brown sugar
3 extra-large eggs, beaten
3 tbsp strong black coffee
1 1/2 cups self-rising flour
1 1/2 tsp baking powder
1 cup walnut pieces
walnut halves, to decorate

frosting

1/2 cup butter
1 3/4 cups confectioners' sugar
1 tbsp strong black coffee
1/2 tsp vanilla extract

method

1 Preheat the oven to 350°F/180°C. Grease and line the bottoms of two 8-inch/20-cm round layer cake pans.

2 Cream together the butter and brown sugar until pale and fluffy. Gradually add the eggs, beating well after each addition. Beat in the coffee.

3 Sift the flour and baking powder into the mixture, then fold in lightly and evenly with a metal spoon. Fold in the walnut pieces.

4 Divide the batter between the prepared cake pans and smooth level. Bake in the preheated oven for 20–25 minutes, or until golden brown and springy to the touch. Turn out onto a wire rack to cool.

5 For the frosting, beat together the butter, confectioners' sugar, coffee, and vanilla extract, mixing until smooth and creamy.

6 Use about half of the frosting to sandwich the cakes together, then spread the remaining frosting on top and swirl with a metal spatula. Decorate with walnut halves.

mocha layer cake

ingredients

SERVES 8

butter, for greasing

generous 1¼ cups self-rising
flour

¼ tsp baking powder

4 tbsp unsweetened cocoa

½ cup superfine sugar

2 eggs

2 tbsp corn syrup

⅔ cup corn oil

⅔ cup milk

filling

1 tsp instant coffee

1 tbsp boiling water

1¼ cups heavy cream

2 tbsp confectioners' sugar

to decorate

1¾ oz/50 g semisweet
chocolate, grated

chocolate curls

confectioners' sugar,
for dusting

method

1 Preheat the oven to 350°F/180°C. Lightly grease three 7-inch/18-cm layer cake pans.

2 Sift the flour, baking powder, and cocoa into a large bowl, then stir in the sugar. Make a well in the center and stir in the eggs, syrup, corn oil, and milk. Beat with a wooden spoon, gradually mixing in the dry ingredients to make a smooth batter. Divide the mixture between the pans.

3 Bake in the preheated oven for 35–45 minutes, or until springy to the touch. Let stand in the pans for 5 minutes, then turn out and let cool completely on a wire rack.

4 To make the filling, dissolve the instant coffee in the boiling water and place in a large bowl with the cream and confectioners' sugar. Whip until the cream is just holding its shape, then use half the cream to sandwich the three cakes together. Spread the remaining cream over the top and sides of the cake. Press the grated chocolate into the cream around the edge of the cake. Transfer the cake to a serving plate. Lay the chocolate curls over the top of the cake. Cut a few thin strips of parchment paper and place on top of the chocolate curls. Dust lightly with confectioners' sugar, then carefully remove the paper. Serve.

coffee caramel cake

ingredients

SERVES 8

3/4 cup butter, softened, plus
    extra for greasing
scant 1 cup golden superfine
    sugar
3 eggs, beaten
generous 1 1/2 cups self-rising
    flour, sifted
scant 1/2 cup strong black
    coffee
chocolate-covered coffee
    beans, to decorate

frosting
1/2 cup milk
generous 1/2 cup butter
3 tbsp golden superfine sugar
5 3/4 cups confectioners' sugar

method

1 Preheat the oven to 350°F/180°C, then grease and line the bottoms of two 8-inch/20-cm layer cake pans. Place the butter and sugar in a bowl and beat together until light and fluffy. Gradually beat in the eggs, then fold in the flour and coffee. Divide the batter between the prepared pans and bake in the preheated oven for 30 minutes, or until well risen and springy when pressed in the center. Let cool in the pans for 5 minutes, then turn out and peel off the lining paper. Transfer to wire racks to cool completely.

2 To make the frosting, place the milk and butter in a saucepan, set over low heat, and stir until the butter has melted. Remove the pan from the heat and set aside. Place the superfine sugar in a separate, heavy-bottom saucepan and set over low heat, stirring continuously, until the sugar dissolves and turns a golden caramel. Remove from the heat and stir in the warm milk mixture. Return to the heat and stir until the caramel dissolves.

3 Remove from the heat and gradually stir in the confectioners' sugar, beating until the frosting is a smooth spreading consistency. Join the cakes together with some of the frosting and spread the rest over the top and sides. Decorate with chocolate-covered coffee beans.

victoria sponge cake

ingredients

SERVES 8–10

3/4 cup butter, at room
temperature

3/4 cup superfine sugar

3 eggs, beaten

13/4 cups self-rising flour

pinch of salt

3 tbsp raspberry jelly and
1 tbsp superfine or
confectioners' sugar, to
serve

method

1 Preheat the oven to 350°F/180°C. Grease two 8-inch/20-cm round layer cake pans and line the bottoms with parchment paper.

2 Cream the butter and sugar together in a mixing bowl using a wooden spoon or a hand-held mixer, until the mixture is pale in color and light and fluffy. Add the egg a little at a time, beating well after each addition.

3 Sift the flour and salt and carefully add to the mixture, folding it in with a metal spoon or a spatula. Divide the mixture between the pans and smooth over with the spatula.

4 Place them on the same shelf in the center of the preheated oven and bake for 25–30 minutes, until well risen, golden brown, and beginning to shrink from the sides of the pans.

5 Remove from the oven and let stand for 1 minute. Loosen the cakes from around the edge of the pans using a palette knife. Turn the cakes out onto a clean dish towel, remove the paper, and invert them onto a wire rack (this prevents the wire rack from marking the top of the cakes).

6 When completely cool, sandwich together with the jelly and sprinkle with the sugar. The cake is delicious when freshly baked, but any remaining cake can be stored in an airtight container for up to 1 week.

sticky toffee cake

ingredients

SERVES 9

1 cup chopped pitted dried
    dates
3/4 cup boiling water
1/2 tsp baking soda
6 tbsp butter, plus extra
    for greasing
3/4 cup superfine sugar
1 extra-large egg, beaten
1/2 tsp vanilla extract
1 1/2 cups self-rising flour

toffee sauce
1/3 cup light brown sugar
3 tbsp butter
2 tbsp light cream or milk

method

1 Preheat the oven to 350°F/180°C. Grease and line an 8-inch/20-cm square cake pan.

2 Put the chopped dates into a small saucepan with the boiling water and baking soda. Heat gently for about 5 minutes, without boiling, until the dates are soft.

3 Cream together the butter and superfine sugar in a bowl until light and fluffy. Beat in the egg, vanilla extract, and date mixture.

4 Fold in the flour using a metal spoon, mixing evenly. Pour the batter into the prepared cake pan. Bake in the preheated oven for 40–45 minutes, or until firm to the touch and just starting to shrink away from the sides of the pan.

5 For the toffee sauce, combine the brown sugar, butter, and cream in a saucepan and heat gently until melted. Simmer gently, stirring, for about 2 minutes.

6 Remove the cake from the oven and prick all over the surface with a skewer or fork. Pour the hot toffee sauce evenly over the surface. Let cool in the pan, then cut into squares.

pound cake

ingredients

SERVES 8–10

3/4 cup unsalted butter, plus
    extra for greasing
scant 1 cup superfine sugar
finely grated rind of 1 lemon
3 extra-large eggs, beaten
1 cup all-purpose flour
1 cup self-rising flour
2–3 tbsp brandy or milk
2 slices of citron peel

method

1 Preheat the oven to 325°F/160°C. Grease and line a 7-inch/18-cm round deep cake pan.

2 Cream together the butter and sugar until pale and fluffy. Add the lemon rind and gradually beat in the eggs. Sift in the flours and fold in evenly, adding enough brandy to make a soft consistency.

3 Spoon the batter into the prepared pan and smooth the surface. Lay the slices of citron peel on top of the cake.

4 Bake in the preheated oven for 1–1$\frac{1}{4}$ hours, or until well risen, golden brown, and springy to the touch.

5 Let cool in the pan for 10 minutes, then turn out and cool completely on a wire rack.

classic cherry cake

ingredients

SERVES 8

generous 1 cup candied
    cherries, quartered

3/4 cup ground almonds

13/4 cups all-purpose flour

1 tsp baking powder

scant 1 cup butter, plus extra
    for greasing

1 cup superfine sugar

3 extra-large eggs

finely grated rind and juice of
    1 lemon

6 sugar cubes, crushed

method

1 Preheat the oven to 350°F/180°C. Grease an 8-inch/20-cm round cake pan and line the bottom and sides with parchment paper.

2 Stir together the candied cherries, ground almonds, and 1 tablespoon of the flour. Sift the remaining flour into a separate bowl with the baking powder.

3 Cream together the butter and sugar until light in color and fluffy in texture. Gradually add the eggs, beating hard with each addition, until evenly mixed.

4 Add the flour mixture and fold lightly and evenly into the creamed mixture with a metal spoon. Add the cherry mixture and fold in evenly. Finally, fold in the lemon rind and juice.

5 Spoon the batter into the prepared cake pan and sprinkle with the crushed sugar cubes. Bake in the preheated oven for 1–11/4 hours, or until risen, golden brown, and the cake is just beginning to shrink away from the sides of the pan.

6 Let cool in the pan for about 15 minutes, then turn out to finish cooling on a wire rack.

rich fruit cake

ingredients

SERVES 8

butter, for greasing

1 cup pitted unsweetened
  dates

3/4 cup no-soak dried prunes

scant 1 cup unsweetened
  orange juice

2 tbsp molasses

1 tsp finely grated lemon rind

1 tsp finely grated orange rind

1 5/8 cups whole wheat self-
  rising flour

1 tsp pumpkin pie spice

3/4 cup seedless raisins

3/4 cup golden raisins

generous 3/4 cup currants

3/4 cup dried cranberries

3 large eggs, separated

1 tbsp apricot jelly, warmed

frosting

1 1/8 cups confectioners' sugar,
  plus extra for dusting

1–2 tsp water

1 tsp vanilla extract

orange rind strips and lemon
  rind strips, to decorate

method

1 Preheat the oven to 325ºF/160ºC. Grease and line a deep 8-inch/20-cm round cake pan. Chop the dates and prunes and place in a saucepan. Pour over the orange juice and let simmer for 10 minutes. Remove the pan from the heat and beat the fruit mixture until puréed. Add the molasses and citrus rinds and cool.

2 Sift the flour and spice into a bowl, adding any bran that remains in the sifter. Add the dried fruits. When the date and prune mixture is cool, whisk in the egg yolks. Whisk the egg whites in a separate, clean bowl until stiff. Spoon the fruit mixture into the dry ingredients and mix together.

3 Gently fold in the egg whites. Transfer to the prepared pan and bake in the preheated oven for 1 1/2 hours. Let cool in the pan.

4 Remove the cake from the pan and brush the top with jelly. To make the frosting, sift the sugar into a bowl and mix with enough water and the vanilla extract to form a soft frosting. Lay the frosting over the top of the cake and trim the edges. Decorate with orange and lemon rind.

crispy-topped fruit loaf

ingredients

SERVES 10

butter, for greasing

12 oz/350 g baking apples

3 tbsp lemon juice

2¹/₂ cups self-rising whole
    wheat flour

1/2 tsp baking powder

1 tsp ground cinnamon, plus
    extra for dusting

3/4 cup prepared blackberries,
    thawed if frozen

3/4 cup light brown sugar

1 egg, beaten

scant 1 cup low-fat plain
    yogurt

2 oz/55 g white or brown sugar
    cubes, lightly crushed

method

1 Preheat the oven to 375°F/190°C. Grease and line a 9 x 5 x 3-inch/23 x 13 x 8-cm loaf pan.

2 Peel, core, and finely dice the apples. Place them in a saucepan with the lemon juice, bring to a boil, cover, and simmer for about 10 minutes, until soft and pulpy. Beat well and set aside to cool.

3 Sift the flour, baking powder, and cinnamon into a bowl, adding any husks that remain in the sifter. Stir in 1/2 cup of the blackberries and the brown sugar.

4 Make a well in the center of the ingredients and add the egg, yogurt, and cooled apple puree. Mix well to incorporate thoroughly. Spoon the batter into the prepared pan and smooth the top.

5 Sprinkle with the remaining blackberries, pressing them down into the cake batter, and top with the crushed sugar cubes. Bake in the preheated oven for 40–45 minutes. Remove from the oven and set aside in the pan to cool.

6 Remove the loaf from the pan and peel away the lining paper. Serve dusted with cinnamon.

gingerbread

ingredients

SERVES 12–16

3 cups all-purpose flour

3 tsp baking powder

1 tsp baking soda

3 tsp ground ginger

$3/4$ cup butter

scant 1 cup brown sugar

$3/4$ cup molasses

$3/4$ cup corn syrup

1 egg, beaten

$1^1/4$ cups milk

cream or warmed corn syrup,
    to serve

method

1 Line a 9-inch/23-cm square cake pan, 2 inches/5 cm deep, with wax paper or parchment paper.

2 Preheat the oven to 325°F/160°C. Sift the dry ingredients into a large mixing bowl.

3 Place the butter, sugar, molasses, and syrup in a medium saucepan and heat over low heat until the butter has melted and the sugar is dissolved. Let cool a little.

4 Mix the beaten egg with the milk and add to the cooled syrup mixture.

5 Add all the liquid ingredients to the flour mixture and beat well using a wooden spoon until the mixture is smooth and glossy.

6 Pour the mixture into the prepared pan and bake in the center of the preheated oven for $1^1/2$ hours, until well risen and just firm to the touch. A skewer inserted into the cake should come out cleanly if it is cooked. This gives a lovely sticky gingerbread, but if you like a firmer cake, cook for an additional 15 minutes.

7 Remove from the oven and let the cake cool in the pan. When cool, remove the cake from the pan with the lining paper. Over wrap with foil and place in an airtight container for up to 1 week to let the flavors mature.

8 Cut into wedges and serve with cream as a dessert. Extra warmed syrup is an added extravagance.

sticky ginger marmalade loaf

ingredients

SERVES 10

3/4 cup butter, softened, plus
   extra for greasing
1/3 cup ginger marmalade
scant 1 cup brown sugar
3 eggs, beaten
generous 1 1/2 cups self-rising
   flour
1/2 tsp baking powder
1 tsp ground ginger
2/3 cup coarsely chopped
   pecans

method

1 Preheat the oven to 350°F/180°C. Grease a 9 x 5 x 3-inch/23 x 13 x 8-cm loaf pan and line with parchment paper. Place 1 tablespoon of the ginger marmalade in a small saucepan and reserve. Place the remaining marmalade in a bowl with the butter, sugar, and eggs.

2 Sift in the flour, baking powder, and ground ginger and beat together until smooth. Stir in three quarters of the nuts. Spoon the mixture into the prepared loaf pan and smooth the top. Sprinkle with the remaining nuts and bake in the preheated oven for 1 hour, or until well risen and a skewer inserted into the center comes out clean.

3 Let cool in the pan for 10 minutes, then turn out and peel off the lining paper. Transfer to a wire rack to cool until warm. Set the pan of reserved marmalade over low heat to warm, then brush over the loaf and serve in slices.

carrot cake

ingredients

SERVES 16

2 eggs

3/4 cup molasses sugar

scant 1 cup sunflower oil

generous 1 1/3 cups coarsely
    grated carrots

2 cups whole wheat flour

1 tsp baking soda

2 tsp ground cinnamon

whole nutmeg, grated

1 cup roughly chopped
    walnuts

topping

1/2 cup half-fat cream cheese

4 tbsp butter, softened

3/4 cup confectioners' sugar

1 tsp grated lemon rind

1 tsp grated orange rind

method

1 Preheat the oven to 375°F/190°C. In a mixing bowl, beat the eggs until well blended and add the sugar and oil. Mix well. Add the grated carrot.

2 Sift in the flour, baking soda, and spices, then add the walnuts. Mix everything together until well incorporated.

3 Spread the mixture into the prepared cake pan and bake in the center of the preheated oven for 40–50 minutes, until the cake is nicely risen, firm to the touch, and has begun to shrink away slightly from the edge of the pan.

4 Remove from the oven and let cool in the pan until just warm, then turn out onto a wire rack.

5 To make the topping, put all the ingredients into a mixing bowl and beat together for 2–3 minutes, until really smooth.

6 When the cake is completely cold, spread with the topping, smooth over with a fork, and let stand to firm up a little before cutting into 16 portions. Store in an airtight container in a cool place for up to 1 week.

banana & chocolate loaf

ingredients

SERVES 8

$^1/_2$ cup butter, softened, plus
extra for greasing
2 ripe bananas
$^3/_8$ cup golden superfine sugar
2 eggs
scant $1^1/_2$ cups self-rising flour
$^1/_4$ cup unsweetened cocoa
1 tsp baking powder
1–2 tbsp milk
generous $^1/_2$ cup semisweet
chocolate chips
butter, to serve (optional)

method

1 Preheat the oven to 350°F/180°C. Grease a 9 x 5 x 3-inch/23 x 13 x 8-cm loaf pan and line with parchment paper. Peel the bananas and place in a large bowl. Mash with a fork.

2 Add the butter, sugar, and eggs, then sift the flour, cocoa, and baking powder into the bowl. Beat vigorously until smooth, adding enough milk to give a reluctant dropping consistency. Stir in the chocolate chips.

3 Spoon the mixture into the prepared pan and bake in the oven for 50–60 minutes, or until well risen and the tip of a knife inserted in the center comes out clean. Let stand in the pan for 5 minutes, then turn out onto a wire rack to cool completely. Serve sliced, with or without butter.

checkerboard sponge cake

ingredients

SERVES 6–8

$^1/_2$ cup butter or margarine,
softened, plus extra
for greasing
generous $^1/_2$ cup superfine
sugar, plus extra
for sprinkling
2 eggs, lightly beaten
1 tsp vanilla extract
1 cup self-rising flour, sifted
a few drops of pink edible food
coloring
2–3 tbsp apricot jam
10$^1/_2$ oz/300 g marzipan

method

1 Preheat the oven to 350°F/180°C. Grease and line a 7-inch/18-cm square shallow baking pan. Cut a strip of double parchment paper and grease it. Use this to divide the pan in half.

2 Cream the butter and sugar in a mixing bowl until pale and fluffy. Gently beat in the eggs and vanilla extract, gradually adding in the flour. Spoon half the batter into a separate bowl and mix in a few drops of food coloring.

3 Spoon the plain batter into one half of the prepared baking pan. Spoon the colored batter into the other half of the pan, making the divide as straight as possible. Bake in the preheated oven for 35–40 minutes. Turn out and let cool on a wire rack.

4 When cool, trim the edges and cut the cake portions lengthwise in half, making four equal parts. Warm the jam in a small saucepan. Brush two sides of each cake portion with some of the jam and stick them together to create a checkerboard effect.

5 Knead the marzipan with a few drops of food coloring to color it a subtle shade of pink. Roll out the marzipan to a rectangle wide enough to wrap around the cake. Brush the outside of the cake with the remaining jam. Place the cake on the marzipan and wrap the marzipan around it, making sure that the seam is on one corner of the cake. Trim the edges, crimp the top edges, and sprinkle with sugar.

angel food cake

ingredients

SERVES 10

sunflower oil, for greasing

8 extra-large egg whites

1 tsp cream of tartar

1 tsp almond extract

1 1/4 cups superfine sugar

1 cup all-purpose flour, plus
   extra for dusting

2 1/4 cups berries, such
   as strawberries and
   raspberries

1 tbsp lemon juice

2 tbsp confectioners' sugar

method

1 Preheat the oven to 325°F/160°C. Brush the inside of a 7 1/2-cup angel cake pan with oil and dust lightly with flour.

2 In a large grease-free bowl, whisk the egg whites until they hold soft peaks. Add the cream of tartar and whisk again until the whites are stiff but not dry.

3 Whisk in the almond extract, then add the sugar a tablespoon at a time, whisking hard between each addition. Sift in the flour and fold in lightly and evenly using a large metal spoon.

4 Spoon the batter into the prepared cake pan and tap on the counter to remove any large air bubbles. Bake in the preheated oven for 40–45 minutes, or until golden brown and firm to the touch.

5 Run the tip of a small knife around the edge of the cake to loosen from the pan. Let cool in the pan for 10 minutes, then turn out onto a wire rack to finish cooling.

6 To serve, place the berries, lemon juice, and confectioners' sugar in a saucepan and heat gently until the sugar has dissolved. Serve with the cake.

moroccan orange & almond cake

ingredients

SERVES 8

1 orange
1/2 cup butter, softened, plus
    extra for greasing
generous 1/2 cup golden
    superfine sugar
2 eggs, beaten
scant 1 cup semolina
generous 1 cup ground
    almonds
1 1/2 tsp baking powder
confectioners' sugar,
    for dusting
Greek-style yogurt, to serve

syrup
1 1/4 cups orange juice
2/3 cup superfine sugar
8 cardamom pods, crushed

method

1 Preheat the oven to 350°F/180°C. Grease and line the bottom of an 8-inch/20-cm cake pan. Grate the rind from the orange, reserving some for the decoration, and squeeze the juice from one half. Place the butter, orange rind, and superfine sugar in a bowl and beat together until light and fluffy. Gradually beat in the eggs. In a separate bowl, mix the semolina, ground almonds, and baking powder, then fold into the creamed mixture with the orange juice. Spoon the batter into the prepared pan and bake in the preheated oven for 30–40 minutes, or until well risen and a skewer inserted into the center comes out clean. Let cool in the pan for 10 minutes.

2 To make the syrup, place the orange juice, sugar, and cardamom pods in a pan over low heat and stir until the sugar has dissolved. Bring to a boil and simmer for 4 minutes, or until syrupy.

3 Turn the cake out into a deep serving dish. Using a skewer, make holes over the surface of the warm cake. Strain the syrup into a separate bowl and spoon three quarters of it over the cake, then let stand for 30 minutes. Dust the cake with confectioners' sugar and cut into slices. Serve with the remaining syrup drizzled around, accompanied by yogurt.

caribbean coconut cake

ingredients

SERVES 8

1 1/4 cups butter, softened,
    plus extra for greasing
scant 1 cup golden superfine
    sugar
3 eggs
1 1/4 cups self-rising flour
1 1/2 tsp baking powder
1/2 tsp freshly grated nutmeg
2/3 cup dry unsweetened
    coconut
5 tbsp coconut cream
2 3/4 cups confectioners' sugar
5 tbsp pineapple jelly
dry unsweetened coconut,
    toasted, to decorate

method

1 Preheat the oven to 350°F/180°C. Grease and line the bottoms of two 8-inch/20-cm sponge cake pans. Place 3/4 cup of the butter in a bowl with the sugar and eggs and sift in the flour, baking powder, and nutmeg. Beat together until smooth, then stir in the coconut and 2 tablespoons of the coconut cream.

2 Divide the mixture between the prepared pans and smooth the tops. Bake in the preheated oven for 25 minutes, or until golden and firm to the touch. Let cool in the pans for 5 minutes, then turn out onto a wire rack, peel off the lining paper, and let cool completely.

3 Sift the confectioners' sugar into a bowl and add the remaining butter and coconut cream. Beat together until smooth. Spread the pineapple jelly on one of the cakes and top with just under half of the buttercream. Place the other cake on top. Spread the remaining buttercream on top of the cake and scatter with the toasted coconut.

honey spice cake

ingredients

SERVES 8

$^2/_3$ cup butter, plus extra for
    greasing
generous $^1/_2$ cup brown sugar
$^1/_2$ cup honey
1 tbsp water
scant $1^1/_2$ cups self-rising flour
$^1/_2$ tsp ground ginger
$^1/_2$ tsp ground cinnamon
$^1/_2$ tsp caraway seeds
seeds from 8 cardamom pods,
    ground
2 eggs, beaten
$3^1/_2$ cups confectioners' sugar

method

1 Preheat the oven to 350°F/180°C. Grease a $3^1/_2$-cup fluted cake pan. Place the butter, sugar, honey, and water in a heavy-bottom saucepan. Set over low heat and stir until the butter has melted and the sugar has dissolved. Remove from the heat and let cool for 10 minutes.

2 Sift the flour into a bowl and mix in the ginger, cinnamon, caraway seeds, and cardamom seeds. Make a well in the center. Pour in the honey mixture and the eggs and beat well until smooth. Pour the batter into the prepared pan and bake in the preheated oven for 40–50 minutes, or until well risen and a skewer inserted into the center comes out clean. Let cool in the pan for 5 minutes, then transfer to a wire rack to cool completely.

3 Sift the confectioners' sugar into a bowl. Stir in enough warm water to make a smooth, flowing frosting. Spoon over the cake, letting it flow down the sides, then let set.

blueberry & lemon drizzle cake

ingredients

SERVES 12

1 cup butter, softened, plus
    extra for greasing
generous 1 cup golden
    superfine sugar
4 eggs, beaten
1³/4 cups self-rising flour, sifted
finely grated rind and juice of
    1 lemon
generous 1/4 cup ground
    almonds
7 oz/200 g fresh blueberries

topping
juice of 2 lemons
generous 1/2 cup golden
    superfine sugar

method

1 Preheat the oven to 350°F/180°C, then grease and line the bottom of an 8-inch/20-cm square cake pan. Place the butter and sugar in a bowl and beat together until light and fluffy. Gradually beat in the eggs, adding a little flour toward the end to prevent curdling. Beat in the lemon rind, then fold in the remaining flour and the almonds with enough of the lemon juice to give a good dropping consistency.

2 Fold in three quarters of the blueberries and turn into the prepared pan. Smooth the surface, then scatter the remaining blueberries on top. Bake in the preheated oven for 1 hour, or until firm to the touch and a skewer inserted into the center comes out clean.

3 To make the topping, place the lemon juice and sugar in a bowl and mix together. As soon as the cake comes out of the oven, prick it all over with a fine skewer and pour over the lemon mixture. Let cool in the pan until completely cold, then cut into 12 squares to serve.

apple streusel cake

ingredients

SERVES 8

1 lb/450 g tart cooking apples

1¼ cups self-rising flour

1 tsp ground cinnamon

pinch of salt

½ cup butter, plus extra for
    greasing

generous ½ cup golden
    superfine sugar

2 eggs

1–2 tbsp milk

confectioners' sugar,
    for dusting

streusel topping

generous ¾ cup self-rising
    flour

6 tbsp butter

scant ½ cup golden superfine
    sugar

method

1 Preheat the oven to 350°F/180°C, then grease a 9-inch/23-cm springform cake pan. To make the streusel topping, sift the flour into a bowl and rub in the butter until the mixture resembles coarse crumbs. Stir in the sugar and set aside.

2 Peel, core, and thinly slice the apples. To make the cake, sift the flour into a bowl with the cinnamon and salt. Place the butter and sugar in a separate bowl and beat together until light and fluffy. Gradually beat in the eggs, adding a little of the flour mixture with the last addition of egg. Gently fold in half the remaining flour mixture, then fold in the rest with the milk.

3 Spoon the batter into the prepared pan and smooth the top. Cover with the sliced apples and sprinkle the streusel topping evenly over the top. Bake in the preheated oven for 1 hour, or until browned and firm to the touch. Let cool in the pan before opening the sides. Dust the cake with confectioners' sugar before serving.

banana & lime cake

ingredients

SERVES 10

butter, for greasing

scant 2 cups all-purpose flour

1 tsp salt

1½ tsp baking powder

generous ¾ cup firmly packed
    brown sugar

1 tsp grated lime rind

1 egg, beaten

1 banana, mashed with 1 tbsp
    lime juice

⅔ cup lowfat mascarpone
    cheese

⅔ cup golden raisins

topping

1 cup confectioners' sugar

1–2 tsp lime juice

½ tsp finely grated lime rind

to decorate

banana chips

finely grated lime rind

method

1 Preheat the oven to 350°F/180°C. Grease a deep 7-inch/18-cm round cake pan and line with parchment paper. Sift the flour, salt, and baking powder into a large bowl and stir in the sugar and lime rind.

2 Make a well in the center of the dry ingredients and add the egg, banana, mascarpone cheese, and golden raisins. Mix well until thoroughly incorporated. Spoon the batter into the pan and smooth the surface.

3 Bake in the preheated oven for 40–45 minutes, until firm to the touch or until a skewer inserted in the center comes out clean. Let the cake cool in the pan for 10 minutes, then turn out onto a wire rack to cool completely.

4 To make the topping, sift the confectioners' sugar into a small bowl and mix with the lime juice to form a soft, but not too runny frosting. Stir in the grated lime rind. Drizzle the frosting over the cake, letting it run down the sides. Decorate the cake with banana chips and lime rind. Let the cake stand for 15 minutes so that the frosting sets.

pear & ginger cake

ingredients

SERVES 6

scant 1 cup unsalted butter,
      softened, plus extra
      for greasing
generous 3/4 cup superfine
      sugar
1 1/4 cups self-rising flour,
      strained
1 tbsp ground ginger
3 eggs, lightly beaten
1 lb/450 g pears, peeled,
      cored, and thinly sliced,
      then brushed with lemon
      juice
1 tbsp brown sugar
ice cream or heavy cream,
      lightly whipped, to serve
      (optional)

method

1 Preheat the oven to 350°F/180°C. Lightly grease a deep 8-inch/20-cm cake pan and line the bottom with parchment paper.

2 Mix all but 2 tablespoons of the butter with the superfine sugar, flour, ginger, and eggs in a bowl. Beat with a whisk until the mixture forms a smooth consistency.

3 Spoon the cake batter into the prepared pan and level out the surface with a spatula.

4 Arrange the pear slices over the cake batter. Sprinkle with the brown sugar and dot with the remaining butter.

5 Bake in the preheated oven for 35–40 minutes, or until the cake is golden on top and feels springy to the touch.

6 Serve warm, with ice cream or whipped cream, if using.

banana loaf

ingredients

SERVES 8

butter, for greasing

scant 1 cup white self-rising
  flour

scant 3/4 cup light brown
  self-rising flour

generous 3/4 cup raw sugar

pinch of salt

1/2 tsp ground cinnamon

1/2 tsp ground nutmeg

2 large ripe bananas, peeled

3/4 cup orange juice

2 eggs, beaten

4 tbsp canola oil

method

1 Preheat the oven to 350°F/180°C. Lightly grease and line a 9 x 5 x 3-inch/23 x 13 x 8-cm loaf pan.

2 Sift the flours, sugar, salt, and spices into a large bowl. In a separate bowl, mash the bananas with the orange juice, then stir in the eggs and oil. Pour into the dry ingredients and mix well.

3 Spoon into the prepared loaf pan and bake in the preheated oven for 1 hour, then test to see if the loaf is cooked by inserting a skewer into the center. If it comes out clean, the loaf is done. If not, bake for an additional 10 minutes and test again.

4 Remove from the oven and let cool in the pan. Turn out the loaf, slice, and serve.

lemon cornmeal cake

ingredients

SERVES 8

scant 1 cup unsalted butter,
    plus extra for greasing
1 cup superfine sugar
finely grated rind and juice of
    1 large lemon
3 eggs, beaten
$1^1/_4$ cups ground almonds
scant $^3/_4$ cup quick-cook
    cornmeal
1 tsp baking powder
sour cream, to serve

syrup

juice of 2 lemons
$^1/_4$ cup superfine sugar
2 tbsp water

method

1 Preheat the oven to 350°F/180°C. Lightly grease an 8-inch/20-cm round deep cake pan and line the bottom with parchment paper.

2 Beat together the butter and sugar until pale and fluffy. Beat in the lemon rind, lemon juice, eggs, and ground almonds. Sift in the cornmeal and baking powder and stir until evenly mixed.

3 Spoon the batter into the prepared pan and spread evenly. Bake in the preheated oven for 30–35 minutes, or until just firm to the touch and golden brown. Remove the cake from the oven and cool in the pan for 20 minutes.

4 For the syrup, place the lemon juice, sugar, and water in a small saucepan. Heat gently, stirring until the sugar has dissolved, then bring to a boil and simmer for 3–4 minutes, or until slightly reduced and syrupy.

5 Turn out the cake onto a wire rack, then drizzle half of the syrup evenly over the surface. Let cool completely.

6 Cut the cake into slices, drizzle the extra syrup over the top, and serve with sour cream.

apple cake with streusel topping

ingredients

SERVES 8

1 lb 2 oz/500 g apples, peeled, cored, and cut into 1/2-inch/1-cm dice

1 tbsp lemon juice

generous 1/2 cup unsalted butter, plus extra for greasing

2/3 cup superfine sugar

2 extra-large eggs, beaten

2 cups all-purpose flour

3 tsp baking powder

1 tsp ground cinnamon

1/2 tsp ground nutmeg

3 tbsp hard cider or apple juice

streusel topping

1/3 cup hazelnuts, skinned and finely chopped

1/3 cup all-purpose flour

2 tbsp light brown sugar

1/2 tsp ground cinnamon

2 tbsp unsalted butter, melted

method

1 Preheat the oven to 350°F/180°C. Grease an 8-inch/20-cm round loose-bottom cake pan and line the bottom with parchment paper. Toss the apples in the lemon juice.

2 Cream together the butter and superfine sugar until pale and fluffy, then gradually add the eggs, beating thoroughly after each addition. Sift together the flour, baking powder, cinnamon, and nutmeg into the mixture and fold in lightly and evenly using a metal spoon. Stir in the hard cider.

3 Stir the apples into the batter to distribute evenly, then spoon into the prepared pan and level the surface.

4 For the streusel topping, combine the hazelnuts, flour, brown sugar, and cinnamon, then stir in the melted butter, mixing until crumbly. Spread over the cake.

5 Bake the cake in the preheated oven for 1–11/4 hours, or until firm and golden brown. Cool for 10 minutes in the pan, then remove carefully and finish cooling on a wire rack.

honey & almond cake

ingredients

SERVES 12–16

generous $2/3$ cup unsalted
    butter, plus extra
    for greasing
$1/2$ cup light brown sugar
$3/4$ cup honey
1 tbsp lemon juice
2 eggs, beaten
$13/4$ cups self-rising flour
1 tbsp slivered almonds
warmed honey, to glaze

method

1 Preheat the oven to 350°F/180°C. Grease an 8-inch/20-cm square deep cake pan and line the bottom with parchment paper.

2 Put the butter, sugar, honey, and lemon juice in a saucepan and stir over medium heat, without boiling, until melted and smooth. Remove the pan from the heat and quickly beat in the eggs with a wooden spoon. Sift in the flour and stir lightly and evenly with a metal spoon.

3 Pour the batter into the prepared pan and sprinkle the slivered almonds over the top. Bake in the preheated oven for 35–40 minutes, until risen, firm, and golden brown.

4 Let cool in the pan for about 15 minutes, then turn out and cool completely on a wire rack. Brush with warmed honey and cut into slices to serve.

pineapple upside-down cake

ingredients

SERVES 10

4 eggs, beaten

1 cup superfine sugar

1 tsp vanilla extract

1³/₄ cups all-purpose flour

2 tsp baking powder

generous ¹/₂ cup unsalted
    butter, melted, plus extra
    for greasing

topping

3 tbsp unsalted butter

4 tbsp dark corn syrup

15 oz/425 g canned pineapple
    rings, drained

4–6 candied cherries, halved

method

1 Preheat the oven to 325°F/160°C. Grease a 9-inch/23-cm round deep cake pan with a solid bottom and line the bottom with parchment paper.

2 For the topping, place the butter and corn syrup in a heavy-bottom saucepan and heat gently until melted. Bring to a boil and boil for 2–3 minutes, stirring, until slightly thickened and taffylike.

3 Pour the syrup into the bottom of the prepared pan. Arrange the pineapple rings and candied cherries in a single layer over the syrup.

4 Place the eggs, sugar, and vanilla extract in a large heatproof bowl set over a saucepan of gently simmering water and beat with an electric mixer for 10–15 minutes, until thick enough to leave a trail when the whisk is lifted. Sift in the flour and baking powder and fold in lightly and evenly with a metal spoon.

5 Fold the melted butter into the mixture with a metal spoon, until evenly mixed. Spoon into the prepared pan and bake in the preheated oven for 1–1¹/₄ hours, or until well risen, firm, and golden brown.

6 Let cool in the pan for 10 minutes, then turn out onto a serving plate. Serve warm or cold.

orange & poppy seed bundt cake

ingredients

SERVES 10

scant 1 cup unsalted butter,
   plus extra for greasing
1 cup superfine sugar
3 extra-large eggs, beaten
finely grated rind of 1 orange
1/4 cup poppy seeds
2 1/4 cups all-purpose flour,
   plus extra for dusting
2 tsp baking powder
2/3 cup milk
1/2 cup orange juice
strips of orange zest,
   to decorate

s y r u p
scant 3/4 cup superfine sugar
2/3 cup orange juice

method

1 Preheat the oven to 325°F/160°C. Grease and lightly flour a Bundt ring pan, about 9 1/2 inches/24 cm in diameter and with a capacity of approximately 8 3/4 cups.

2 Cream together the butter and sugar until pale and fluffy, then add the eggs gradually, beating thoroughly after each addition. Stir in the orange rind and poppy seeds. Sift in the flour and baking powder, then fold in evenly.

3 Add the milk and orange juice, stirring to mix evenly. Spoon the batter into the prepared pan and bake in the preheated oven for 45–50 minutes, or until firm and golden brown. Cool in the pan for 10 minutes, then turn out onto a wire rack to cool.

4 For the syrup, place the sugar and orange juice in a saucepan and heat gently until the sugar melts. Bring to a boil and simmer for about 5 minutes, until reduced and syrupy.

5 Spoon the syrup over the cake while it is still warm. Top with the strips of orange zest and serve warm or cold.

hummingbird cake

ingredients

SERVES 10

2 1/4 cups all-purpose flour

1 1/4 cups superfine sugar

1 tsp ground cinnamon

1 tsp baking soda

3 eggs, beaten

scant 1 cup sunflower oil,
plus extra for greasing

scant 1 cup pecans, coarsely
chopped, plus extra
to decorate

1 cup mashed ripe bananas
(about 3 bananas)

3 oz/85 g canned crushed
pineapple (drained weight),
plus 4 tbsp juice from
the can

frosting

3/4 cup cream cheese

1/4 cup unsalted butter

1 tsp vanilla extract

3 1/2 cups confectioners' sugar

method

1 Preheat the oven to 350°F/180°C. Lightly grease three 9-inch/23-cm layer cake pans with oil and line the bottoms with parchment paper.

2 Sift together the flour, superfine sugar, cinnamon, and baking soda into a large bowl. Add the eggs, oil, pecans, bananas, and pineapple with the juice and stir with a wooden spoon until evenly mixed.

3 Divide the batter among the prepared pans, spreading it evenly. Bake in the preheated oven for 25–30 minutes, or until golden brown and firm to the touch.

4 Remove the cakes from the oven and let cool for 10 minutes in the pans before turning out onto wire racks to cool.

5 For the frosting, beat together the cream cheese, butter, and vanilla extract in a bowl until smooth. Sift in the confectioners' sugar and mix until smooth.

6 Sandwich the cakes together with half of the frosting, spread the remaining frosting over the top, then sprinkle with pecans to decorate.

strawberry roulade

ingredients

SERVES 8

3 eggs

2/3 cup superfine sugar

scant 1 cup all-purpose flour

1 tbsp hot water

1 tbsp toasted slivered
   almonds, to decorate

filling

3/4 cup low-fat mascarpone
   cheese

1 tsp almond extract

1 1/2 cups small strawberries

method

1 Preheat the oven to 425°F/220°C. Line a 14 x 10-inch/35 x 25-cm jelly roll pan with parchment paper.

2 Place the eggs in a heatproof bowl with the sugar. Place the bowl over a saucepan of hot water and whisk until pale and thick.

3 Remove the bowl from the pan. Sift in the flour and fold into the egg mixture along with the hot water. Pour the batter into the prepared pan and bake in the preheated oven for 8–10 minutes, until golden and springy to the touch.

4 Turn out the cake onto a sheet of parchment paper. Peel off the lining paper and roll up the cake tightly along with the parchment paper. Wrap in a clean dish towel and let cool.

5 For the filling, mix together the mascarpone cheese and the almond extract. Wash, hull, and slice the strawberries. Chill the mascarpone mixture and the strawberries in the refrigerator until ready to use.

6 Unroll the cake, spread the mascarpone mixture over the surface, and sprinkle with sliced strawberries. Roll up the cake again (without the parchment paper this time) and transfer to a serving plate. Sprinkle with slivered almonds and serve.

citrus mousse cake

ingredients

SERVES 12

3/4 cup butter, plus extra
    for greasing
3/4 cup superfine sugar
4 eggs, lightly beaten
1 3/4 cups self-rising flour
1 tbsp unsweetened cocoa
1 3/4 oz/50 g orange-flavored
    semisweet chocolate,
    melted
peeled orange segments,
    to decorate

m o u s s e
2 eggs, separated
4 tbsp superfine sugar
3/4 cup freshly squeezed
    orange juice
2 tsp gelatin
3 tbsp water
1 1/4 cups heavy cream

method

1 Preheat the oven to 350°F/180°C. Grease an 8-inch/20-cm springform round cake pan and line the bottom with parchment paper.

2 Beat the butter and sugar in a bowl until light and fluffy. Gradually add the eggs, beating well after each addition. Sift together the flour and cocoa and then fold into the creamed mixture. Fold in the melted chocolate.

3 Pour into the prepared pan and level the top. Bake in the preheated oven for 40 minutes, or until springy to the touch. Let cool for 5 minutes in the pan, then turn out onto a wire rack and let cool completely. Cut the cake into two layers.

4 To make the orange mousse, beat the egg yolks and sugar until pale, then whisk in the orange juice. Sprinkle the gelatin over the water in a small heatproof bowl and let it go spongy, then place over a saucepan of hot water and stir until dissolved. Stir into the egg yolk mixture.

5 Whip the cream until holding its shape. Fold the remainder into the mousse, reserving a little for decoration. Whisk the egg whites until soft peaks form, then fold in. Let stand in a cool place until starting to set, stirring occasionally.

6 Place one half of the cake in the pan. Pour in the mousse and press the second half of the cake on top. Chill until set. Transfer to a plate, then spoon teaspoonfuls of cream around the top and arrange orange segments in the center.

chocolate fudge cake

ingredients

SERVES 9

3/4 cup unsalted butter, softened, plus extra for greasing

3/4 cup golden superfine sugar

3 eggs, beaten

3 tbsp corn syrup

1/4 cup ground almonds

13/4 cups self-rising flour

pinch of salt

1/4 cup unsweetened cocoa

frosting

8 oz/225 g semisweet chocolate, broken into pieces

1/4 cup dark brown sugar

1 cup unsalted butter, diced

5 tbsp evaporated milk

1/2 tsp vanilla extract

method

1 Grease and line the bottoms of two 8-inch/ 20-cm round cake pans. To make the frosting, place the chocolate, sugar, butter, evaporated milk, and vanilla extract in a heavy-bottom saucepan. Heat gently, stirring continuously, until melted. Pour into a bowl and let cool. Cover and chill in the refrigerator for 1 hour, or until spreadable.

2 Preheat the oven to 350°F/180°C. Place the butter and sugar in a bowl and beat together until light and fluffy. Gradually beat in the eggs. Stir in the syrup and ground almonds. Sift the flour, salt, and cocoa into a separate bowl, then fold into the mixture. Add a little water, if necessary, to make a dropping consistency. Spoon the mixture into the prepared pans and bake in the preheated oven for 30–35 minutes, or until springy to the touch and a skewer inserted in the center comes out clean.

3 Let the cakes cool in the pans for 5 minutes, then turn out onto wire racks to cool completely. When the cakes are cold, sandwich them together with half the frosting. Spread the remaining frosting over the top and sides of the cake.

chocolate truffle torte

ingredients

SERVES 10

butter, for greasing

generous 1/4 cup golden
    superfine sugar

2 eggs

scant 1/4 cup all-purpose flour

1/4 cup unsweetened cocoa,
    plus extra to decorate

1/4 cup cold strong black
    coffee

2 tbsp brandy

topping

2 1/2 cups whipping cream

15 oz/425 g semisweet
    chocolate, melted and
    cooled

confectioners' sugar,
    to decorate

method

1 Preheat the oven to 425°F/220°C. Grease a 9-inch/23-cm springform cake pan with butter and line the bottom with parchment paper. Place the sugar and eggs in a heatproof bowl and set over a saucepan of hot water. Whisk together until pale and mousselike. Sift the flour and cocoa into a separate bowl, then fold gently into the cake batter. Pour into the prepared pan and bake in the oven for 7–10 minutes, or until risen and firm to the touch.

2 Transfer to a wire rack to cool. Wash and dry the pan and replace the cooled cake in the pan. Mix the coffee and brandy together and brush over the cake. To make the topping, place the cream in a bowl and whip until very soft peaks form. Carefully fold in the cooled chocolate. Pour the chocolate mixture over the sponge. Let chill in the refrigerator for 4–5 hours, or until set.

3 To decorate the torte, sift cocoa over the top and remove carefully from the pan. Using strips of thin cardboard or wax paper, sift bands of confectioners' sugar over the torte to create a striped pattern. To serve, cut into slices with a hot knife.

rich chocolate cake

ingredients

SERVES 10–12

generous ½ cup raisins

finely grated rind and juice of
1 orange

¼ cup butter, diced, plus
extra for greasing the pan

3½ oz/100 g semisweet
chocolate, at least 70%
cocoa solids, broken up

4 large eggs, beaten

½ cup superfine sugar

1 tsp vanilla extract

⅜ cup all-purpose flour

generous ½ cup ground
almonds

½ tsp baking powder

pinch of salt

scant ½ cup blanched
almonds, toasted and
chopped

confectioners' sugar, sifted,
to decorate

method

1 Put the raisins in a small bowl, add the orange juice, and let soak for 20 minutes. Line a deep 10-inch/25-cm round loose-bottomed cake pan with wax paper and grease the paper; set aside.

2 Melt the butter and chocolate together in a small saucepan over medium heat, stirring. Remove from the heat and set aside to cool.

3 Preheat the oven to 350°F/180°C. Using an electric mixer beat the eggs, sugar, and vanilla together for about 3 minutes until light and fluffy. Stir in the cooled chocolate mixture.

4 Drain the raisins if they haven't absorbed all the orange juice. Sift over the flour, ground almonds, baking powder, and salt. Add the raisins, orange rind, and almonds, and fold everything together.

5 Spoon into the cake pan and smooth the surface. Bake in the preheated oven for about 40 minutes, or until a toothpick inserted into the center comes out clean and the cake starts to come away from the side of the pan. Let cool in the pan for 10 minutes, then remove from the pan and let cool completely on a wire rack. Dust the surface with confectioners' sugar before serving.

devil's food cake

ingredients

SERVES 10–12

3¹/₂ oz/100 g semisweet
    chocolate
generous 1¹/₂ cups self-rising
    flour
1 tsp baking soda
1 cup butter, plus extra for
    greasing
2 cups firmly packed dark
    brown sugar
1 tsp vanilla extract
3 eggs
¹/₂ cup buttermilk
1 cup boiling water
candied orange peel,
    to decorate

frosting
1¹/₂ cups superfine sugar
2 egg whites
1 tbsp lemon juice
3 tbsp orange juice

method

1 Preheat the oven to 375°F/190°C. Lightly grease two 8-inch/20-cm shallow round cake pans and line the bottoms. Melt the chocolate. Sift the flour and baking soda together.

2 Place the butter and sugar in a large bowl and beat until pale and fluffy. Beat in the vanilla extract and the eggs, one at a time, beating well after each addition. Add a little flour if the mixture starts to curdle. Fold the melted chocolate into the mixture until well blended. Fold in the remaining flour, then stir in the buttermilk and boiling water.

3 Divide the mixture between the pans and level the tops. Bake in the preheated oven for 30 minutes, or until springy to the touch. Let cool in the pan for 5 minutes, then transfer to a wire rack and let cool completely.

4 Place the frosting ingredients in a large bowl set over a saucepan of simmering water. Using an electric mixer, beat until thick and forming soft peaks. Remove from the heat and beat until the mixture is cool.

5 Sandwich the two cakes together with a little of the frosting, then spread the remainder over the sides and top of the cake. Decorate with candied orange peel.

chocolate ganache cake

ingredients

SERVES 10

3/4 cup butter, plus extra for
    greasing
3/4 cup superfine sugar
4 eggs, beaten lightly
13/4 cups self-rising flour
1 tbsp unsweetened cocoa
13/4 oz/50 g semisweet
    chocolate, melted

ganache
2 cups heavy cream
13 oz/375 g semisweet
    chocolate, broken into
    pieces
7 oz/200 g chocolate-flavored
    cake covering, to finish

method

1 Preheat the oven to 350°F/180°C. Lightly grease an 8-inch/20-cm springform cake pan and line the bottom. Beat the butter and sugar until light and fluffy. Gradually add the eggs, beating well. Sift the flour and cocoa together. Fold into the cake mixture, then fold in the melted chocolate.

2 Pour into the prepared pan and smooth the top. Bake in the preheated oven for 40 minutes or until springy to the touch. Let cool for 5 minutes in the pan, then turn out onto a wire rack. Cut the cold cake into two layers.

3 To make the ganache, place the cream in a saucepan and bring to a boil, stirring. Add the chocolate and stir until melted and combined. Pour into a bowl and whisk for about 5 minutes, or until the ganache is fluffy and cool.

4 Set aside one third of the ganache. Use the remaining ganache to sandwich the cake together and spread smoothly and evenly over the top and sides of the cake.

5 Melt the cake covering and spread it over a large sheet of parchment paper. Let cool until just set. Cut into strips a little wider than the height of the cake. Place the strips around the edge of the cake, overlapping them slightly.

6 Using a pastry bag fitted with a fine tip, pipe the reserved ganache in tear drops or shells to cover the top of the cake. Let the finished cake chill for 1 hour in the refrigerator before serving.

chocolate cake with coffee syrup

ingredients

SERVES 12

1/2 cup unsalted butter, plus extra for greasing
8 oz/225 g semisweet chocolate, broken into pieces
1 tbsp strong black coffee
4 large eggs
2 egg yolks
generous 1/2 cup golden superfine sugar
generous 1/3 cup all-purpose flour
2 tsp ground cinnamon
scant 1/2 cup ground almonds
chocolate-covered coffee beans, to decorate

syrup
1 1/4 cups strong black coffee
generous 1/2 cup golden superfine sugar
1 cinnamon stick

method

1 Preheat the oven to 375°F/190°C. Grease and line the bottom of a deep 8-inch/20-cm round cake pan. Place the chocolate, butter, and coffee in a heatproof bowl and set over a saucepan of gently simmering water until melted. Stir to blend, then remove from the heat and let cool slightly.

2 Place the whole eggs, egg yolks, and sugar in a separate bowl and whisk together until thick and pale. Sift the flour and cinnamon over the egg mixture. Add the almonds and the chocolate mixture and fold in carefully. Spoon the cake batter into the prepared pan. Bake in the oven for 35 minutes, or until the tip of a knife inserted into the center comes out clean. Let cool slightly before turning out onto a serving plate.

3 Meanwhile, make the syrup. Place the coffee, sugar, and cinnamon stick in a heavy-bottom saucepan and heat gently, stirring, until the sugar has dissolved. Increase the heat and boil for 5 minutes, or until reduced and thickened slightly. Keep warm. Pierce the surface of the cake with a toothpick, then drizzle over half the coffee syrup. Decorate with chocolate-covered coffee beans and serve, cut into wedges, with the remaining coffee syrup.

white truffle cake

ingredients

SERVES 12

butter, for greasing
2 eggs
4 tbsp superfine sugar
1/3 cup all-purpose flour
1 3/4 oz/50 g white chocolate,
    melted
semisweet, light, or white
    chocolate curls
unsweetened cocoa,
    for dusting

truffle topping

1 1/4 cups heavy cream
12 oz/350 g white chocolate,
    broken into pieces
9 oz/250 g mascarpone
    cheese

method

1 Preheat the oven to 350°F/180°C. Grease an 8-inch/20-cm round springform cake pan and line with parchment paper.

2 Whisk the eggs and superfine sugar in a mixing bowl for 10 minutes, or until the mixture is very light and foamy and the whisk leaves a trail that lasts a few seconds when lifted. Sift the flour and fold in with a metal spoon. Fold in the melted white chocolate. Pour into the pan and bake in the preheated oven for 25 minutes, or until springy to the touch. Let cool slightly, then transfer to a wire rack until completely cold. Return the cold cake to the pan.

3 To make the topping, place the cream in a saucepan and bring to a boil, stirring to prevent it from sticking to the bottom of the pan. Cool slightly, then add the white chocolate pieces and stir until melted and combined. Remove from the heat and stir until almost cool, then stir in the mascarpone cheese. Pour the mixture on top of the cake and let chill for 2 hours.

4 Remove the cake from the pan and transfer to a plate. Decorate the top of the cake with chocolate curls. Dust with cocoa.

double chocolate gâteau

ingredients

SERVES 10

1 cup butter, softened, plus
    extra for greasing
generous 1 cup golden
    superfine sugar
4 eggs, beaten
generous 1 cup self-rising
    flour
generous 1/2 cup unsweetened
    cocoa
few tbsp milk (optional)

filling

generous 1 cup whipping
    cream
8 oz/225 g white chocolate,
    broken into pieces

frosting

12 oz/350 g semisweet
    chocolate, broken into
    pieces
1/2 cup butter
1/3 cup heavy cream

to decorate

chocolate curls, chilled
2 tsp confectioner's sugar
2 tsp unsweetened cocoa

method

1 Grease and line the bottom of an 8-inch/ 20-cm deep round cake pan. To make the filling, heat the cream to almost boiling. Place the white chocolate in a food processor and chop coarsely. With the motor running, pour the cream through the feed tube. Process for 10–15 seconds, or until the mixture is smooth. Transfer to a bowl and let cool. Cover and let chill for 2 hours, or until firm. Whisk until just starting to hold soft peaks.

2 Preheat the oven to 350°F/180°C. To make the sponge, beat the butter and sugar together until light and fluffy. Gradually beat in the eggs. Sift the flour and cocoa into another bowl, then fold into the batter, adding a little milk, if necessary, to make a dropping consistency. Spoon into the prepared pan, level the surface, and bake in the preheated oven for 45–50 minutes, or until springy to the touch and the tip of a knife inserted into the center comes out clean. Let stand in the pan for 5 minutes, then let cool on a wire rack.

3 For the frosting, melt the chocolate. Stir in the butter and cream. Let cool, stirring frequently, until the mixture is a spreading consistency. Slice the cake into three layers. Sandwich the layers together with the filling. Cover the cake with frosting, put chocolate curls on top, and sift confectioners' sugar and cocoa over the cake.

double chocolate roulade

ingredients

SERVES 8

4 eggs, separated

generous 1/2 cup golden
   superfine sugar

4 oz/115 g semisweet
   chocolate, melted and
   cooled

1 tsp instant coffee granules,
   dissolved in 2 tbsp hot
   water, cooled

confectioners' sugar,
   to decorate

unsweetened cocoa,
   for dusting

fresh raspberries, to serve

filling

generous 1 cup whipping
   cream

5 oz/140 g white chocolate,
   broken into pieces

3 tbsp Tia Maria

method

1 Preheat the oven to 350°F/180°C. Line a
9 x 13-inch/23 x 33-cm jelly roll pan with
nonstick parchment paper. Whisk the egg yolks
and sugar in a bowl until pale and mousselike.
Fold in the chocolate, then the coffee. Place the
egg whites in a clean bowl and whisk until stiff
but not dry. Stir a little of the egg whites into the
chocolate mixture, then fold in the remainder.
Pour into the prepared pan and bake in the
preheated oven for 15–20 minutes, or until
firm. Cover with a damp dish towel and let
stand in the pan for 8 hours, or overnight.

2 Meanwhile, make the filling. Heat the cream
until almost boiling. Place the chocolate in a
food processor and chop coarsely. With the
motor running, pour the cream through the
feed tube. Process until smooth. Stir in the Tia
Maria. Transfer to a bowl and let cool. Let chill
for 8 hours, or overnight.

3 To assemble the roulade, whip the chocolate
cream until soft peaks form. Cut a sheet of
wax paper larger than the roulade, place on
a counter and sift confectioners' sugar over.
Turn out the roulade onto the paper. Peel away
the lining paper. Spread the chocolate cream
over the roulade and roll up from the short
side nearest to you. Transfer to a dish, seam-
side down. Let chill for 2 hours, then dust with
cocoa. Serve with raspberries.

chocolate & walnut cake

ingredients

SERVES 8

butter, for greasing

4 eggs

²/₃ cup superfine sugar

2³/₄ oz/75 g semisweet
   chocolate, broken into
   pieces

scant 1 cup all-purpose flour

1 tbsp unsweetened cocoa

2 tbsp butter, melted

1 cup walnuts, chopped finely

frosting

2³/₄ oz/75 g semisweet
   chocolate

¹/₂ cup butter

1¹/₂ cups confectioners' sugar

2 tbsp milk

walnut halves, to decorate

method

1 Preheat the oven to 325°F/160°C. Grease and line a 7-inch/18-cm deep round cake pan. Place the eggs and sugar in a bowl and beat with an electric mixer for 10 minutes, or until foamy, and a trail is left when the beaters are dragged across the surface. Put the chocolate in a heatproof bowl set over a saucepan of gently simmering water, until melted.

2 Sift the flour and cocoa together and fold into the eggs and sugar with a spoon or a spatula. Fold in the melted butter, melted chocolate, and chopped walnuts. Pour into the prepared pan and bake in the preheated oven for 30–35 minutes, or until springy to the touch.

3 Let cool in the pan for 5 minutes, then transfer to a wire rack and let cool completely.

4 To make the frosting, melt the chocolate and let cool slightly. Beat together the butter, confectioners' sugar, and milk until the mixture is pale and fluffy. Whisk in the melted chocolate.

5 Cut the cake into two layers of equal thickness. Place the bottom half on a serving plate, spread with some of the frosting, and put the other half on top. Smooth the remaining frosting over the top of the cake with a spatula, swirling it slightly as you do so for a decorative effect. Decorate the cake with walnut halves and serve.

chocolate slab cake

ingredients

SERVES 6

generous ³/₄ cup butter, plus
    extra for greasing
3¹/₂ oz/100 g bittersweet
    chocolate, broken into
    pieces
¹/₃ cup water
2¹/₂ cups all-purpose flour
2 tsp baking powder
1¹/₃ cups brown sugar
¹/₃ cup sour cream
2 eggs, beaten

frosting

7 oz/200 g bittersweet
    chocolate
6 tbsp water
3 tbsp light cream
1 tbsp butter, chilled

method

1 Preheat the oven to 375°F/190°C. Grease a 13 x 8-inch/33 x 20-cm square cake pan and line the bottom with parchment paper. Melt the butter and chocolate with the water in a saucepan over low heat, stirring frequently.

2 Sift the flour and baking powder into a mixing bowl and stir in the sugar.

3 Pour the hot chocolate liquid into the bowl and then beat well until all of the ingredients are evenly mixed. Stir in the sour cream, followed by the eggs.

4 Pour the cake batter into the cake pan and bake in the preheated oven for 40–45 minutes, until springy to the touch.

5 Let the cake cool slightly in the pan before turning it out on to a wire rack. Let cool completely.

6 To make the frosting, melt the chocolate with the water in a saucepan over very low heat, stir in the cream, and remove from the heat. Stir in the chilled butter, then pour the frosting over the cooled cake, using a spatula to spread it evenly over the top of the cake.

chocolate passion cake

ingredients

SERVES 6

butter, for greasing

5 eggs

generous 3/4 cup superfine
  sugar

1 cup all-purpose flour

generous 3/8 cup unsweetened
  cocoa

1 2/3 cups carrots, peeled,
  finely grated, and
  squeezed until dry

scant 1/2 cup chopped walnuts

2 tbsp corn oil

1 1/2 cups medium-fat soft
  cheese

1 1/2 cups confectioners' sugar

6 oz/175 g milk or semisweet
  chocolate, melted

method

1 Preheat the oven to 375°F/190°C. Lightly grease and line the bottom of an 8-inch/20-cm deep round cake pan.

2 Place the eggs and sugar in a large heatproof bowl set over a saucepan of gently simmering water and, using an electric mixer, beat until the mixture is very thick and the beaters leave a trail that lasts a few seconds when lifted.

3 Remove the bowl from the heat. Sift the flour and cocoa into the bowl and carefully fold in. Fold in the carrots, walnuts, and oil until the cake batter is just blended.

4 Pour into the prepared pan and bake in the preheated oven for 45 minutes. Let cool slightly, then turn out onto a wire rack to cool completely.

5 Beat the soft cheese and confectioners' sugar together until blended, then beat in the melted chocolate. Split the cake in half and sandwich together again with half the chocolate mixture. Cover the top of the cake with the remainder of the chocolate mixture, swirling it with a knife. Let chill in the refrigerator until required, or serve immediately.

chocolate & orange cake

ingredients

SERVES 8

3/4 cup superfine sugar

3/4 cup butter or block margarine, plus extra for greasing

3 eggs, beaten

1 1/2 cups self-rising flour, sifted

2 tbsp unsweetened cocoa, sifted

2 tbsp milk

3 tbsp orange juice

grated rind of 1/2 orange

frosting

1 1/2 cups confectioners' sugar

2 tbsp orange juice

a little melted chocolate

method

1 Preheat the oven to 375°F/190°C. Lightly grease an 8-inch/20-cm deep round cake pan. Beat the sugar and butter or margarine together in a bowl until light and fluffy. Gradually add the eggs, beating well after each addition. Carefully fold in the flour.

2 Divide the mixture in half. Add the unsweetened cocoa and milk to one half, stirring until well combined. Flavor the other half with the orange juice and grated orange rind.

3 Place spoonfuls of each mixture into the prepared pan and swirl together with a skewer to create a marbled effect. Bake in the preheated oven for 25 minutes, or until the cake is springy to the touch. Let the cake cool in the pan for a few minutes before transferring to a wire rack to cool completely.

4 To make the frosting, sift the sugar into a mixing bowl and mix in enough of the orange juice to form a smooth frosting. Spread the frosting over the top of the cake and let set. Pipe fine lines of melted chocolate in a decorated pattern over the top.

date & chocolate cake

ingredients

SERVES 6

4 oz/115 g semisweet
   chocolate

1 tbsp grenadine

1 tbsp corn syrup

1/2 cup unsalted butter, plus
   extra for greasing

generous 1/4 cup superfine
   sugar

2 large eggs

1/2 cup self-rising flour, plus
   extra for dusting

2 tbsp ground rice

1 tbsp confectioners' sugar,
   to decorate

filling

2/3 cup dried dates, chopped

1 tbsp orange juice

1 tbsp raw sugar

1/8 cup blanched almonds,
   chopped

2 tbsp apricot jelly

method

1 Preheat the oven to 350°F/180°C. Grease two 7-inch/18-cm sandwich cake pans and dust with flour. Break the chocolate into pieces, then place the chocolate, grenadine, and syrup in the top of a double boiler or in a heatproof bowl set over a saucepan of barely simmering water. Stir over low heat until the chocolate has melted and the mixture is smooth. Remove the pan from the heat and let cool.

2 Beat the butter and superfine sugar together in a bowl until pale and fluffy. Gradually beat in the eggs, then beat in the chocolate mixture. Sift the flour into another bowl and stir in the ground rice. Fold the two mixtures together.

3 Divide the cake batter between the prepared pans and level the surface. Bake in a hot oven for 20–25 minutes, or until golden and firm to the touch. Turn out onto a wire rack to cool.

4 To make the filling, put all the ingredients into a saucepan and stir over low heat for 4–5 minutes, or until fully blended. Remove from the heat, let cool, then use the filling to sandwich the cakes together. Dust the top of the cake with confectioners' sugar and serve.

chocolate marshmallow cake

ingredients

SERVES 6

6 tbsp unsalted butter, plus
    extra for greasing
generous 1 cup superfine
    sugar
1/2 tsp vanilla extract
2 eggs, beaten lightly
3 oz/85 g semisweet
    chocolate, broken into
    pieces
2/3 cup buttermilk
11/4 cups self-rising flour
1/2 tsp baking soda
pinch of salt

frosting
6 oz/175 g white
    marshmallows
1 tbsp milk
2 egg whites
2 tbsp superfine sugar
grated milk chocolate, to
    decorate

method

1 Preheat the oven to 325°F/160°C. Grease a 3³/₄-cup ovenproof bowl with butter. Cream the butter, sugar, and vanilla extract together in a dish until pale and fluffy, then gradually beat in the eggs.

2 Melt the chocolate in a heatproof bowl over a saucepan of simmering water. When the chocolate has melted, stir in the buttermilk gradually, until well combined. Remove the pan from the heat and cool slightly.

3 Sift the flour, baking soda, and salt into a separate bowl. Add the chocolate mixture and the flour mixture alternately to the creamed mixture, a little at a time. Spoon the mixture into the ovenproof dish and smooth the surface. Bake in the preheated oven for 50 minutes, until a skewer inserted into the center of the cake comes out clean. Turn out onto a wire rack to cool.

4 To make the frosting, put the marshmallows and milk in a small saucepan and heat very gently until the marshmallows have melted. Remove from the heat and set aside to cool. Whisk the egg whites until soft peaks form, add the sugar, and continue whisking until stiff peaks form. Fold the egg white into the marshmallow mixture and set aside for 10 minutes. Cover the top and sides of the cake with the frosting. Top with grated chocolate.

family chocolate cake

ingredients

SERVES 8

1/2 cup soft margarine, plus extra for greasing

1/2 cup superfine sugar

2 eggs

1 tbsp light corn syrup

1 cup self-rising flour, sifted

2 tbsp unsweetened cocoa, sifted

a little light or white chocolate, melted (optional)

filling and topping

4 tbsp confectioners' sugar, sifted

2 tbsp butter

3 1/2 oz/100 g white or light chocolate

method

1 Preheat the oven to 375°F/190°C. Grease and line the bottoms of two 8-inch/20-cm round cake pans. Place all of the ingredients for the cake in a large mixing bowl and beat with a wooden spoon or electric mixer to form a smooth mixture.

2 Divide the mixture between the prepared pans and smooth the tops. Bake in the preheated oven for 20 minutes, or until springy to the touch. Let the cakes cool for a few minutes in the pans before transferring to a wire rack to cool completely.

3 To make the filling, beat the confectioners' sugar and butter together in a bowl until light and fluffy. Melt the chocolate and beat half into the sugar mixture. Use the filling to sandwich the cakes together.

4 Spread the remaining melted cooking chocolate over the top of the cake. Pipe circles of contrasting melted chocolate and feather into the chocolate with a toothpick, if desired. Let set before serving.

dark & white chocolate torte

ingredients

SERVES 6

4 eggs
1/2 cup superfine sugar
3/4 cup all-purpose flour

filling

11/4 cups heavy cream
51/2 oz/150 g semisweet
    chocolate, broken into
    small pieces

topping

23/4 oz/75 g white chocolate
1 tbsp butter
1 tbsp milk
4 tbsp confectioners' sugar

method

1 Preheat the oven to 350°F/180°C. Grease and line the bottom of an 8-inch/20-cm round springform cake pan. Whisk the eggs and superfine sugar in a large bowl with an electric whisk for 10 minutes, or until the mixture is very light and foamy and the whisk leaves a trail that lasts a few seconds when lifted.

2 Sift the flour and fold in with a metal spoon or spatula. Pour into the prepared pan and bake in the oven for 35–40 minutes, or until springy to the touch. Let cool slightly, then transfer to a wire rack to cool completely.

3 For the filling, place the cream in a pan and bring to a boil, stirring. Add the chocolate and stir until melted. Remove from the heat, transfer to a bowl, and let cool. Beat with a wooden spoon until thick.

4 Slice the cold cake horizontally into 2 layers. Sandwich the layers together with the semisweet chocolate cream and place on a wire rack.

5 For the topping, melt the chocolate and butter together and stir until blended. Whisk in the milk and confectioners' sugar. Continue whisking for a few minutes until the frosting is cool. Pour it over the cake and spread with a spatula to coat the top and sides. Let set.

chocolate brandy torte

ingredients

SERVES 12

base

9 oz/250 g gingersnaps

2³/4 oz/75 g semisweet
    chocolate

¹/2 cup butter, plus extra for
    greasing

filling

8 oz/225 g semisweet
    chocolate

generous 1 cup mascarpone
    cheese

2 eggs, separated

3 tbsp brandy

1¹/4 cups heavy cream

4 tbsp superfine sugar

to decorate

1¹/4 cups heavy cream

chocolate-covered coffee
    beans

method

1 Grease a 9-inch/23-cm springform cake pan. Place the gingersnaps in a plastic bag and crush with a rolling pin. Transfer to a bowl. Put the chocolate and butter into a small saucepan and heat gently until melted, then pour over the crushed cookies. Mix well, then press into the prepared pan. Chill the base while preparing the filling.

2 To make the filling, place the chocolate in a heatproof bowl and set over a saucepan of simmering water, stirring until melted. Remove from the heat and beat in the mascarpone cheese, egg yolks, and brandy. Whip the cream until just holding its shape. Fold in the chocolate mixture.

3 Whisk the egg whites in a spotlessly clean, grease-free bowl until soft peaks form. Add the sugar, a little at a time, and whisk until thick and glossy. Fold into the chocolate mixture, in two batches, until just mixed.

4 Spoon the mixture into the prepared base and let chill in the refrigerator for at least 2 hours. Carefully transfer to a serving plate. To decorate, whip the cream and pipe onto the cheesecake, add the chocolate-covered coffee beans, and serve.

chocolate & almond torte

ingredients

SERVES 10

8 oz/225 g semisweet
    chocolate, broken into
    pieces

3 tbsp water

1 cup brown sugar

3/4 cup butter, softened, plus
    extra for greasing

1/4 cup ground almonds

3 tbsp self-rising flour

5 eggs, separated

2/3 cup finely chopped
    blanched almonds

confectioners' sugar,
    for dusting

heavy cream, to serve

method

1 Preheat the oven to 350°F/180°C. Grease a 9-inch/23-cm loose-bottom cake pan and line the bottom with parchment paper. Melt the chocolate with the water in a saucepan set over very low heat, stirring until smooth. Add the sugar and stir until dissolved, taking the pan off the heat to prevent it from overheating.

2 Add the butter in small amounts until it has melted into the chocolate. Remove from the heat and lightly stir in the ground almonds and flour. Add the egg yolks one at a time, beating well after each addition.

3 Whisk the egg whites in a large mixing bowl, until they stand in soft peaks, then fold them into the chocolate mixture with a metal spoon. Stir in the chopped almonds. Pour the mixture into the prepared cake pan and smooth the surface.

4 Bake in the preheated oven for 40–45 minutes, until well risen and firm (the cake will crack on the surface during cooking).

5 Let cool in the pan for 30–40 minutes, then turn out onto a wire rack to cool completely. Dust with confectioners' sugar and serve in slices with cream.

chocolate orange mousse cake

ingredients

SERVES 8

1/2 cup superfine sugar
scant 1/2 cup margarine, plus
    extra for greasing
2 eggs, lightly beaten
3/4 cup all-purpose flour
1 tsp baking powder
2 tbsp unsweetened cocoa
finely pared strips of orange
    rind, to decorate

m o u s s e
7 oz/200 g good-quality
    semisweet chocolate
grated rind of 2 oranges
juice of 1 orange
4 eggs, separated

method

1 Preheat the oven to 350°F/180°C. Grease a 9-inch/23-cm round, loose-bottom cake pan and line the bottom. Cream the sugar and margarine together in a mixing bowl until pale and fluffy. Gradually add the eggs, beating well with a wooden spoon between each addition. Sift the flour, baking powder, and unsweetened cocoa together, fold half into the egg mixture, then fold in the remainder. Spoon the mixture into the prepared pan and level the surface with the back of a spoon. Bake in the preheated oven for 20 minutes, until risen and firm to the touch. Let cool completely in the pan.

2 Meanwhile, melt the chocolate in a heatproof bowl placed over a saucepan of gently simmering water. Let cool, then stir in the orange rind, orange juice, and the egg yolks.

3 Whisk the egg whites in a large bowl until they form stiff peaks. Gently fold a large spoonful of the egg whites into the chocolate mixture, then fold in the remainder. Spoon the mixture on top of the cooked, cooled sponge and level the top with the back of a spoon. Alternatively, remove the sponge from the pan, slice through, and sandwich with the mousse. Place in the refrigerator to set. Remove the sides of the pan (though not the bottom) before decorating with the orange rind strips and serving.

sicilian cassata

ingredients

SERVES 8

generous 1 cup self-rising
    flour

2 tbsp unsweetened cocoa

1 tsp baking powder

3/4 cup butter, softened, plus
    extra for greasing

scant 1 cup golden superfine
    sugar

3 eggs

confectioners' sugar,
    for dusting

chocolate curls to decorate

filling

2 cups ricotta cheese

3 1/2 oz/100 g semisweet
    chocolate, grated

generous 1/2 cup golden
    superfine sugar

3 tbsp Marsala

1/3 cup chopped candied peel

2 tbsp almonds, chopped

method

1 Preheat the oven to 375°F/190°C. Grease and line the bottom of a 7-inch/18-cm round cake pan. Sift the flour, unsweetened cocoa, and baking powder into a large bowl. Add the butter, sugar, and eggs and beat together thoroughly until smooth and creamy. Pour the cake batter into the prepared pan and bake in the preheated oven for 30–40 minutes, or until well risen and firm to the touch. Let stand in the pan for 5 minutes, then turn out onto a wire rack to cool completely.

2 Wash and dry the cake pan and grease and line it again. To make the filling, rub the ricotta cheese through a strainer into a bowl. Add the grated chocolate, sugar, and Marsala and beat together until the mixture is light and fluffy. Stir in the candied peel and almonds.

3 Cut the thin crust off the top of the cake and discard. Cut the cake horizontally into 3 layers. Place the first slice in the prepared pan and cover with half the ricotta mixture. Repeat the layers, finishing with a cake layer. Press down lightly, cover with a plate and a weight, and let chill in the refrigerator for 8 hours, or overnight. To serve, turn the cake out onto a serving plate. Dust with confectioners' sugar and decorate with chocolate curls.

chocolate fudge gâteau

ingredients

SERVES 10

1 tsp sunflower oil, for oiling

1 cup butter, softened

1 cup dark brown sugar

4 eggs, beaten

1 1/2 cups self-rising flour

3 oz/85 g semisweet
   chocolate, melted and
   kept warm

generous 1/2 cup ground
   almonds

4 oz/115 g soft vanilla fudge,
   chopped small

2 oz/55 g semisweet
   chocolate, grated

cocoa-dusted truffles,
   to decorate

frosting

3/4 cup butter, softened

2 1/2 cups confectioners' sugar,
   sifted

3–4 tbsp light cream

1/4 cup dark brown sugar

1 tbsp unsweetened cocoa,
   sifted

method

1 Preheat the oven to 350°F/180°C. Lightly oil two 8-inch/20-cm shallow cake pans and line the bottoms with parchment paper. Cream the butter and sugar together until light and fluffy, then gradually add the eggs, beating well between each addition and adding a little flour after each addition. Stir in the chocolate and then the remaining flour and mix lightly together.

2 Stir in the almonds with 1–2 tablespoons of cooled boiled water. Mix to form a soft dropping consistency. Stir in the fudge pieces, then divide between the prepared pans and smooth the tops. Bake in the preheated oven for 35–40 minutes, or until the tops spring back when touched lightly with a finger. Remove and let cool before turning out onto wire racks and discarding the lining paper. Let cool completely.

3 Beat the butter for the frosting until soft and creamy, then gradually beat in the confectioners' sugar, adding the cream as the mixture becomes stiff. Add the brown sugar and cocoa and stir. Add enough cream to give a soft, spreadable frosting.

4 Place the grated chocolate on a sheet of nonstick parchment paper. Split the cakes in half horizontally and sandwich together with a third of the frosting. Spread another third around the sides, then roll the cake in the grated chocolate. Place on a plate. Spread the top with the remaining frosting, piping rosettes around the outside edge. Decorate with truffles.

chocolate chestnut gâteau

ingredients

SERVES 8

1 tsp sunflower oil, for oiling

1 cup butter, softened

1 cup superfine sugar

4 eggs, beaten

1¹/₂ cups self-rising flour

2 oz/55 g white chocolate, grated

chestnut frosting

4 oz/115 g canned or fresh sweetened chestnut paste

4 tbsp butter, softened

3 cups confectioners' sugar, sifted

1–2 tbsp milk

1 tsp vanilla extract

2 oz/55 g semisweet chocolate, melted and kept warm

to decorate

¹/₃ cup chopped hazelnuts, toasted

2 oz/55 g semisweet chocolate

1 tbsp butter

2 tsp corn syrup

few marrons glacés

method

1 Preheat the oven to 350°F/180°C. Oil two 8-inch/20-cm shallow cake pans and line the bottoms with nonstick parchment paper. Cream the butter and sugar together until light and fluffy, then add the eggs a little at a time, beating well between each addition and adding a little flour after each addition. Stir in the remaining flour with 1–2 tablespoons of cooled boiled water.

2 Stir in the grated chocolate, mix lightly, and divide among the prepared pans. Smooth the tops and bake in the preheated oven for 25 minutes, or until the top springs back when touched. Let cool before turning out and discarding the lining paper. Let stand until cold, then split each cake horizontally in half.

3 For the frosting, cream the chestnut paste and butter together until smooth, then gradually beat in the sifted sugar with a little milk. Stir in the vanilla extract and the chocolate. Set aside 2–3 tablespoons, then use half the frosting to sandwich the cakes together. Place the hazelnuts on a sheet of parchment paper. Spread the remaining frosting around the sides of the cake and roll in the nuts. Place on a plate and use the reserved frosting to pipe small rosettes round the top edge of the cake.

4 Place the remaining ingredients in a saucepan and heat gently, stirring until the chocolate and butter have melted. Let cool until starting to thicken, then spoon over the top of the cake. Decorate with marrons glacés and serve.

chocolate cherry gâteau

ingredients

SERVES 6

2 lb/900 g fresh cherries,
　　pitted and halved
generous 1¼ cups superfine
　　sugar
scant ½ cup cherry brandy
¾ cup all-purpose flour
½ cup unsweetened cocoa
½ tsp baking powder
4 eggs
3 tbsp unsalted butter, melted,
　　plus extra for greasing
4 cups heavy cream
grated semisweet chocolate
　　whole fresh cherries,
　　to decorate

method

1 Preheat the oven to 350°F/180°C. Grease and line a 9-inch/23-cm springform cake pan. Put the halved cherries into a saucepan, add 3 tablespoons of the sugar and the cherry brandy. Simmer for 5 minutes. Drain, reserving the syrup. In another bowl, sift together the flour, cocoa, and baking powder.

2 Put the eggs in a heatproof bowl and beat in a generous ¾ cup of the sugar. Place the bowl over a pan of simmering water and beat for 6 minutes until thickened. Remove from the heat, then gradually fold in the flour mixture and melted butter. Spoon into the cake pan. Bake for 40 minutes.

3 Remove from the oven and let cool. Turn out the cake and cut in half horizontally. Mix the cream with the remaining sugar. Spread the reserved syrup over the cut sides of the cake. Arrange the cherries over one half, top with a layer of cream, and place the other half on top. Cover with cream, press grated chocolate all over, and decorate with cherries.

white chocolate coffee gâteau

ingredients

SERVES 8–10

3 tbsp unsalted butter,
   plus extra for greasing
3 oz/85 g white chocolate
2/3 cup superfine sugar
4 extra-large eggs, beaten
2 tbsp very strong black coffee
1 tsp vanilla extract
generous 1 cup all-purpose
   flour
white chocolate curls,
   to decorate

frosting

6 oz/175 g white chocolate
6 tbsp unsalted butter
generous 1/2 cup sour cream
generous 1 cup confectioners'
   sugar, sifted
1 tbsp coffee liqueur or very
   strong black coffee

method

1 Preheat the oven to 350°F/180°C. Grease two 8-inch/20-cm layer cake pans and line the bottoms with parchment paper. Place the butter and chocolate in a bowl set over a saucepan of hot water over very low heat until melted. Stir to mix, then remove from the heat.

2 Place the sugar, eggs, coffee, and vanilla extract in a large bowl set over a saucepan of hot water and mix hard with an electric mixer until the mixture is pale, and thick enough to leave a trail when the beaters are lifted. Remove from the heat, sift in the flour, and fold in lightly and evenly. Quickly fold in the butter and chocolate mixture, then divide the batter between the prepared pans. Bake in the preheated oven for 25–30 minutes, until risen, golden brown, and springy to the touch. Let cool for 2 minutes, then run a knife around the edges to loosen. Let cool on a wire rack.

3 For the frosting, place the chocolate and butter in a bowl set over a saucepan of hot water and heat gently until melted. Remove from the heat, stir in the sour cream, add the sugar and coffee liqueur, and mix until smooth. Chill for at least 30 minutes, stirring occasionally, until thick and glossy. Use one third to sandwich the cakes together. Spread the remainder over the top and sides, arrange the chocolate curls over the top, and let set.

german chocolate & hazelnut gâteau

ingredients

SERVES 8

3/4 cup unsalted butter,
   softened, plus extra
   for greasing

3/4 cup dark brown sugar

scant 1 cup self-rising flour,
   plus extra for dusting

1 tbsp unsweetened cocoa

1 tsp allspice

3 eggs, beaten

1 cup ground hazelnuts

2 tbsp black coffee

confectioners' sugar,
   for dusting

method

1 Preheat the oven to 350°F/180°C. Grease a 7¹/₂-inch/19-cm Bundt ring and dust with flour. Place the butter and brown sugar in a large mixing bowl and beat together until light and fluffy. Sift the flour, cocoa, and allspice into a separate bowl.

2 Beat the eggs into the creamed batter, one at a time, adding 1 tablespoon of the flour mixture with the second and third eggs. Fold in the remaining flour mixture, the hazelnuts, and the coffee.

3 Turn into the prepared pan and bake in the preheated oven for 45–50 minutes, or until the cake springs back when lightly pressed. Let stand in the pan for 10 minutes, then turn out onto a wire rack to cool completely. Dust with confectioners' sugar before serving.

muffins & cupcakes

Cupcakes are so called because they were originally baked in a small cup. Nowadays, we are more likely to use paper or foil liners. In Britain, they are also sometimes called fairy cakes, clearly a reference to their size but perhaps also to their lightness. Muffins are like slightly larger cupcakes made with a thicker batter. They are usually less sweet and not quite so rich as cupcakes but because they contain baking powder, they rise much higher. Cupcakes are almost always frosted but this is not so common with muffins. Note that traditional English muffins are very different from the American version because they are made from yeast dough and cooked on a griddle.

Both cupcakes and muffins are understandably well-liked by children, and muffins, in particular, make a good addition to a school lunch. While chocolate is a favorite flavoring, those made with fresh or dried fruit are just as delicious and a healthier option. Of course, adults like cupcakes and muffins too and there are plenty of recipes to suit the more sophisticated palate, flavored with edible flowers, coffee, lemon, and even brandy and liqueurs. Muffins are also a good choice for breakfast for all the family because they are tempting and easy to eat,

go well with tea, coffee, and milk and, if you must, you can eat them on the run. If they're served still warm from the oven, they are irresistible. In fact, they make great snacks any time of day although try not to be too greedy because they are high in calories.

drizzled honey cupcakes

ingredients

MAKES 12

generous $1/2$ cup self-rising white flour
$1/4$ tsp ground cinnamon
pinch of ground cloves
pinch of grated nutmeg
6 tbsp butter, softened
scant $1/2$ cup superfine sugar
1 tbsp honey
finely grated rind of 1 orange
2 eggs, lightly beaten
$3/4$ cup walnut pieces, minced

topping
$1/8$ cup walnut pieces, minced
$1/4$ tsp ground cinnamon
2 tbsp honey
juice of 1 orange

method

1 Preheat the oven to 375°F/190°C. Put 12 paper baking liners in a muffin pan, or put 12 double-layer paper liners on a baking sheet.

2 Sift the flour, cinnamon, cloves, and nutmeg together into a bowl. Put the butter and sugar in a separate bowl and beat together until light and fluffy. Beat in the honey and orange rind, then gradually add the eggs, beating well after each addition. Using a metal spoon, fold in the flour mixture. Stir in the walnuts, then spoon the batter into the paper liners.

3 Bake the cupcakes in the preheated oven for 20 minutes, or until well risen and golden brown. Transfer to a wire rack and let cool.

4 To make the topping, mix together the walnuts and cinnamon. Put the honey and orange juice in a saucepan and heat gently, stirring, until combined.

5 When the cupcakes have almost cooled, prick the tops all over with a fork or skewer and then drizzle with the warm honey mixture. Sprinkle the walnut mixture over the top of each cupcake and serve warm or cold.

frosted peanut butter cupcakes

ingredients

MAKES 16

4 tbsp butter, softened, or soft
    margarine
scant 1¼ cups firmly packed
    brown sugar
generous ⅓ cup crunchy
    peanut butter
2 eggs, lightly beaten
1 tsp vanilla extract
generous 1½ cups all-purpose
    flour
2 tsp baking powder
generous ⅓ cup milk

frosting

scant 1 cup full-fat cream
    cheese
2 tbsp butter, softened
2 cups confectioners' sugar

method

1 Preheat the oven to 350°F/180°C. Put 16 paper baking liners in a muffin pan.

2 Put the butter, sugar, and peanut butter in a bowl and beat together for 1–2 minutes, or until well mixed. Gradually add the eggs, beating well after each addition, then add the vanilla extract. Sift in the flour and baking powder and then, using a metal spoon, fold them into the mixture, alternating with the milk. Spoon the batter into the paper liners.

3 Bake the cupcakes in the preheated oven for 25 minutes, or until well risen and golden brown. Transfer to a wire rack and let cool.

4 To make the frosting, put the cream cheese and butter in a large bowl and, using an electric handheld mixer, beat together until smooth. Sift the confectioners' sugar into the mixture, then beat together until well mixed.

5 When the cupcakes are cold, spread the frosting on top of each cupcake, swirling it with a round-bladed knife. Store the cupcakes in the refrigerator until ready to serve.

rose petal cupcakes

ingredients

MAKES 12

$^1/_2$ cup butter, softened
generous $^1/_2$ cup superfine
    sugar
2 eggs, lightly beaten
1 tbsp milk
few drops extract of rose oil
$^1/_4$ tsp vanilla extract
scant 1$^1/_4$ cups self-rising
    white flour

frosting

6 tbsp butter, softened
1$^1/_2$ cups confectioners' sugar
pink or purple food coloring
    (optional)
silver dragées (cake decoration
    balls), to decorate

candied rose petals

12–24 rose petals
lightly beaten egg white,
    for brushing
superfine sugar, for sprinkling

method

1 To make the candied rose petals, gently rinse the petals and dry well with paper towels. Using a pastry brush, paint both sides of a rose petal with egg white, then coat well with superfine sugar. Place on a sheet and repeat with the remaining petals. Cover the sheet with foil and let dry overnight.

2 Preheat the oven to 400°F/200°C. Put 12 paper baking liners in a muffin pan, or put 12 double-layer paper liners on a baking sheet.

3 Put the butter and sugar in a bowl and beat together until light and fluffy. Gradually add the eggs, beating well after each addition. Stir in the milk, rose oil extract, and vanilla extract then, using a metal spoon, fold in the flour. Spoon the batter into the paper liners.

4 Bake the cupcakes in the preheated oven for 12–15 minutes, until well risen and golden brown. Transfer to a wire rack and let cool.

5 To make the frosting, put the butter in a large bowl and beat until fluffy. Sift in the confectioners' sugar and mix well together. If liked, add a few drops of pink or purple food coloring to complement the rose petals.

6 When the cupcakes are cold, spread the frosting on top of each cake. Top with 1–2 candied rose petals and decorate with silver dragées.

sticky gingerbread cupcakes

ingredients

MAKES 16

generous ³/₄ cup all-purpose
    flour

2 tsp ground ginger

³/₄ tsp ground cinnamon

1 piece preserved ginger,
    minced

³/₄ tsp baking soda

4 tbsp milk

6 tbsp butter, softened, or soft
    margarine

generous ¹/₃ cup firmly packed
    brown sugar

2 tbsp molasses

2 eggs, lightly beaten

pieces of preserved ginger,
    to decorate

frosting

6 tbsp butter, softened

1¹/₂ cups confectioners' sugar

2 tbsp ginger syrup from the
    preserved ginger jar

method

1 Preheat the oven to 325°F/160°C. Put 16 paper baking liners in a muffin pan, or place 16 double-layer paper liners on a baking sheet.

2 Sift the flour, ground ginger, and cinnamon together into a bowl. Add the chopped ginger and toss in the flour mixture until well coated. In a separate bowl, dissolve the baking soda in the milk.

3 Put the butter and sugar in a bowl and beat together until fluffy. Beat in the molasses, then gradually add the eggs, beating well after each addition. Beat in the flour mixture, then gradually beat in the milk. Spoon the batter into the paper liners.

4 Bake the cupcakes in the preheated oven for 20 minutes, or until well risen and golden brown. Transfer to a wire rack and let cool.

5 To make the frosting, put the butter in a bowl and beat until fluffy. Sift in the confectioners' sugar, add the ginger syrup, and beat together until smooth and creamy. Slice the preserved ginger into thin slivers or chop finely.

6 When the cupcakes are cold, spread the frosting on top of each cupcake, then decorate with pieces of ginger.

fudge nut muffins

ingredients

MAKES 12

generous 1¾ cups all-purpose
   flour
4 tsp baking powder
scant ½ cup superfine sugar
6 tbsp crunchy peanut butter
1 large egg, beaten
4 tbsp butter, melted
¾ cup milk
5½ oz/150 g vanilla fudge,
   cut into small pieces
3 tbsp coarsely chopped
   unsalted peanuts

method

1 Preheat the oven to 400°F/200°C. Line a 12-cup muffin pan with double paper baking liners. Sift the flour and baking powder together into a bowl. Stir in the sugar, add the peanut butter, and stir until the mixture resembles bread crumbs.

2 Place the egg, butter, and milk in a separate bowl and beat until blended, then stir into the dry ingredients until just blended. Lightly stir in the fudge pieces. Divide the batter evenly between the muffin liners.

3 Sprinkle the chopped peanuts on top and bake in the oven for 20–25 minutes, until well risen and firm to the touch. Remove the muffins from the oven and let cool for 2 minutes, then place them on a wire rack to cool completely.

fig & almond muffins

ingredients

MAKES 12

generous 1¾ cups all-purpose
    flour
1 tsp baking soda
½ tsp salt
1 cup raw sugar
generous ½ cup dried figs,
    chopped
1 cup almonds, chopped, plus
    2 tbsp chopped almonds,
    to decorate
2 tbsp sunflower oil or peanut
    oil, plus extra for oiling (if
    using)
1 cup water
1 tsp almond extract

method

1 Preheat the oven to 375°F/190°C. Oil a 12-cup muffin pan or line it with 12 paper baking liners. Sift the flour, baking soda, and salt into a mixing bowl, then add the sugar and stir.

2 In a separate bowl, mix the figs, almonds, and oil together. Stir in the water and almond extract. Add the fruit and nut mixture to the flour mixture and gently stir together. Do not overstir—it is fine for it to be a little lumpy.

3 Divide the muffin batter evenly between the 12 cups in the muffin pan or the paper liners (they should be about two-thirds full), then sprinkle over the remaining chopped almonds to decorate. Bake in the preheated oven for 25 minutes, or until risen and golden. Remove the muffins from the oven and serve warm, or place them on a wire rack and let cool.

banana & pecan cupcakes

ingredients

MAKES 12

generous 1¹/₂ cups all-purpose
    flour
1¹/₄ tsp baking powder
¹/₄ tsp baking soda
2 ripe bananas
¹/₂ cup butter, softened,
    or soft margarine
generous ¹/₂ cup superfine
    sugar
¹/₂ tsp vanilla extract
2 eggs, lightly beaten
4 tbsp sour cream
¹/₂ cup pecans, coarsely
    chopped

topping

¹/₂ cup butter, softened
1 cup confectioners' sugar
¹/₄ cup pecans, chopped

method

1 Preheat the oven to 375ºF/190ºC. Put 24 paper baking liners in a muffin pan, or put 24 double-layer paper liners on a baking sheet.

2 Sift together the flour, baking powder, and baking soda. Peel the bananas, put them in a bowl, and mash with a fork.

3 Put the butter, sugar, and vanilla extract in a bowl and beat together until light and fluffy. Gradually add the eggs, beating well after each addition. Stir in the mashed bananas and sour cream. Using a metal spoon, fold in the sifted flour mixture and chopped nuts, then spoon the batter into the paper liners.

4 Bake the cupcakes in the preheated oven for 20 minutes, or until well risen and golden brown. Transfer to a wire rack and let cool.

5 To make the topping, put the butter in a bowl and beat until fluffy. Sift in the confectioners' sugar and mix together well. Spread the frosting on top of each cupcake and sprinkle with the chopped pecans before serving.

apple & cinnamon muffins

ingredients

MAKES 6

scant ²/₃ cup all-purpose
 whole wheat flour
¹/₂ cup all-purpose white flour
1¹/₂ tsp baking powder
pinch of salt
1 tsp ground cinnamon
scant ¹/₄ cup golden superfine
 sugar
2 small apples, peeled, cored,
 and finely chopped
¹/₂ cup milk
1 egg, beaten
4 tbsp butter, melted

topping

12 brown sugar lumps,
 coarsely crushed
¹/₂ tsp ground cinnamon

method

1 Preheat the oven to 400°F/200°C. Place 6 paper baking liners in a muffin pan.

2 Sift both flours, baking powder, salt, and cinnamon together into a large bowl and stir in the sugar and chopped apples. Place the milk, egg, and butter in a separate bowl and mix. Add the wet ingredients to the dry ingredients and gently stir until just combined.

3 Divide the batter evenly between the paper liners. To make the topping, mix the crushed sugar lumps and cinnamon together and sprinkle over the muffins. Bake in the preheated oven for 20–25 minutes, or until risen and golden.

4 Remove the muffins from the oven and serve warm or place them on a wire rack and let cool.

warm molten-centered chocolate cupcakes

ingredients

MAKES 8

4 tbsp soft margarine

generous 1/4 cup superfine
    sugar

1 large egg

generous 1/2 cup self-rising
    flour

1 tbsp unsweetened cocoa

2 oz/55 g semisweet chocolate

sifted confectioners' sugar,
    for dusting

method

1 Preheat the oven to 375°F/190°C. Put 8 paper baking liners in a muffin pan, or put 8 double-layer paper liners on a baking sheet.

2 Put the margarine, sugar, egg, flour, and cocoa in a large bowl and, using an electric handheld mixer, beat together until just smooth.

3 Spoon half of the batter into the paper liners. Using a teaspoon, make an indentation in the center of each cake. Break the chocolate evenly into 8 squares and place a piece in each indentation, then spoon the remaining cake batter on top.

4 Bake the cupcakes in the preheated oven for 20 minutes, or until well risen and springy to the touch. Leave the cupcakes for 2–3 minutes before serving warm, dusted with confectioners' sugar.

spiced chocolate muffins

ingredients

MAKES 12

scant 1/2 cup butter, softened

scant 3/4 cup superfine sugar

1/2 cup firmly packed brown
    sugar

2 large eggs

2/3 cup sour cream

5 tbsp milk

generous 13/4 cups all-purpose
    flour

1 tsp baking soda

2 tbsp unsweetened cocoa

1 tsp allspice

generous 1 cup semisweet
    chocolate chips

method

1 Preheat the oven to 375°F/190°C. Line a
12-cup muffin pan with paper baking liners.

2 Place the butter, superfine sugar, and brown
sugar in a bowl and beat well. Beat in the eggs,
sour cream, and milk until thoroughly mixed.
Sift the flour, baking soda, cocoa, and allspice
into a separate bowl and stir into the mixture.
Add the chocolate chips and mix well. Divide
the batter evenly between the paper liners.
Bake in the preheated oven for 25–30 minutes.

3 Remove from the oven and let cool for
10 minutes. Place them on a wire rack
and let cool completely. Store in an airtight
container until required.

devil's food cakes with chocolate frosting

ingredients

MAKES 18

3¹/₂ tbsp soft margarine

generous ¹/₂ cup firmly packed brown sugar

2 large eggs

generous ³/₄ cup all-purpose flour

¹/₂ tsp baking soda

generous ¹/₄ cup unsweetened cocoa

¹/₂ cup sour cream

frosting

4¹/₂ oz/125 g semisweet chocolate

2 tbsp superfine sugar

²/₃ cup sour cream

chocolate curls (optional)

3¹/₂ oz/100 g semisweet chocolate

method

1 Preheat the oven to 350°F/180°C. Put 18 paper baking liners in a muffin pan, or put 18 double-layer paper liners on a baking sheet.

2 Put the margarine, sugar, eggs, flour, baking soda, and cocoa in a large bowl and, using an electric handheld mixer, beat together until just smooth. Using a metal spoon, fold in the sour cream. Spoon the batter into the paper liners.

3 Bake the cupcakes in the preheated oven for 20 minutes, or until well risen and firm to the touch. Transfer to a wire rack to cool.

4 To make the frosting, break the chocolate into a heatproof bowl. Set the bowl over a saucepan of gently simmering water and heat until melted, stirring occasionally. Remove from the heat and let cool slightly, then whisk in the sugar and sour cream until combined. Spread the frosting over the tops of the cupcakes and let set in the refrigerator before serving. If liked, serve decorated with chocolate curls.

cranberry & cheese muffins

ingredients

MAKES 18

butter, for greasing

generous 1 1/2 cups all-purpose
flour

2 tsp baking powder

1/2 tsp salt

1/4 cup superfine sugar

4 tbsp butter, melted

2 large eggs, lightly beaten

3/4 cup milk

generous 1 cup fresh
cranberries

1/4 cup freshly grated
Parmesan cheese

method

1 Preheat the oven to 400°F/200°C. Lightly grease two 9-cup muffin pans with butter.

2 Sift the flour, baking powder, and salt into a mixing bowl. Stir in the sugar.

3 In a separate bowl, combine the butter, beaten eggs, and milk, then pour into the bowl of dry ingredients. Mix lightly together until all of the ingredients are evenly combined, then stir in the fresh cranberries.

4 Divide the batter evenly between the prepared 18 cups in the muffin pans. Sprinkle the grated Parmesan cheese over the top. Transfer to the preheated oven and bake for 20 minutes, or until the muffins are well risen and a golden brown color.

5 Remove the muffins from the oven and let them cool slightly in the pans. Place the muffins on a wire rack and let cool completely.

dried cherry cheesecake muffins

ingredients

MAKES 12 MUFFINS

scant ¾ cup butter, plus extra
    for greasing
scant 1 cup cream cheese
generous ¾ cup superfine
    sugar
3 large eggs, lightly beaten
2 cups self-rising flour
generous ½ cup dried
    cherries, chopped
confectioners' sugar,
    for dusting

method

1 Preheat the oven to 350°F/180°C. Grease a deep 12-cup muffin pan.

2 Melt the butter and let cool slightly. In a large bowl, beat the cream cheese and sugar together, add the eggs one at a time until well combined, and then stir in the melted butter.

3 Mix the flour and cherries together in a bowl, then stir gently into the batter. Spoon into the prepared muffin pan, filling each hole to about two-thirds full, and bake in the preheated oven for 12–15 minutes, or until golden brown. Remove from the oven and let cool on a wire rack. Eat warm or cold, dusted lightly with confectioners' sugar.

banana pecan muffins

ingredients

MAKES 8

generous 1 cup all-purpose
 flour
1$\frac{1}{2}$ tsp baking powder
pinch of salt
$\frac{1}{3}$ cup golden superfine sugar
1 cup shelled pecans, coarsely
 chopped
2 large ripe bananas, mashed
5 tbsp milk
2 tbsp butter, melted
1 large egg, beaten
$\frac{1}{2}$ tsp vanilla extract

method

1 Preheat the oven to 375°F/190°C. Place 8 paper baking liners in a muffin pan. Sift the flour, baking powder, and salt into a bowl, add the sugar and pecans, and stir to combine.

2 Place the mashed bananas, milk, butter, egg, and vanilla extract in a separate bowl and mix together. Add the wet ingredients to the dry ingredients and gently stir until just combined.

3 Divide the batter evenly between the paper liners and bake in the preheated oven for 20–25 minutes, until risen and golden. Remove the muffins from the oven, place them on a wire rack, and let cool.

nectarine & banana muffins

ingredients

MAKES 12

generous 1¾ cups all-purpose
   flour

1 tsp baking soda

¼ tsp salt

¼ tsp allspice

½ cup superfine sugar

½ cup shelled almonds,
   chopped

6 oz/175 g ripe nectarine,
   peeled and chopped

1 ripe banana, sliced

2 large eggs

generous ⅓ cup sunflower oil
   or peanut oil, plus extra for
   oiling (if using)

⅓ cup thick Greek-style
   or banana-flavored yogurt

1 tsp almond extract

method

1 Preheat the oven to 400°F/200°C. Oil a
12-cup muffin pan or line it with 12 paper
baking liners. Sift the flour, baking soda, salt,
and allspice into a mixing bowl. Then add the
sugar and almonds and stir together.

2 In a separate large bowl, mash the nectarine
and banana together, then stir in the eggs, oil,
yogurt, and almond extract. Add the mashed
fruit mixture to the flour mixture and then gently
stir together until just combined. Do not overstir
the batter—it is fine for it to be a little lumpy.

3 Divide the muffin batter evenly between the
12 cups in the muffin pan or the paper liners
(they should be about two-thirds full). Transfer
to the preheated oven and bake for 20 minutes,
or until risen and golden. Remove the muffins
from the oven and serve warm, or place them
on a wire rack and let cool.

tropical coconut muffins

ingredients

MAKES 12

1 tbsp sunflower oil or peanut
   oil, for oiling (if using)
generous 1³/₄ cups all-purpose
   flour
1 tsp baking powder
1 tsp baking soda
¹/₂ tsp allspice
¹/₂ cup butter
1 cup firmly packed brown
   sugar
2 large eggs, beaten
2 tbsp thick plain, banana, or
   pineapple-flavored yogurt
1 tbsp rum
1 ripe banana, sliced
2³/₄ oz/75 g canned pineapple
   rings, drained and
   chopped
scant ¹/₂ cup dry unsweetened
   coconut

coconut topping
4 tbsp raw sugar
1 tsp allspice
scant ¹/₄ cup dry unsweetened
   coconut

method

1 Preheat the oven to 400°F/200°C. Oil a 12-cup muffin pan or line it with 12 paper baking liners. Sift the flour, baking powder, baking soda, and allspice into a mixing bowl.

2 In a separate large bowl, cream together the butter and brown sugar, then stir in the eggs, yogurt, and rum. Add the banana, pineapple, and dry unsweetened coconut and mix together gently. Add the pineapple mixture to the flour mixture and then gently stir together until just combined. Do not overstir the batter—it is fine for it to be a little lumpy.

3 Divide the muffin batter evenly between the 12 cups in the muffin pan or the paper liners (they should be about two-thirds full). To make the topping, mix the sugar and allspice together and sprinkle over the muffins. Sprinkle over the dry unsweetened coconut, then transfer to the preheated oven. Bake for 20 minutes, or until risen and golden. Remove the muffins from the oven and serve warm, or place them on a wire rack and let cool.

apple streusel cupcakes

ingredients

MAKES 14

1/2 tsp baking soda

1 1/4 cups applesauce

4 tbsp butter, softened, or soft
    margarine

scant 1/2 cup raw sugar

1 large egg, lightly beaten

scant 1 1/4 cups self-rising
    white flour

1/2 tsp ground cinnamon

1/2 tsp freshly ground nutmeg

topping

generous 1/3 cup all-purpose
    flour

1/4 cup raw sugar

1/4 tsp ground cinnamon

1/4 tsp freshly grated nutmeg

2 1/2 tbsp butter

method

1 Preheat the oven to 350ºF/180ºC. Put 14 paper baking liners in a muffin pan, or put 14 double-layer paper liners on a baking sheet.

2 First make the topping. Put the flour, sugar, cinnamon, and nutmeg in a bowl or in the bowl of a food processor. Cut the butter into small pieces, then either rub it in by hand or blend in the processor until the mixture resembles fine bread crumbs. Set aside while you make the cakes.

3 To make the cupcakes, add the baking soda to the applesauce and stir until dissolved. Put the butter and sugar in a bowl and beat together until light and fluffy. Gradually beat in the egg. Sift in the flour, cinnamon, and nutmeg and, using a large metal spoon, fold into the mixture, alternating with the applesauce.

4 Spoon the batter into the paper liners. Sprinkle the topping over each cupcake to cover the tops and press down gently.

5 Bake the cupcakes in the preheated oven for 20 minutes, or until well risen and golden brown. Let the cakes stand for 2–3 minutes before serving warm, or transfer to a wire rack and let cool.

carrot & orange cupcakes with mascarpone frosting

ingredients

MAKES 12

1/2 cup butter, softened, or soft
   margarine
generous 1/2 cup firmly packed
   brown sugar
juice and finely grated rind of
   1 small orange
2 large eggs, lightly beaten
3 carrots, grated
1/4 cup walnut pieces, coarsely
   chopped
scant 1 cup all-purpose flour
1 tsp ground pumpkin pie
   spice
1 1/2 tsp baking powder

frosting

1 1/4 cups mascarpone cheese
4 tbsp confectioners' sugar
grated rind of 1 large orange

method

1 Preheat the oven to 350°F/180°C. Put 12 paper baking liners in a muffin pan.

2 Put the butter, sugar, and orange rind in a bowl and beat together until light and fluffy. Gradually add the eggs, beating well after each addition. Squeeze any excess liquid from the carrots and add to the mixture with the walnuts and orange juice. Stir into the mixture until well mixed. Sift in the flour, pumpkin pie spice, and baking powder and then, using a metal spoon, fold into the mixture. Spoon the batter into the paper liners.

3 Bake the cupcakes in the preheated oven for 25 minutes, or until well risen, firm to the touch, and golden brown. Transfer to a wire rack and let cool.

4 To make the frosting, put the mascarpone cheese, confectioners' sugar, and orange rind in a large bowl and beat together until well mixed.

5 When the cupcakes are cold, spread the frosting on top of each cupcake, swirling it with a round-bladed knife. Store the cupcakes in the refrigerator until ready to serve.

shredded orange cupcakes

ingredients

MAKES 12

6 tbsp butter, softened,
   or soft margarine
scant ¹/₂ cup superfine sugar
1 large egg, lightly beaten
generous ¹/₂ cup self-rising
   flour
generous ¹/₄ cup ground
   almonds
grated rind and juice of
   1 small orange

orange topping

1 orange
generous ¹/₄ cup superfine
   sugar
2 tbsp toasted slivered
   almonds

method

1 Preheat the oven to 350°F/180°C. Put 12 paper baking liners in a muffin pan, or put 12 double-layer paper liners on a baking sheet.

2 Put the butter and sugar in a bowl and beat together until light and fluffy. Gradually beat in the egg. Add the flour, ground almonds, and orange rind and, using a large metal spoon, fold into the mixture. Fold in the orange juice.

3 Spoon the batter into the paper liners. Bake the cupcakes in the preheated oven for 20–25 minutes, or until well risen and golden brown.

4 Meanwhile, make the topping. Using a citrus zester, pare the rind from the orange, then squeeze the juice. Put the rind, juice, and sugar in a saucepan and heat gently, stirring, until the sugar has dissolved, then let simmer for 5 minutes.

5 When the cupcakes have cooked, prick them all over with a skewer. Spoon the warm syrup and rind over each cupcake, then sprinkle the slivered almonds on top. Transfer to a wire rack and let cool.

cranberry cupcakes

ingredients

MAKES 14

5$\frac{1}{2}$ tbsp butter, softened, or
soft margarine

$\frac{1}{2}$ cup superfine sugar

1 large egg

2 tbsp milk

$\frac{3}{4}$ cup self-rising flour

1 tsp baking powder

scant $\frac{3}{4}$ cup cranberries,
frozen

method

1 Preheat the oven to 350°F/180°C. Put 14 paper baking liners in a muffin pan, or put 14 double-layer paper liners on a baking sheet.

2 Put the butter and sugar in a bowl and beat together until light and fluffy. Gradually beat in the egg, then stir in the milk. Sift in the flour and baking powder and, using a large metal spoon, fold them into the mixture. Gently fold in the frozen cranberries. Spoon the batter into the paper liners.

3 Bake the cupcakes in the preheated oven for 15–20 minutes, or until well risen and golden brown. Transfer to a wire rack and let cool.

coconut cherry cupcakes

ingredients

MAKES 12

1/2 cup butter, softened, or soft
    margarine
generous 1/2 cup superfine
    sugar
2 tbsp milk
2 eggs, lightly beaten
generous 1/2 cup self-rising
    white flour
1/2 tsp baking powder
2/3 cup dry unsweetened
    coconut
4 oz/115 g candied cherries,
    quartered
1/2 cup candied cherries,
    maraschino cherries, or
    fresh cherries, to decorate

frosting

4 tbsp butter, softened
1 cup confectioners' sugar
1 tbsp milk

method

1 Preheat the oven to 350°F/180°C. Put 12 paper baking liners in a muffin pan, or put 12 double-layer paper liners on a baking sheet.

2 Put the butter and sugar in a bowl and beat together until light and fluffy. Stir in the milk. Gradually add the eggs, beating well after each addition. Sift in the flour and baking powder and fold them in with the coconut. Gently fold in most of the quartered cherries. Spoon the batter into the paper liners and sprinkle the remaining quartered cherries on top.

3 Bake the cupcakes in the preheated oven for 20–25 minutes, or until well risen, golden brown, and firm to the touch. Transfer to a wire rack and let cool.

4 To make the buttercream frosting, put the butter in a bowl and beat until fluffy. Sift in the confectioners' sugar and beat together until well mixed, gradually beating in the milk.

5 To decorate the cupcakes, using a pastry bag fitted with a large star tip, pipe the buttercream on top of each cupcake, then add a candied cherry to decorate.

tropical pineapple cupcakes with citrus cream frosting

ingredients

MAKES 12

2 slices of canned pineapple in natural juice

6 tbsp butter, softened, or soft margarine

scant 1/2 cup superfine sugar

1 large egg, lightly beaten

generous 1/2 cup self-rising white flour

1 tbsp juice from the canned pineapple

frosting

2 tbsp butter, softened

scant 1/2 cup cream cheese

grated rind of 1 lemon or lime

scant 1 cup confectioners' sugar

1 tsp lemon juice or lime juice

method

1 Preheat the oven to 350°F/180°C. Put 12 paper baking liners in a muffin pan, or put 12 double-layer paper liners on a baking sheet.

2 Finely chop the pineapple slices. Put the butter and sugar in a bowl and beat together until light and fluffy. Gradually beat in the egg. Add the flour and, using a large metal spoon, fold into the mixture. Fold in the chopped pineapple and the pineapple juice. Spoon the batter into the paper liners.

3 Bake the cupcakes in the preheated oven for 20 minutes, or until well risen and golden brown. Transfer to a wire rack and let cool.

4 To make the frosting, put the butter and cream cheese in a large bowl and, using an electric handheld mixer, beat together until smooth. Add the rind from the lemon or lime. Sift the confectioners' sugar into the mixture, then beat together until well mixed. Gradually beat in the juice from the lemon or lime, adding enough to form a spreading consistency.

5 When the cupcakes are cold, spread the frosting on top of each cake, or fill a pastry bag fitted with a large star tip and pipe the frosting on top. Store the cupcakes in the refrigerator until ready to serve.

warm strawberry cupcakes baked in a teacup

ingredients

MAKES 6

4 tbsp strawberry conserve

1/2 cup butter, softened, plus extra for greasing

generous 1/2 cup superfine sugar

2 eggs, lightly beaten

1 tsp vanilla extract

generous 3/4 cup self-rising white flour

1 lb/450 g small whole fresh strawberries

confectioners' sugar, for dusting

method

1 Preheat the oven to 350°F/180°C. Grease six heavy, round teacups with butter. Spoon 2 teaspoons of the strawberry conserve into the bottom of each teacup.

2 Put the butter and sugar in a bowl and beat together until light and fluffy. Gradually add the eggs, beating well after each addition, then add the vanilla extract. Sift in the flour and, using a large metal spoon, fold it into the mixture. Spoon the batter into the teacups.

3 Stand the cups in a roasting pan, then pour in enough hot water to come one third up the sides of the cups. Bake the cupcakes in the preheated oven for 40 minutes, or until well risen and golden brown, and a skewer, inserted in the center, comes out clean. If the cupcakes begin to brown too much, cover them with a sheet of foil. Let cool for 2–3 minutes, then carefully lift the cups from the pan and place them on saucers.

4 Place a few of the whole strawberries on each cake, then dust them with sifted confectioners' sugar. Serve warm with the remaining strawberries.

double chocolate muffins

ingredients

MAKES 12

scant 1$\frac{1}{2}$ cups all-purpose
    flour
$\frac{1}{3}$ cup unsweetened cocoa,
    plus extra for dusting
1 tbsp baking powder
1 tsp ground cinnamon
generous $\frac{1}{2}$ cup golden
    superfine sugar
6$\frac{1}{2}$ oz/185 g white chocolate,
    broken into pieces
2 large eggs
generous $\frac{1}{3}$ cup sunflower oil
    or peanut oil
1 cup milk

method

1 Preheat the oven to 400°F/200°C. Line a 12-cup muffin pan with paper baking liners. Sift the flour, cocoa, baking powder, and cinnamon into a large mixing bowl. Stir in the sugar and 4$\frac{1}{2}$ oz/125 g of the chocolate.

2 Place the eggs and oil in a separate bowl and beat until frothy, then gradually beat in the milk. Stir into the dry ingredients until just blended. Divide the batter evenly between the paper liners, filling each three-quarters full. Bake in the preheated oven for 20 minutes, or until well risen and springy to the touch. Remove the muffins from the oven, let cool in the pan for 2 minutes, then remove them and place them on a wire rack to cool completely.

3 Place the remaining chocolate in a heatproof bowl, set the bowl over a saucepan of barely simmering water, and heat until melted. Spread over the top of the muffins. Let set, then dust the tops with a little cocoa and serve.

chocolate chip muffins

ingredients

MAKES 12

3 tbsp soft margarine

1 cup superfine sugar

2 large eggs

2/3 cup plain yogurt

5 tbsp milk

2 cups all-purpose flour

1 tsp baking soda

1 cup semisweet chocolate
chips

method

1 Preheat the oven to 400°F/200°C. Line a 12-cup muffin pan with paper baking liners. Place the margarine and sugar in a mixing bowl and beat with a wooden spoon until light and fluffy. Beat in the eggs, yogurt, and milk until combined.

2 Sift the flour and baking soda into the batter. Stir until just blended.

3 Stir in the chocolate chips, then divide the batter evenly between the paper liners and bake in the preheated oven for 25 minutes, or until risen and golden. Remove the muffins from the oven and let cool in the pan for 5 minutes, then place them on a wire rack to cool completely.

chocolate orange muffins

ingredients

MAKES 10

sunflower oil or peanut oil, for oiling

scant 1 cup self-rising white flour

scant 1 cup self-rising whole wheat flour

generous 1/4 cup ground almonds

generous 1/4 cup firmly packed brown sugar

rind and juice of 1 orange

3/4 cup cream cheese

2 large eggs

1/3 cup semisweet chocolate chips

method

1 Preheat the oven to 375°F/190°C. Thoroughly oil 10 cups of a 12-cup muffin pan.

2 Sift both flours into a mixing bowl and stir in the ground almonds and sugar.

3 Mix the orange rind and juice, cream cheese, and eggs together in a separate bowl. Make a well in the center of the dry ingredients and stir in the wet ingredients, then add the chocolate chips. Beat well to combine all the ingredients.

4 Divide the batter evenly between the cups, filling each no more than three-quarters full. Bake in the preheated oven for 20–25 minutes, until well risen and golden brown.

5 Remove from the oven and let cool slightly on a wire rack, but eat them as fresh as possible.

dark & white fudge cupcakes

ingredients

MAKES 20

scant 1 cup water

6 tbsp butter

scant $1/2$ cup superfine sugar

1 tbsp corn syrup

3 tbsp milk

1 tsp vanilla extract

1 tsp baking soda

generous $1^1/2$ cups all-purpose flour

2 tbsp unsweetened cocoa

topping

$1^3/4$ oz/50 g semisweet chocolate

4 tbsp water

$3^1/2$ tbsp butter

$1^3/4$ oz/50 g white chocolate

3 cups confectioners' sugar

chocolate curls

$3^1/2$ oz/100 g semisweet chocolate

$3^1/2$ oz/100 g white chocolate

method

1 Preheat the oven to 350°F/180°C. Put 20 paper baking liners in two muffin pans, or put 20 double-layer paper liners on two baking sheets. Put the water, butter, sugar, and syrup in a saucepan. Heat gently, stirring, until the sugar has dissolved, then bring to a boil. Reduce the heat and cook gently for 5 minutes. Remove from the heat and let cool.

2 Meanwhile, put the milk and vanilla extract in a bowl. Add the baking soda and stir to dissolve. Sift the flour and cocoa into a separate bowl and add the syrup mixture. Stir in the milk and beat until smooth. Spoon the batter into the paper liners to two-thirds full. Bake the cupcakes in the preheated oven for 20 minutes, until well risen and firm to the touch. Transfer to a wire rack and let cool.

3 To make the topping, break the semisweet chocolate into a small heatproof bowl, add half the water and half the butter, and set the bowl over a saucepan of gently simmering water until melted. Stir until smooth and let stand over the water. Using another bowl, repeat with the white chocolate and remaining water and butter. Sift half the sugar into each bowl and beat until smooth and thick. Top the cupcakes with the frostings and let set. Serve decorated with chocolate curls made by shaving the chocolate with a potato peeler.

jumbo chocolate chip cupcakes

ingredients

MAKES 8

7 tbsp soft margarine

1/2 cup superfine sugar

2 large eggs

scant 3/4 cup self-rising white flour

generous 1/2 cup semisweet chocolate chips

method

1 Preheat the oven to 375ºF/190ºC. Put 8 paper baking liners in a muffin pan.

2 Put the margarine, sugar, eggs, and flour in a large bowl and, using an electric handheld mixer, beat together until just smooth. Fold in the chocolate chips. Spoon the batter into the paper liners.

3 Bake the cupcakes in the preheated oven for 20–25 minutes, or until well risen and golden brown. Transfer to a wire rack to cool.

mocha cupcakes with whipped cream

ingredients

MAKES 20

2 tbsp instant espresso coffee powder

6 tbsp butter

scant 1/2 cup superfine sugar

1 tbsp honey

scant 1 cup water

generous 1 1/2 cups all-purpose flour

2 tbsp unsweetened cocoa

1 tsp baking soda

3 tbsp milk

1 large egg, lightly beaten

topping

1 cup whipping cream

sifted unsweetened cocoa, for dusting

method

1 Preheat the oven to 350°F/180°C. Put 20 paper baking liners in two muffin pans, or put 20 double-layer paper liners on two baking sheets.

2 Put the coffee powder, butter, sugar, honey, and water in a saucepan and heat gently, stirring, until the sugar has dissolved. Bring to a boil, then reduce the heat and let simmer for 5 minutes. Pour into a large heatproof bowl and let cool.

3 When the mixture has cooled, sift in the flour and cocoa. Dissolve the baking soda in the milk, then add to the mixture with the egg and beat together until smooth. Spoon the batter into the paper liners.

4 Bake the cupcakes in the preheated oven for 15–20 minutes, or until well risen and firm to the touch. Transfer to a wire rack to cool.

5 For the topping, whisk the cream in a bowl until it holds its shape. Just before serving, spoon heaping teaspoonfuls of cream on top of each cake, then dust lightly with cocoa. Store the cupcakes in the refrigerator until ready to serve.

chocolate cupcakes with cream cheese frosting

ingredients

MAKES 18

6 tbsp butter, softened, or soft margarine

$1/2$ cup superfine sugar

2 eggs, lightly beaten

2 tbsp milk

$1/3$ cup semisweet chocolate chips

generous $1^1/2$ cups self-rising white flour

generous $1/4$ cup unsweetened cocoa

frosting

8 oz/225 g white chocolate

generous $2/3$ cup lowfat cream cheese

method

1 Preheat the oven to 400°F/200°C. Put 18 paper baking liners into two muffin pans.

2 Put the butter and sugar in a bowl and beat together until light and fluffy. Gradually add the eggs, beating well after each addition.

3 Add the milk, then fold in the chocolate chips. Sift in the flour and cocoa, then fold into the mixture. Spoon the batter into the paper liners and smooth the tops.

4 Bake the cupcakes in the preheated oven for 20 minutes, or until well risen and springy to the touch. Transfer to a wire rack and let cool.

5 To make the frosting, break the chocolate into a small heatproof bowl and set the bowl over a saucepan of gently simmering water until melted. Let cool slightly. Put the cream cheese in a bowl and beat until softened, then beat in the slightly cooled chocolate.

6 Spread a little of the frosting over the top of each cupcake, then let chill in the refrigerator for 1 hour before serving.

tiny chocolate cupcakes with ganache frosting

ingredients

MAKES 20

4 tbsp butter, softened

generous 1/4 cup superfine sugar

1 large egg, lightly beaten

scant 1/2 cup white self-rising flour

2 tbsp unsweetened cocoa

1 tbsp milk

20 chocolate-coated coffee beans, to decorate (optional)

frosting

3 1/2 oz/100 g semisweet chocolate

generous 1/3 cup heavy cream

method

1 Preheat the oven to 375°F/190°C. Put 20 double-layer mini paper liners on two baking sheets.

2 Put the butter and sugar in a bowl and beat together until light and fluffy. Gradually beat in the egg. Sift in the flour and cocoa and then, using a metal spoon, fold them into the mixture. Stir in the milk.

3 Fill a pastry bag, fitted with a large plain tip, with the batter and pipe it into the paper liners, filling each one halfway.

4 Bake the cakes in the preheated oven for 10–15 minutes, or until well risen and firm to the touch. Transfer to a wire rack to cool.

5 To make the frosting, break the chocolate into a saucepan and add the cream. Heat gently, stirring all the time, until the chocolate has melted. Pour into a large heatproof bowl and, using an electric handheld mixer, beat the mixture for 10 minutes, or until thick, glossy, and cool.

6 Fill a pastry bag, fitted with a large star tip, with the frosting and pipe a swirl on top of each cupcake. Alternatively, spoon the frosting over the top of each cupcake. Chill in the refrigerator for 1 hour before serving. Serve decorated with a chocolate-coated coffee bean, if using.

frosted lavender muffins

ingredients

MAKES 12

1 large baking apple, peeled, cored, and thinly sliced

3 tbsp water

1 cup all-purpose flour

1 tsp baking powder

1 tsp baking soda

pinch of salt

4 tbsp butter

4 tbsp superfine sugar

1 large egg, beaten

1/2 tsp vanilla extract

1 tbsp dried lavender flowers, plus extra to decorate

lavender frosting

scant 1 cup confectioners' sugar

1 tbsp dried lavender flowers, stripped from the stalk

1 tbsp liquid glucose

1–2 tbsp milk

method

1 Make the frosting a day in advance. Place the sugar in a bowl, add the dried lavender flowers, cover with plastic wrap, and let stand overnight.

2 To make the muffins, place the apple and water in a saucepan and bring to a boil, then cover and simmer for 15–20 minutes, stirring occasionally, until the water has been absorbed. Remove from the heat and let cool. Transfer to a food processor and process until smooth.

3 Preheat the oven to 400°F/200°C. Line a 12-cup muffin pan with paper liners. Sift the flour, baking powder, baking soda, and salt into a mixing bowl. In a separate large bowl, cream together the butter and sugar, then stir in the egg, vanilla extract, apple puree, and dried lavender flowers. Stir the egg mixture into the flour mixture until just combined. Do not overstir—it is fine for the batter to be a little lumpy. Divide the batter evenly between the 12 paper liners to two-thirds full. Transfer to the preheated oven and bake for 20 minutes, or until risen and golden.

4 Meanwhile, remove the plastic wrap from the confectioners' sugar/lavender mixture, sift the mixture into a bowl, and discard the lavender. Stir in the liquid glucose and enough milk to make the frosting easy to spread. Cover with plastic wrap until ready to use. When the muffins are cooked, let cool on a wire rack. Spread each muffin with some of the lavender frosting, add some lavender flowers, and serve.

irish coffee muffins

ingredients

MAKES 12

1 tbsp sunflower oil or peanut
   oil, for oiling (if using)
2 cups all-purpose flour
1 tbsp baking powder
pinch of salt
7 tbsp butter
scant 1/2 cup raw sugar
1 large egg, beaten
1/2 cup heavy cream
1 tsp almond extract
2 tbsp strong coffee
2 tbsp coffee-flavored liqueur
4 tbsp Irish whiskey or similar
   whiskey

method

1 Preheat the oven to 400°F/200°C. Oil a 12-cup muffin pan or line it with 12 paper baking liners. Sift the flour, baking powder, and salt into a large mixing bowl.

2 In a separate large bowl, cream the butter and sugar together, then stir in the egg. Pour in the heavy cream, almond extract, coffee, liqueur, and whiskey and stir together. Add the whiskey mixture to the flour mixture and then gently stir together until just combined. Do not overstir the batter—it is fine for it to be a little lumpy.

3 Divide the muffin batter evenly between the 12 cups in the muffin pan or the paper liners (they should be about two-thirds full). Transfer to the preheated oven and bake for 20 minutes, or until risen and golden. Remove the muffins from the oven and serve warm, or place them on a wire rack and let cool.

mocha muffins

ingredients

MAKES 12

1 tbsp sunflower oil or peanut
   oil, for oiling (if using)
generous 1 3/4 cups all-purpose
   flour
1 tbsp baking powder
2 tbsp unsweetened cocoa
pinch of salt
1/2 cup butter, melted
scant 3/4 cup raw sugar
1 large egg, beaten
1 cup milk
1 tsp almond extract
2 tbsp strong coffee
1 tbsp instant coffee powder
generous 1/4 cup semisweet
   chocolate chips
scant 1/3 cup raisins

cocoa topping

3 tbsp raw sugar
1 tbsp unsweetened cocoa
1 tsp allspice

method

1 Preheat the oven to 375°F/190°C. Oil a 12-cup muffin pan or line it with 12 paper baking liners. Sift the flour, baking powder, cocoa, and salt into a large mixing bowl.

2 In a separate large bowl, cream the butter and raw sugar together, then stir in the beaten egg. Pour in the milk, almond extract, and coffee, then add the coffee powder, chocolate chips, and raisins and gently mix together. Add the raisin mixture to the flour mixture and then gently stir together until just combined. Do not overstir the batter—it is fine for it to be a little lumpy.

3 Divide the muffin batter evenly between the 12 cups in the muffin pan or the paper liners (they should be about two-thirds full). To make the topping, place the raw sugar in a bowl, add the cocoa and allspice, and mix together well. Sprinkle the topping over the muffins, then transfer to the preheated oven and bake for 20 minutes, or until risen and golden. Remove the muffins from the oven and serve warm, or place them on a wire rack and let cool.

triple chocolate muffins

ingredients

MAKES 12

generous 1³/₄ cups all-purpose flour

¹/₃ cup unsweetened cocoa

2 tsp baking powder

¹/₂ tsp baking soda

generous ¹/₂ cup semisweet chocolate chips

generous ¹/₂ cup white chocolate chips

2 large eggs, beaten

1¹/₄ cups sour cream

scant ¹/₂ cup firmly packed brown sugar

3 tbsp butter, melted

method

1 Preheat the oven to 400°F/200°C. Line a 12-cup muffin pan with paper baking liners. Sift the flour, cocoa, baking powder, and baking soda into a large bowl, add the chocolate chips, and stir.

2 Place the eggs, sour cream, sugar, and melted butter in a separate mixing bowl and mix well. Add the wet ingredients to the dry ingredients and stir gently until just combined.

3 Using 2 spoons, divide the batter evenly between the paper liners and bake in the preheated oven for 20 minutes, or until well risen and firm to the touch. Remove from the oven and serve warm, or place on a wire rack and let cool.

rice muffins with amaretto

ingredients

MAKES 9

butter, for greasing

1 cup all-purpose flour

1 tbsp baking powder

1/2 tsp baking soda

1/2 tsp salt

1 large egg

4 tbsp honey

1/2 cup milk

2 tbsp sunflower oil or
      peanut oil

1/2 tsp almond extract

3/4 cup cooked risotto rice

2–3 amaretti cookies, coarsely
      crushed

amaretto butter

1 tbsp honey

1–2 tbsp amaretto

1/2 cup mascarpone cheese

method

1 Preheat the oven to 400°F/200°C. Grease nine cups of a 12-cup muffin pan with butter. Sift the flour, baking powder, baking soda, and salt into a large bowl and stir. Make a well in the center.

2 In a separate bowl, beat the egg, honey, milk, oil, and almond extract with an electric whisk for about 2 minutes, or until light and foamy. Gradually beat in the rice. Pour into the well in the dry ingredients and, using a fork, stir lightly until just combined. Do not beat too long or the batter can become lumpy.

3 Divide the batter evenly between the prepared cups in the muffin pan. Sprinkle each with some of the amaretti crumbs and bake in the preheated oven for 15 minutes, until risen and golden. The tops should spring back when pressed. Remove from the oven and let cool in the pan for about 1 minute. Carefully remove the muffins and let cool slightly.

4 To make the amaretto butter, place the honey, amaretto, and mascarpone cheese in a small bowl and beat together. Spoon into a small serving bowl and serve with the warm muffins.

brandied cherry muffins

ingredients

MAKES 12

1 tbsp sunflower oil or peanut
    oil, for oiling (if using)
generous 1½ cups all-purpose
    flour
1 tbsp baking powder
pinch of salt
3 tbsp butter
2 tbsp superfine sugar
1 large egg, beaten
scant 1 cup milk
2 tsp cherry brandy
10½ oz/300 g drained canned
    cherries, chopped

method

1 Preheat the oven to 400°F/200°C. Oil a 12-cup muffin pan or line it with 12 paper baking liners. Sift the flour, baking powder, and salt into a large mixing bowl.

2 In a separate large bowl, cream the butter and superfine sugar together, then stir in the beaten egg. Pour in the milk and cherry brandy, then add the chopped cherries and gently stir together. Add the cherry mixture to the flour mixture and then gently stir together until just combined. Do not overstir the batter—it is fine for it to be a little lumpy.

3 Divide the muffin batter evenly between the 12 cups in the muffin pan or the paper liners (they should be about two-thirds full). Transfer to the oven and bake for 20–25 minutes until risen and golden. Remove the muffins from the oven and serve warm, or place them on a wire rack and let cool.

apricot muffins with cointreau

ingredients

MAKES 12

1 tbsp sunflower oil or peanut
 oil, for oiling (if using)
scant 1 cup self-rising flour
2 tsp baking powder
3/4 cup butter
scant 2/3 cup superfine sugar
2 large eggs, beaten
1/2 cup milk
4 tbsp light cream
1 tbsp Cointreau
generous 1/2 cup no-soak
 dried apricots, chopped
generous 1/2 cup plumped
 dried dates, pitted
 and chopped

cinnamon topping

3 tbsp raw sugar
1 tsp ground cinnamon
1 tbsp freshly grated orange
 rind

method

1 Preheat the oven to 375°F/190°C. Oil a 12-cup muffin pan or line it with 12 paper baking liners.

2 Sift the flour and baking powder into a large mixing bowl.

3 In a separate large bowl, cream together the butter and sugar, then stir in the eggs. Pour in the milk, cream, and Cointreau, then add the chopped apricots and dates and gently mix together. Add the fruit mixture to the flour mixture and gently stir together until just combined. Do not overstir the batter—it is fine for it to be a little lumpy.

4 Divide the muffin batter evenly between the 12 cups in the muffin pan or the paper liners (they should be about two-thirds full). To make the topping, place the raw sugar in a small bowl, then mix in the cinnamon and orange rind. Sprinkle the topping over the muffins, then transfer to the preheated oven and bake for 20 minutes, or until risen and golden. Remove the muffins from the oven and serve warm, or place them on a wire rack and let cool.

marshmallow muffins

ingredients

MAKES 12

5 tbsp butter

2 cups all-purpose flour

6 tbsp unsweetened cocoa

3 tsp baking powder

scant 1/2 cup superfine sugar

generous 1/2 cup milk
    chocolate chips

1/4 cup multicolored mini
    marshmallows

1 large egg, beaten

1 1/4 cups milk

method

1 Preheat the oven to 375°F/190°C. Line a 12-cup muffin pan with paper baking liners. Melt the butter in a saucepan.

2 Sift the flour, cocoa, and baking powder together into a large bowl. Stir in the sugar, chocolate chips, and marshmallows until thoroughly mixed.

3 Whisk the egg, milk, and melted butter together in a separate bowl, then gently stir into the flour to form a stiff batter. Divide the batter evenly between the paper liners.

4 Bake in the preheated oven for 20–25 minutes until well risen and golden brown. Remove from the oven and let cool in the pan for 5 minutes, then place on a wire rack and let cool completely.

lime & poppy seed muffins

ingredients

MAKES 12

1¹/₂ cups all-purpose flour

1 tsp baking powder

¹/₂ tsp salt

scant 1¹/₄ cups superfine
    sugar

1 large egg

1 large egg white

³/₄ cup sunflower oil or peanut
    oil, plus extra for oiling (if
    using)

²/₃ cup milk

1 tbsp lime juice

1 tbsp grated lime rind

2 tsp poppy seeds

to decorate

2 tsp grated lime rind

1–2 tsp poppy seeds

method

1 Preheat the oven to 375°F/190°C. Oil a 12-cup muffin pan or line it with 12 muffin paper liners. Sift the flour, baking powder, and salt into a mixing bowl. Then add the sugar and stir together.

2 In a separate bowl, whisk the egg, egg white, oil, and milk together, then stir in the lime juice and grated lime rind. Add the egg mixture to the flour mixture, then add the poppy seeds and gently stir together. Do not overstir the batter—it is fine for it to be a little lumpy.

3 Divide the muffin batter evenly between the 12 cups in the muffin pan or the paper liners (they should be about two-thirds full). Sprinkle over the grated lime rind and poppy seeds to decorate, then bake in the preheated oven for 25 minutes, or until risen and golden. Remove the muffins from the oven and serve warm, or place them on a wire rack and let cool.

doughnut muffins

ingredients

MAKES 12

3/4 cup butter, softened, plus
    extra for greasing
1 cup superfine sugar
2 large eggs, lightly beaten
generous 2 1/2 cups all-purpose
    flour
3/4 tbsp baking powder
1/4 tsp baking soda
pinch of salt
1/2 tsp freshly grated nutmeg
generous 1 cup milk

topping
1/2 cup superfine sugar
1 tsp ground cinnamon
2 tbsp butter, melted

method

1 Preheat the oven to 350°F/180°C. Grease a deep 12-cup muffin pan. In a large bowl, beat the butter and sugar together until light and creamy. Add the eggs, a little at a time, beating well between additions.

2 Sift the flour, baking powder, baking soda, salt, and nutmeg together. Add half to the creamed mixture with half of the milk.

3 Gently fold the ingredients together before incorporating the remaining flour and milk. Spoon the mixture into the prepared muffin pan, filling each hole to about two-thirds full.

4 Bake in the preheated oven for 15–20 minutes, or until the muffins are lightly browned and firm to the touch.

5 For the topping, mix the sugar and cinnamon together. While the muffins are still warm from the oven, brush lightly with melted butter, and sprinkle over the cinnamon and sugar mixture. Eat warm or cold.

marbled chocolate cupcakes

ingredients

MAKES 21

3/4 cup soft margarine

generous 3/4 cup superfine
   sugar

3 eggs

scant 1 1/4 cups self-rising
   white flour

2 tbsp milk

2 oz/55 g semisweet
   chocolate, melted

method

1 Preheat the oven to 350°F/180°C. Put 21 paper baking liners in a muffin pan, or put 21 double-layer paper liners on a baking sheet.

2 Put the margarine, sugar, eggs, flour, and milk in a large bowl and, using an electric handheld mixer, beat together until just smooth.

3 Divide the batter between two bowls. Add the melted chocolate to one bowl and stir together until well mixed. Using a teaspoon, and alternating the chocolate batter with the plain batter, put four half-teaspoons into each paper liner.

4 Bake the cupcakes in the preheated oven for 20 minutes, or until well risen and springy to the touch. Transfer to a wire rack and let cool.

banana & date muffins

ingredients

MAKES 12

vegetable oil cooking spray,
    for oiling (if using)

1½ cups all-purpose flour

2 tsp baking powder

¼ tsp salt

½ tsp allspice

5 tbsp superfine sugar

2 large egg whites

2 ripe bananas, sliced

⅜ cup plumped dried dates,
    pitted and chopped

4 tbsp skim milk

5 tbsp maple syrup

method

1 Preheat the oven to 400°F/200°C. Spray a 12-cup muffin pan with oil or line it with 12 paper baking liners. Sift the flour, baking powder, salt, and allspice into a mixing bowl. Add the sugar and mix together.

2 In a separate bowl, whisk the egg whites together. Mash the bananas in a separate bowl, then add them to the egg whites. Add the dates, then pour in the milk and maple syrup and stir together gently to mix. Add the banana and date mixture to the flour mixture and then gently stir together until just combined. Do not overstir the batter—it is fine for it to be a little lumpy.

3 Divide the muffin batter evenly between the 12 cups in the muffin pan or the paper liners (they should be about two-thirds full). Transfer to the preheated oven and bake for 25 minutes, or until risen and golden. Remove the muffins from the oven and serve warm, or place them on a wire rack and let cool.

apple & raspberry muffins

ingredients

MAKES 12

3 large baking apples, peeled and cored

generous 1½ cups water

1½ tsp allspice

vegetable oil cooking spray, for oiling (if using)

generous 2 cups all-purpose whole wheat flour

1 tbsp baking powder

¼ tsp salt

3 tbsp superfine sugar

generous 1 cup fresh raspberries

method

1 Thinly slice two baking apples and place them in a saucepan with 6 tablespoons of the water. Bring to a boil, then reduce the heat. Stir in ½ teaspoon of the allspice, cover the pan, and let simmer, stirring occasionally, for 15–20 minutes, until the water has been absorbed. Remove from the heat and let cool. Transfer to a food processor and blend until smooth. Stir in the remaining water and mix well.

2 Preheat the oven to 400°F/200°C. Spray a 12-cup muffin pan with oil or line it with 12 paper baking liners. Sift the flour, baking powder, salt, and remaining allspice into a mixing bowl, then stir in the sugar.

3 Chop the remaining apple and add to the flour mixture. Add the raspberries, then combine gently with the flour mixture until lightly coated. Finally, gently stir in the cooled apple/water mixture. Do not overstir the batter—it is fine for it to be a little lumpy.

4 Divide the muffin batter evenly between the 12 cups in the muffin pan or the paper liners (they should be about two-thirds full). Transfer to the oven and bake for 25 minutes, or until risen and golden. Remove the muffins from the oven and serve warm, or place them on a wire rack and let cool.

dairy-free berry muffins

ingredients

MAKES 12

1 large baking apple, peeled, cored, and thinly sliced

3 tbsp water

1 tsp allspice

2 tbsp sunflower oil or peanut oil, plus extra for oiling (if using)

1 1/2 cups all-purpose white or whole wheat flour

1 tbsp baking powder

1/4 tsp salt

6 tbsp wheat germ

scant 1/4 cup fresh raspberries

scant 1/2 cup fresh strawberries, hulled and chopped

6 tbsp maple syrup

3/4 cup apple juice

method

1 Place the sliced baking apple and water in a saucepan and bring to a boil. Reduce the heat and stir in half of the allspice, then cover the pan and let simmer, stirring occasionally, for 15–20 minutes until the water has been absorbed. Remove the pan from the heat and let cool. Transfer the apple mixture to a food processor and blend until smooth.

2 Preheat the oven to 375°F/190°C. Lightly oil a 12-cup muffin pan or line it with 12 paper baking liners.

3 Sift the flour, baking powder, salt, and remaining allspice into a mixing bowl, then stir in the wheat germ.

4 In a separate bowl, mix the raspberries, strawberries, maple syrup, oil, pureed apple, and the apple juice together. Add the fruit mixture to the flour mixture and then gently stir together until just combined. Do not overstir the batter—it is fine for it to be a little lumpy.

5 Divide the muffin batter evenly between the 12 cups in the muffin pan or the paper liners (they should be about two-thirds full). Transfer to the preheated oven and bake for 25 minutes, or until risen and golden. Remove the muffins from the oven and serve warm, or place them on a wire rack and let cool.

blueberry muffins

ingredients

MAKES 12

vegetable oil cooking spray,
    for oiling (if using)
generous 1$\frac{1}{2}$ cups all-purpose
    flour
1 tsp baking soda
$\frac{1}{4}$ tsp salt
1 tsp allspice
generous $\frac{3}{4}$ cup superfine
    sugar
3 large egg whites
3 tbsp lowfat margarine
$\frac{2}{3}$ cup thick, lowfat, plain or
    blueberry-flavored yogurt
1 tsp vanilla extract
$\frac{3}{4}$ cup fresh blueberries

method

1 Preheat the oven to 375°F/190°C. Spray a 12-cup muffin pan with oil or line it with 12 paper baking liners. Sift the flour, baking soda, salt, and half of the allspice into a large mixing bowl. Add 6 tablespoons of the superfine sugar and mix together.

2 In a separate bowl, whisk the egg whites together. Add the margarine, yogurt, and vanilla extract and mix together well, then stir in the blueberries until thoroughly mixed. Add the fruit mixture to the flour mixture and then gently stir together until just combined. Do not overstir the batter—it is fine for it to be a little lumpy.

3 Divide the muffin batter evenly between the 12 cups in the muffin pan or the paper liners (they should be about two-thirds full). Mix the remaining sugar with the remaining allspice, then sprinkle the mixture over the muffins. Transfer to the preheated oven and bake for 25 minutes, or until risen and golden. Remove the muffins from the oven and serve warm, or place them on a wire rack and let cool.

fruity muffins

ingredients

MAKES 10

2 cups self-rising whole wheat
   flour
2 tsp baking powder
2 tbsp brown sugar
generous 1/2 cup plumped
   dried apricots, finely
   chopped
1 banana, mashed with
1 tbsp orange juice
1 tsp finely grated orange rind
1 1/4 cups skim milk
1 large egg, beaten
3 tbsp sunflower oil or peanut
   oil
2 tbsp rolled oats
fruit spread, honey, or maple
   syrup, to serve

method

1 Preheat the oven to 400°F/200°C. Line
10 cups of a 12-cup muffin pan with paper
baking liners. Sift the flour and baking powder
into a mixing bowl, adding any husks that
remain in the sifter. Stir in the sugar and
chopped apricots.

2 Make a well in the center and add the mashed
banana, orange rind, milk, egg, and oil. Mix the
banana, orange juice, orange rind, milk, egg,
and oil.

3 Sprinkle with a few rolled oats and bake in the
preheated oven for 25–30 minutes, until well
risen and firm to the touch, or until a toothpick
inserted into the center comes out clean.

4 Remove the muffins from the oven and place
them on a wire rack to cool slightly. Serve the
muffins while still warm with a little fruit spread,
honey, or maple syrup.

honey & lemon muffins

ingredients

MAKES 12

1/4 cup unrefined superfine sugar

2 tbsp unsalted butter, melted and cooled slightly

2/3 cup buttermilk

2 eggs, beaten

4 tbsp flower honey

finely grated rind of 1 lemon and juice of 1/2 lemon

generous 1 1/2 cups all-purpose flour

2 3/4 cups oat bran

1 1/2 tbsp baking powder

method

1 Preheat the oven to 350°F/180°C. Line a 12-hole muffin pan with paper baking liners. Put the sugar into a pitcher and add the butter, buttermilk, eggs, half the honey, and lemon rind. Mix briefly to combine.

2 Sift the flour into a large mixing bowl, add the oat bran and baking powder, and stir to combine. Make a well in the center of the flour mixture and add the buttermilk mixture. Quickly mix together—do not overmix; the batter should be slightly lumpy.

3 Spoon the batter into the paper liners and bake in the preheated oven for 25 minutes. Turn out onto a wire rack.

4 Mix the lemon juice with the remaining honey in a small bowl or pitcher and drizzle over the muffins while they are still hot. Let the muffins stand for 10 minutes before serving.

easter cupcakes

ingredients

MAKES 12

1/2 cup butter, softened, or soft
    margarine
generous 1/2 cup superfine
    sugar
2 eggs, lightly beaten
generous 1/2 cup self-rising
    white flour
generous 1/4 cup unsweetened
    cocoa

topping

6 tbsp butter, softened
1 1/2 cups confectioners' sugar
1 tbsp milk
2–3 drops vanilla extract
9 1/2 oz/260 g mini chocolate
    candies
shell eggs

method

1 Preheat the oven to 350°F/180°C. Put 12 paper baking liners in a muffin pan, or put 12 double-layer paper liners on a baking sheet.

2 Put the butter and sugar in a bowl and beat together until light and fluffy. Gradually add the eggs, beating well after each addition. Sift in the flour and cocoa and, using a large metal spoon, fold into the mixture. Spoon the batter into the paper liners.

3 Bake the cupcakes in the preheated oven for 15–20 minutes, or until well risen and firm to the touch. Transfer to a wire rack and let cool.

4 To make the topping, put the butter in a bowl and beat until fluffy. Sift in the confectioners' sugar and beat together until well mixed, adding the milk and vanilla extract.

5 When the cupcakes are cold, put the frosting in a pastry bag, fitted with a large star tip, and pipe a circle around the edge of each cupcake to form a nest. Place chocolate eggs in the center of each nest to decorate.

halloween cupcakes

ingredients

MAKES 12

1/2 cup soft margarine

generous 1/2 cup superfine sugar

2 eggs

generous 3/4 cup self-rising white flour

topping

7 oz/200 g orange ready-to-roll colored fondant frosting

confectioners' sugar, for dusting

2 oz/55 g black ready-to-roll colored fondant frosting

black cake writing frosting

white cake writing frosting

method

1 Preheat the oven to 350ºF/180ºC. Put 12 paper baking liners in a muffin pan, or put 12 double-layer paper liners on a baking sheet.

2 Put the margarine, sugar, eggs, and flour in a bowl and, using an electric handheld mixer, beat together until smooth. Spoon the batter into the liners.

3 Bake the cupcakes in the preheated oven for 15–20 minutes, or until well risen, golden brown, and firm to the touch. Transfer to a wire rack and let cool.

4 When the cupcakes are cold, knead the orange frosting until pliable, then roll out on a counter dusted with confectioners' sugar. Using the palm of your hand, lightly rub confectioners' sugar into the frosting to prevent it from spotting. Using a 21/4-inch/ 5.5-cm plain round cutter, cut out 12 circles, rerolling the frosting as necessary. Place a circle on top of each cupcake.

5 Roll out the black frosting on a counter lightly dusted with confectioners' sugar. Using the palm of your hand, lightly rub confectioners' sugar into the frosting to prevent it from spotting. Using a 11/4-inch/3-cm plain round cutter, cut out 12 circles and place them on the center of the cupcakes. Using the black writing frosting, pipe eight legs onto each spider and, using the white writing frosting, draw two eyes and a mouth.

christmas cupcakes

ingredients

MAKES 16

generous 1 cup butter,
softened
1 cup superfine sugar
4–6 drops almond extract
4 eggs, lightly beaten
generous 1 cup self-rising
white flour
1³/₄ cups ground almonds

topping
1 lb/450 g white ready-to-roll
fondant frosting
2 oz/55 g green ready-to-roll
colored fondant frosting
1 oz/25 g red ready-to-roll
colored fondant frosting
confectioners' sugar,
for dusting

method

1 Preheat the oven to 350°F/180°C. Put 16 paper baking liners in a muffin pan.

2 Put the butter, sugar, and almond extract in a bowl and beat together until light and fluffy. Gradually add the eggs, beating well after each addition. Add the flour and, using a large metal spoon, fold it into the mixture, then fold in the ground almonds. Spoon the batter into the paper liners to fill them halfway.

3 Bake the cakes in the preheated oven for 20 minutes, or until well risen, golden brown, and firm to the touch. Transfer to a wire rack and let cool.

4 When the cakes are cold, knead the white frosting until pliable, then roll out on a counter lightly dusted with confectioners' sugar. Using a 2³/₄-inch/7-cm plain round cutter, cut out 16 circles, rerolling the frosting as necessary. Place a circle on top of each cupcake.

5 Roll out the green frosting on a counter lightly dusted with confectioners' sugar. Using the palm of your hand, rub confectioners' sugar into the frosting to prevent it from spotting. Using a holly leaf-shaped cutter, cut out 32 leaves, rerolling the frosting as necessary. Brush each leaf with a little cooled boiled water and place 2 leaves on top of each cake. Roll the red frosting between the palms of your hands to form 48 berries and place in the center of the leaves.

valentine heart cupcakes

ingredients

MAKES 6

6 tbsp butter, softened, or soft
    margarine
scant 1/2 cup superfine sugar
1/2 tsp vanilla extract
2 eggs, lightly beaten
1/2 cup all-purpose flour
1 tbsp unsweetened cocoa
1 tsp baking powder

marzipan hearts
1 1/4 oz/35 g marzipan
red food coloring (liquid
    or paste)
confectioners' sugar,
    for dusting

topping
4 tbsp butter, softened
1 cup confectioners' sugar
1 oz/25 g semisweet
    chocolate, melted
6 chocolate flower decorations

method

1 To make the hearts, knead the marzipan until pliable, then add a few drops of red coloring and knead until evenly colored red. Roll out the marzipan to a thickness of 1/4 inch/5 mm on a counter dusted with confectioners' sugar. Using a small heart-shaped cutter, cut out six hearts. Put these on a cookie sheet lined with wax paper and dusted with confectioners' sugar. Let dry for 3–4 hours.

2 To make the cupcakes, preheat the oven to 350°F/180°C. Put six paper baking liners in a muffin pan.

3 Put the butter, sugar, and vanilla extract in a bowl and beat together until light and fluffy. Gradually add the eggs, beating well after each addition. Sift in the flour, cocoa, and baking powder and, using a large metal spoon, fold into the mixture. Spoon the batter into the paper liners. Bake the cupcakes in the preheated oven for 20–25 minutes, or until well risen and firm to the touch. Transfer to a wire rack and let cool.

4 To make the topping, put the butter in a large bowl and beat until fluffy. Sift in the confectioners' sugar and beat together until smooth. Add the melted chocolate and beat together until well mixed. When the cakes are cold, spread the frosting on top of each cake and decorate with a chocolate flower.

cupcake wedding cake

ingredients

MAKES 48

2 cups butter, softened
1³/₄ cups superfine sugar
2 tsp vanilla extract
8 large eggs, lightly beaten
3 cups self-rising flour
²/₃ cup milk

topping

scant 5 cups confectioners'
 sugar
3–4 tbsp hot water
48 ready-made sugar roses,
 or 48 small fresh rosebuds
 gently rinsed and left to dry
 on paper towels

to assemble the cake

4 silver cake boards or
 1 x 20-inch/50-cm,
 1 x 16-inch/40-cm,
 1 x 12-inch/30-cm, and
 1 x 8-inch/20-cm
 sandblasted glass disks
 with polished edges
13 white or Perspex cake
 pillars
1 small bouquet of fresh
 flowers in a small vase

method

1 Preheat the oven to 350°F/180°C. Put 48 paper baking liners in a muffin pan, or put 48 double-layer paper liners on a baking sheet.

2 Put the butter, sugar, and vanilla extract in a bowl and beat together until light and fluffy. Gradually add the eggs, beating well after each addition. Add the flour and, using a large metal spoon, fold into the mixture with the milk. Spoon the batter into the paper liners.

3 Bake the cupcakes in the preheated oven for 15–20 minutes, or until well risen and firm to the touch. Transfer to a wire rack and let cool.

4 To make the topping, sift the confectioners' sugar into a large bowl. Add the hot water and stir until the mixture is smooth and thick enough to coat the back of a wooden spoon. Spoon the frosting on top of each cupcake. Store the cupcakes in an airtight container for up to one day.

5 To serve, carefully place a sugar rose or rosebud on top of each cupcake. To arrange the cupcakes, place the largest cake board on a table where the finished display is to be. Stand five pillars on the board and arrange some of the cupcakes on the base. Continue with the remaining boards, pillars (using only four pillars to support each remaining tier), and cupcakes to make four tiers, standing the bouquet in the center of the top tier.

christening cupcakes

ingredients

MAKES 24

1 3/4 cups butter, softened
2 cups superfine sugar
finely grated rind of 2 lemons
8 eggs, lightly beaten
generous 2 3/4 cups self-rising
    white flour

topping

3 cups confectioners' sugar
6–8 tbsp hot water
red or blue food coloring
    (liquid or paste)
24 sugared almonds

method

1 Preheat the oven to 350°F/180°C. Put 24 paper baking liners in a muffin pan.

2 Put the butter, sugar, and lemon rind in a bowl and beat together until light and fluffy. Gradually add the eggs, beating well after each addition. Add the flour and, using a large metal spoon, fold into the mixture. Spoon the batter into the paper liners, filling them halfway.

3 Bake the cupcakes in the preheated oven for 20–25 minutes, or until well risen, golden brown, and firm to the touch. Transfer to a wire rack and let cool.

4 When the cakes are cold, make the topping. Sift the confectioners' sugar into a bowl. Add the hot water and stir until the mixture is smooth and thick enough to coat the back of a wooden spoon. Dip a skewer into the red or blue food coloring, then stir it into the frosting until it is evenly colored pink or pale blue.

5 Spoon the frosting on top of each cupcake. Top each with a sugared almond and let set for about 30 minutes before serving.

birthday party cupcakes

ingredients

MAKES 24

1 cup soft margarine

scant 1¹/₄ cups superfine
sugar

4 eggs

generous 1¹/₂ cups self-rising
white flour

topping

³/₄ cup butter, softened

3 cups confectioners' sugar

a variety of small candies
and chocolates, sugar-
coated chocolates, dried
fruits, edible sugar flower
shapes, cake decorating
sprinkles, silver dragées
(cake decoration balls),
and sugar strands

various colored tubes of
writing frosting

24 birthday cake candles
(optional)

method

1 Preheat the oven to 350°F/180°C. Put
24 paper baking liners in a muffin pan, or put
24 double-layer paper liners on a baking sheet.

2 Put the margarine, sugar, eggs, and flour in
a large bowl and, using an electric handheld
mixer, beat together until just smooth. Spoon
the batter into the paper liners.

3 Bake the cupcakes in the preheated oven
for 15–20 minutes, or until well risen, golden
brown, and firm to the touch. Transfer to a wire
rack and let cool.

4 To make the frosting, put the butter in a bowl
and beat until fluffy. Sift in the confectioners'
sugar and beat together until smooth and
creamy.

5 When the cupcakes are cold, spread the
frosting on top of each cupcake, then decorate
to your choice and, if desired, place a candle in
the top of each.

gold & silver anniversary cupcakes

ingredients

MAKES 24

1 cup butter, softened
generous 1 cup superfine
    sugar
1 tsp vanilla extract
4 large eggs, lightly beaten
generous 1½ cups self-rising
    flour
5 tbsp milk

topping

¾ cup unsalted butter
3 cups confectioners' sugar
silver or gold dragées
    (cake decoration balls)

method

1 Preheat the oven to 350°F/180°C. Put 24 silver or gold foil cake liners in muffin pans, or arrange them on baking sheets.

2 Put the butter, sugar, and vanilla extract in a bowl and beat together until light and fluffy. Gradually add the eggs, beating well after each addition. Add the flour and, using a large metal spoon, fold into the mixture with the milk. Spoon the batter into the foil liners.

3 Bake the cupcakes in the preheated oven for 15–20 minutes, or until well risen and firm to the touch. Transfer to a wire rack and let cool.

4 To make the topping, put the butter in a large bowl and beat until fluffy. Sift in the confectioners' sugar and beat together until well mixed. Put the topping in a pastry bag fitted with a medium star-shaped tip.

5 When the cupcakes are cold, pipe frosting on top of each cupcake to cover the tops. Sprinkle over the dragées before serving.

feather-frosted coffee cupcakes

ingredients

MAKES 16

1 tbsp instant coffee granules

1 tbsp boiling water

1/2 cup butter, softened, or soft margarine

generous 1/2 cup firmly packed brown sugar

2 eggs

generous 3/4 cup self-rising white flour

1/2 tsp baking powder

2 tbsp sour cream

frosting

2 cups confectioners' sugar

4 tsp warm water

1 tsp instant coffee granules, dissolved in 2 tsp boiling water

method

1 Preheat the oven to 375°F/190°C. Put 16 paper baking liners in a muffin pan, or put 16 double-layer paper liners on a baking sheet.

2 Put the coffee granules in a cup or small bowl, add the boiling water, and stir until dissolved. Let cool slightly.

3 Put the butter, sugar, and eggs in a bowl. Sift in the flour and baking powder, then beat the ingredients together until smooth. Add the dissolved coffee and the sour cream and beat together until well mixed. Spoon the batter into the paper liners. Bake the cupcakes in the preheated oven for 20 minutes, until well risen and golden brown. Let cool on a wire rack.

4 To make the frosting, sift 3/4 cup of the confectioners' sugar into a bowl, then gradually mix in the warm water to make a coating consistency that will cover the back of a wooden spoon. Sift the remaining confectioners' sugar into a bowl, then stir in the dissolved coffee granules. Spoon the frosting into a pastry bag fitted with a piping tip. When the cupcakes are cold, coat the tops with the white frosting, then quickly pipe the coffee frosting in parallel lines on top. Using a skewer, draw it across the piped lines in both directions and let set.

small bites

Brownies, squares, slices, bars, tartlets and all kinds of little cakes are quick and easy to make—and even quicker and easier to eat. These tasty sweet snacks run the gamut of textures and flavors—rich gooey chocolate, light zesty citrus, chewy crunchy nuts, moist crumbly spices, and fragrant succulent berries. There is certainly something for everyone from after-school snacks to a coffee morning with the neighbors.

Many of these recipes are so simple and have such speedy results that they are a great way to introduce children to cooking and to occupy a rainy afternoon—real quality time. They also make the perfect contribution to the cake stall at fund-raisers, especially as many of them can be cooked in advance and frozen. A batch of homemade brownies can be rustled up in no time, yet will make visitors feel welcome and right at home and they make fabulous picnic or lunch-box treats. Pretty little frosted cakes, fruit tartlets, shortcake, and éclairs require slightly more effort and time, but it's well spent and they may even tempt you to reintroduce the old-fashioned custom of afternoon tea—you don't have to have a silver teapot and a butler to make this a truly delightful occasion.

Because these small bites usually bake quickly, it is important to keep an eye on them. Even a few minutes too long in the oven can result in unattractive crusty edges. If using a fan oven, reduce the oven temperature slightly and don't switch the fan on until halfway through the cooking time.

chocolate brownies

ingredients

MAKES 12

butter, for greasing

1/3 cup unsweetened pitted dates, chopped

1/3 cup plumped dried prunes, chopped

6 tbsp unsweetened apple juice

4 eggs, beaten

1 1/2 cups firmly packed brown sugar

1 tsp vanilla extract

4 tbsp lowfat drinking chocolate powder, plus extra for dusting

2 tbsp unsweetened cocoa

1 1/4 cups all-purpose flour

1/3 cup semisweet chocolate chips

frosting

generous 1 cup confectioners' sugar

1–2 tsp water

1 tsp vanilla extract

method

1 Preheat the oven to 350°F/180°C. Grease and line a 7 x 11 inch/18 x 28 cm cake pan with parchment paper. Place the dates and prunes in a small saucepan and add the apple juice. Bring to a boil, cover, and let simmer for 10 minutes, until soft. Beat to form a smooth paste, then let cool.

2 Place the cooled fruit in a mixing bowl and stir in the eggs, sugar, and vanilla extract. Sift in the drinking chocolate powder, cocoa, and flour, and fold in along with the chocolate chips until well incorporated.

3 Spoon the batter into the prepared pan and smooth over the top. Bake in the preheated oven for 25–30 minutes, until firm to the touch or until a skewer inserted into the center comes out clean. Cut into 12 bars and let cool in the pan for 10 minutes. Transfer to a wire rack to cool completely.

4 To make the frosting, sift the sugar into a bowl and mix with enough water and the vanilla extract to form a soft, but not too runny, frosting. Drizzle the frosting over the chocolate brownies and let set. Dust with chocolate powder before serving.

super mocha brownies

ingredients

MAKES 12

5 1/2 oz/150 g good-quality
     semisweet chocolate
scant 1/2 cup dairy-free
     margarine, plus extra
     for greasing
1 tsp strong instant coffee
1 tsp vanilla extract
1 cup ground almonds
scant 1 cup superfine sugar
4 eggs, separated
confectioners' sugar,
     to decorate (optional)

method

1 Preheat the oven to 350°F/180°C. Grease an 8-inch/20-cm square cake pan and line the bottom.

2 Melt the chocolate and margarine in a heatproof bowl placed over a saucepan of gently simmering water, making sure that the bottom of the bowl does not touch the water. Stir very occasionally, until the chocolate and margarine have melted and are smooth.

3 Carefully remove the bowl from the heat. Let cool slightly, then stir in the coffee and vanilla extract. Add the almonds and sugar and mix well until combined. Lightly beat the egg yolks in a separate bowl, then stir into the chocolate mixture.

4 Beat the egg whites in a large bowl until stiff peaks form. Gently fold a large spoonful of the egg whites into the chocolate mixture, then fold in the remainder until completely incorporated.

5 Spoon the mixture into the prepared pan and bake in the preheated oven for 35–40 minutes, or until risen and firm on top but still slightly gooey in the center. Let cool in the pan, then turn out, remove the lining paper, and cut into 12 pieces. Dust with confectioners' sugar before serving, if liked.

pecan brownies

ingredients

MAKES 20

2¹/2 oz/70 g bittersweet
    chocolate
scant 1 cup all-purpose flour
³/4 tsp baking soda
¹/4 tsp baking powder
¹/3 cup pecans
1 cup unsalted butter, plus
    extra for greasing
¹/2 cup raw sugar
¹/2 tsp almond extract
1 egg
1 tsp milk

method

1 Preheat the oven to 350°F/180°C. Grease a large baking dish and line it with parchment paper.

2 Put the chocolate in a heatproof bowl set over a saucepan of gently simmering water and heat until it is melted. Meanwhile, sift together the flour, baking soda, and baking powder into a large bowl.

3 Finely chop the pecans and set aside. In a separate bowl, beat together the butter and sugar, then mix in the almond extract and the egg. Remove the chocolate from the heat and stir into the butter mixture. Add the flour mixture, milk, and chopped nuts to the bowl and stir until well combined.

4 Spoon the mixture into the prepared dish and smooth it. Transfer to the preheated oven and cook for 30 minutes, or until firm to the touch (it should still be a little soft in the center). Remove from the oven and let cool completely. Cut into 20 squares and serve.

no-bake chocolate squares

ingredients

MAKES 16

9 1/2 oz/275 g semisweet
  chocolate
3/4 cup butter
4 tbsp golden syrup
2 tbsp dark rum (optional)
6 oz/175 g plain cookies
1/3 cup toasted rice cereal
generous 1/4 cup chopped
  walnuts or pecans
generous 1/2 cup candied
  cherries, coarsely chopped
1 oz/25 g white chocolate,
  to decorate

method

1 Line a 7-inch/18-cm square cake pan with parchment paper. Place the semisweet chocolate in a large bowl with the butter, syrup, and rum, if using, and set over a saucepan of gently simmering water until melted, stirring continuously, until blended.

2 Break the cookies into small pieces and stir into the chocolate mixture with the rice cereal, nuts, and cherries.

3 Pour the batter into the pan and level the top, pressing down well with the back of a spoon. Let chill in the refrigerator for 2 hours.

4 To decorate, melt the white chocolate and drizzle it over the top of the cake in a random pattern. Let set. To serve, carefully turn out of the pan and remove the parchment paper. Cut into 16 squares and serve.

chocolate peanut butter squares

ingredients

MAKES 20

10 1/2 oz/300 g milk chocolate
2 1/2 cups all-purpose flour
1 tsp baking powder
1 cup butter
1 3/4 cups light brown sugar
2 cups rolled oats
1/2 cup chopped mixed nuts
1 egg, beaten
1 1/3 cups canned sweetened
    condensed milk
1/3 cup crunchy peanut butter

method

1 Preheat the oven to 350°F/180°C.

2 Finely chop the chocolate. Sift the flour and baking powder into a large bowl. Add the butter to the flour mixture and rub in using your fingertips, until the mixture resembles bread crumbs. Stir in the sugar, oats, and nuts.

3 Put a quarter of the mixture into a bowl and stir in the chocolate. Set aside.

4 Stir the egg into the remaining mixture and press into the bottom of a 12 x 8-inch/ 30 x 20-cm cake pan. Bake in the preheated oven for 15 minutes. Meanwhile, mix the condensed milk and peanut butter together. Pour into the cake pan and spread evenly, then sprinkle the reserved chocolate mixture on top and press down lightly.

5 Return to the oven and bake for an additional 20 minutes, until golden brown. Let cool in the pan, then cut into squares.

chocolate caramel shortbread

ingredients

MAKES 12

1/2 cup butter, plus extra for greasing

generous 1 cup all-purpose flour

generous 1/4 cup superfine sugar

filling and topping

3/4 cup butter

generous 1/2 cup superfine sugar

3 tbsp dark corn syrup

1 1/3 cups canned sweetened condensed milk

7 oz/200 g semisweet chocolate, broken into pieces

method

1 Preheat the oven to 350°F/180°C. Grease a 9-inch/23-cm shallow square cake pan and line the bottom with parchment paper.

2 Place the butter, flour, and sugar in a food processor and process until it starts to bind together. Press into the prepared pan and level the top. Bake in the preheated oven for 20–25 minutes, or until golden.

3 Meanwhile, make the caramel. Place the butter, sugar, corn syrup, and condensed milk in a heavy-bottom saucepan. Heat gently until the sugar has dissolved. Bring to a boil, then reduce the heat and let simmer for 6–8 minutes, stirring, until very thick. Pour over the shortbread and let chill in the refrigerator for 2 hours, or until firm.

4 Place the chocolate in a heatproof bowl set over a saucepan of gently simmering water and stir until melted. Let cool slightly, then spread over the caramel. Let chill in the refrigerator for 2 hours, or until set. Cut the shortbread into 12 pieces using a sharp knife and serve.

chocolate peppermint slices

ingredients

MAKES 16

4 tbsp unsalted butter, plus
   extra for greasing
1/4 cup superfine sugar
2/3 cup all-purpose flour
1 1/4 cups confectioners' sugar
1–2 tbsp warm water
1/2 tsp peppermint extract
6 oz/175 g bittersweet
   chocolate, broken
   into pieces

method

1 Preheat the oven to 350°F/180°C. Grease an 8 x 12-inch/20 x 30-cm jelly roll pan and line with parchment paper. Beat the butter and sugar together until pale and fluffy. Stir in the flour until the mixture binds together.

2 Knead the mixture to form a smooth dough, then press into the prepared pan. Prick the surface all over with a fork. Bake in the preheated oven for 10–15 minutes, or until lightly browned and just firm to the touch. Remove from the oven and let cool in the pan.

3 Sift the confectioners' sugar into a bowl. Gradually add the water, then add the peppermint extract. Spread the frosting over the base, then let set.

4 Melt the chocolate in a heatproof bowl set over a saucepan of gently simmering water, then remove from the heat and spread over the frosting. Let set, then cut into slices.

chocolate butterfly cakes

ingredients

MAKES 12

8 tbsp soft margarine

$\frac{1}{2}$ cup superfine sugar

generous 1$\frac{1}{2}$ cups self-rising white flour

2 large eggs

2 tbsp unsweetened cocoa

1 oz/25 g semisweet chocolate, melted

sifted confectioners' sugar, for dusting

filling

6 tbsp butter, softened

1$\frac{1}{2}$ cups confectioners' sugar

1 oz/25 g semisweet chocolate, melted

method

1 Preheat the oven to 350°F/180°C. Put 12 paper baking liners in a muffin pan, or put 12 double-layer paper liners on a baking sheet.

2 Put the margarine, sugar, flour, eggs, and cocoa in a large bowl and, using an electric handheld mixer, beat together until just smooth. Beat in the melted chocolate. Spoon the batter into the paper liners, filling them three-quarters full.

3 Bake the cupcakes in the preheated oven for 15 minutes, or until springy to the touch. Transfer to a wire rack and let cool.

4 To make the filling, put the butter in a bowl and beat until fluffy. Sift in the confectioners' sugar and beat together until smooth. Add the melted chocolate and beat together until well mixed.

5 When the cupcakes are cold, use a serrated knife to cut a circle from the top of each cake and then cut each circle in half. Spread or pipe a little of the buttercream into the center of each cupcake and press the two semicircular halves into it at an angle to resemble butterfly wings. Dust with confectioners' sugar before serving.

chocolate tartlets

ingredients

MAKES 4

1 quantity sweet pie dough
5$\frac{1}{2}$ squares bittersweet
  chocolate, broken into
  pieces
scant $\frac{1}{2}$ cup butter
scant $\frac{1}{2}$ cup whipping cream
1 large egg
scant $\frac{1}{8}$ cup superfine sugar
unsweetened cocoa,
  to decorate
sour cream, to serve

method

1 Preheat the oven to 400°F/200°C with a baking sheet inside. Prepare the pastry, roll it out, and use to line four 4$\frac{1}{2}$-inch/12-cm loose-bottom tart pans, leaving the excess pastry hanging over the edges. Line the pastry shells with larger pieces of wax paper, then fill with dried beans. Put the pans on the baking sheet and bake in the preheated oven for 5 minutes, or until the pastry rims look set. Remove the paper and beans and return the pastry shells to the oven for an additional 5 minutes, or until the pastry looks dry. Remove the tart shells from the oven, then let them stand on the baking sheet and reduce the oven temperature to 350°F/180°C.

2 Meanwhile, place the chocolate in a heatproof bowl set over a saucepan of simmering water. Add the butter and cream and leave until the chocolate and butter melt. Beat the egg and sugar together until light and fluffy. Remove the chocolate mixture from the heat and stir until smooth, then stir it into the egg mixture. Carefully pour the filling into the tart shells, then transfer to the oven and bake for 15 minutes, or until the filling is set. If the pastry looks as though it is becoming too brown, cover with foil.

3 Transfer to a wire rack to cool completely before rolling a rolling pin over the edges to remove the excess pastry. To serve, remove from the pans, transfer to individual plates, dust with cocoa, and serve with sour cream.

chocolate temptations

ingredients

MAKES 24

12$\frac{1}{2}$ oz/350 g bittersweet
     chocolate
$\frac{3}{4}$ cup unsalted butter, plus
     extra for greasing
1 tsp strong coffee
2 eggs
$\frac{3}{4}$ cup soft brown sugar
scant 1$\frac{1}{4}$ cups all-purpose
     flour
$\frac{1}{4}$ tsp baking powder
pinch of salt
2 tsp almond extract
$\frac{1}{2}$ cup Brazil nuts, chopped
$\frac{1}{2}$ cup hazelnuts, chopped
1$\frac{1}{2}$ oz/40 g white chocolate

method

1 Preheat the oven to 350°F/180°C. Place 8 oz/225 g of the bittersweet chocolate, the butter, and coffee in a heatproof bowl set over a saucepan of gently simmering water and heat until the chocolate is almost melted.

2 Meanwhile, beat the eggs in a bowl until fluffy. Gradually whisk in the sugar until thick. Remove the chocolate from the heat and stir until smooth. Add to the egg mixture and stir until combined.

3 Sift the flour, baking powder, and salt into a bowl, then stir into the chocolate mixture. Chop 3 oz/85 g of the remaining bittersweet chocolate into pieces and stir into the mixture. Stir in the almond extract and chopped nuts.

4 Put 24 tablespoonfuls of the mixture onto one or two large, greased cookie sheets, then transfer to the preheated oven and bake for 16 minutes. Remove from the oven and transfer to a wire rack to cool.

5 To decorate, melt the remaining chocolate in turn, then spoon into a pastry bag and pipe thin lines onto the cookies.

chocolate fudge brownies

ingredients

MAKES 16

scant 1 cup lowfat cream
  cheese
$1/2$ tsp vanilla extract
generous 1 cup superfine
  sugar
2 eggs
generous $1/3$ cup butter, plus
  extra for greasing
3 tbsp unsweetened cocoa
$3/4$ cup self-rising flour, sifted
$1/3$ cup chopped pecans

frosting
4 tbsp butter
1 tbsp milk
$2/3$ cup confectioners' sugar
2 tbsp unsweetened cocoa
pecans, to decorate (optional)

method

1 Preheat the oven to 350°F/180°C. Lightly grease an 8-inch/20-cm square shallow cake pan and line the bottom.

2 Beat together the cheese, vanilla extract, and 5 teaspoons of sugar until smooth, then set aside.

3 Beat the eggs and remaining sugar together until light and fluffy. Place the butter and cocoa in a small saucepan and heat gently, stirring until the butter melts and the mixture combines, then stir it into the egg mixture. Fold in the flour and nuts.

4 Pour half of the cake batter into the pan and smooth the top. Carefully spread the cream cheese over it, then cover it with the remaining cake batter. Bake in the preheated oven for 40–45 minutes. Let cool in the pan.

5 To make the frosting, melt the butter in the milk. Stir in the sugar and cocoa. Spread the frosting over the brownies and decorate with pecans, if using. Let the frosting set, then cut into squares to serve.

chocolate crispy bites

ingredients

MAKES 16

white layer

4 tbsp butter, plus extra for
    greasing
1 tbsp corn syrup
$5^1/_2$ oz/150 g white chocolate
2 cups toasted rice cereal

dark layer

4 tbsp butter
2 tbsp corn syrup
$4^1/_2$ oz/125 g semisweet
    chocolate, broken into
    small pieces
3 cups toasted rice cereal

method

1 Grease an 8-inch/20-cm square cake pan and line with parchment paper.

2 To make the white layer, melt the butter, corn syrup, and chocolate in a bowl set over a saucepan of gently simmering water.

3 Remove from the heat and stir in the rice cereal until it is well combined.

4 Press into the prepared pan and smooth the surface.

5 To make the dark layer, melt the butter, corn syrup, and semisweet chocolate in a bowl set over a saucepan of gently simmering water.

6 Remove from the heat and stir in the rice cereal. Pour the semisweet chocolate over the hardened white chocolate layer, let cool, then let chill until hardened.

7 Turn out of the cake pan and cut into small squares, using a sharp knife.

chocolate parfait slices

ingredients

MAKES 4

3 large egg whites

3/4 cup superfine sugar

5 oz/140 g white chocolate, grated

13/4 cups whipping cream, whipped

12 oz/350 g prepared puff pastry sheets

melted semisweet chocolate, for drizzling

method

1 To make the parfait, beat the egg whites and the sugar together in a heatproof bowl, then set the bowl over a saucepan of gently simmering water. Using an electric mixer, beat the whites over the heat until you have a light and fluffy meringue. This will take up to 10 minutes. Remove from the heat, add the chocolate, and keep beating to cool. Fold in the whipping cream.

2 Spoon the parfait into a shallow rectangular freezerproof container and freeze for 5–6 hours.

3 Meanwhile, preheat the oven to 350°F/180°C and line a cookie sheet with parchment paper. Cut the dough into regular-size rectangles to accommodate a slice of the parfait. Place the rectangles on the sheet and top with another cookie sheet, which will keep the pastry flat but crisp. Bake in the preheated oven for 15 minutes, transfer to a wire rack, and let cool.

4 About 20 minutes before you are ready to serve, remove the parfait from the freezer. When it has softened, cut the parfait into slices and put each slice between two pieces of pastry to make a "sandwich." Drizzle with semisweet chocolate before serving.

italian fruit cake

ingredients

SERVES 12–16

butter, for greasing

1/4 cup candied cherries, quartered

2/3 cup mixed candied orange and lemon peel, finely chopped

2 tbsp candied ginger, coarsely chopped

1 cup slivered almonds

3/4 cup hazelnuts, toasted and coarsely ground

3/8 cup all-purpose flour

1/4 cup unsweetened cocoa

1 tsp ground cinnamon

1/4 tsp ground cloves

1/4 tsp ground nutmeg

1/4 tsp ground coriander

1/3 cup honey

generous 1/2 cup golden superfine sugar

1 tsp orange flower water

confectioners' sugar, for dusting

method

1 Preheat the oven to 325°F/160°C. Thoroughly grease the bottom of an 8-inch/20-cm loose-bottom cake pan or tart pan. Line the bottom with nonstick parchment paper. Place the cherries, candied peel, ginger, almonds, and hazelnuts in a bowl. Sift in the flour, cocoa, cinnamon, cloves, nutmeg, and coriander and mix. Set aside.

2 Place the honey, sugar, and orange flower water in a saucepan and heat gently until the sugar has dissolved. Bring the mixture to a boil and boil steadily until a temperature of 241°F/116°C has been reached on a sugar thermometer, or a small amount of the mixture forms a soft ball when dropped into cold water.

3 Quickly remove the pan from the heat and stir in the dry ingredients. Mix thoroughly and turn into the prepared pan. Spread evenly and bake in the preheated oven for 30 minutes. Let cool in the pan. Turn out and carefully peel away the lining paper. Dust confectioners' sugar lightly over the top and cut into wedges to serve.

refrigerator cake

ingredients

MAKES 12

1/3 cup raisins

2 tbsp brandy

4 oz/115 g semisweet
    chocolate, broken into
    pieces

4 oz/115 g milk chocolate,
    broken into pieces

4 tbsp butter, plus extra
    for greasing

2 tbsp corn syrup

6 oz/175 g graham crackers,
    coarsely broken

1/2 cup slivered almonds,
    lightly toasted

1/8 cup candied cherries,
    chopped

topping

3 1/2 oz/100 g semisweet
    chocolate, broken into
    pieces

scant 2 tbsp butter

method

1 Grease a 7-inch/18-cm shallow square pan
and line the bottom. Place the raisins and
brandy in a bowl and let soak for 30 minutes.
Put the chocolate, butter, and syrup in a
saucepan and heat gently until melted.

2 Stir in the graham crackers, almonds, cherries,
raisins, and brandy. Turn into the prepared pan
and let cool. Cover and let chill in the refrigerator
for 1 hour.

3 To make the topping, place the chocolate and
butter in a small heatproof bowl and set over
a saucepan of gently simmering water until
melted. Stir and pour the chocolate mixture
over the cookie base. Let chill in the refrigerator
for 8 hours, or overnight. Cut into bars or
squares to serve.

malted chocolate wedges

ingredients

MAKES 16

6 tbsp butter, plus extra
   for greasing
2 tbsp corn syrup
2 tbsp malted chocolate drink
8 oz/225 g malted milk
   cookies
2³/₄ oz/75 g light or semisweet
   chocolate, broken into
   pieces
2 tbsp confectioners' sugar
2 tbsp milk

method

1 Grease a shallow 7-inch/18-cm round cake pan or tart pan and line the bottom.

2 Place the butter, corn syrup, and malted chocolate drink in a small saucepan and heat gently, stirring all the time, until the butter has melted and the mixture is well combined.

3 Crush the cookies in a plastic bag with a rolling pin, or process them in a food processor. Stir the cookie crumbs into the chocolate mixture and mix well.

4 Press the mixture into the prepared pan and chill in the refrigerator until firm.

5 Place the chocolate pieces in a small heatproof bowl with the sugar and the milk. Place the bowl over a saucepan of gently simmering water and stir until the chocolate melts and the mixture is combined.

6 Spread the chocolate frosting over the cookie base and let the frosting set in the pan. Using a sharp knife, cut into wedges to serve.

white chocolate brownies

ingredients

MAKES 9

8 squares white chocolate

3/4 cup walnut pieces

1/2 cup unsalted butter, plus
    extra for greasing

2 eggs

generous 1/2 cup soft brown
    sugar

generous 2/3 cup self-rising
    flour

method

1 Preheat the oven to 350°F/180°C. Lightly grease a 7-inch/18-cm square cake pan.

2 Coarsely chop six squares of white chocolate and all the walnuts. Put the remaining chocolate and the butter in a heatproof bowl set over a saucepan of gently simmering water. When melted, stir together, then set aside to cool slightly.

3 Beat the eggs and sugar together, then beat in the cooled chocolate mixture until well mixed. Fold in the flour, chopped chocolate, and walnuts. Turn the mixture into the prepared pan and smooth the surface.

4 Transfer the pan to the preheated oven and bake for 30 minutes, or until just set. The mixture should still be a little soft in the center. Remove from the oven and let cool in the pan, then cut into nine squares before serving.

white chocolate tarts

ingredients

MAKES 12

generous 1 cup all-purpose
    flour, plus extra for dusting
2 tbsp golden superfine sugar
scant 3/4 cup chilled butter,
    diced
2 egg yolks
2 tbsp cold water
semisweet chocolate curls,
    to decorate
unsweetened cocoa,
    for dusting

filling

1 vanilla bean
1 3/4 cups heavy cream
12 oz/350 g white chocolate,
    broken into pieces

method

1 Place the flour and sugar in a bowl. Add the butter and rub it in until the mixture resembles fine bread crumbs. Place the egg yolks and water in a separate bowl and mix together. Stir into the dry ingredients and mix to form a dough. Knead for 1 minute, or until smooth. Wrap in plastic wrap and let chill for 20 minutes.

2 Preheat the oven to 400°F/200°C. Roll out the dough on a floured counter and use to line 12 tartlet molds. Prick the bottoms, cover, and let chill for 15 minutes. Line the shells with foil and dried beans and bake for 10 minutes. Remove the beans and foil and cook for an additional 5 minutes. Let cool.

3 To make the filling, split the vanilla bean lengthwise and scrape out the black seeds with a knife. Place the seeds in a saucepan with the cream and heat until almost boiling. Place the chocolate in a heatproof bowl and pour over the hot cream. Keep stirring until smooth. Beat the mixture with an electric mixer until thickened and the beaters leave a trail when lifted. Let chill in the refrigerator for 30 minutes, then beat until soft peaks form. Divide the filling between the pastry shells and let chill for 30 minutes. Decorate with chocolate curls and dust with cocoa.

mocha brownies

ingredients

MAKES 16

4 tbsp butter, plus extra
  for greasing
4 oz/115 g semisweet
  chocolate, broken into
  pieces
scant 1 cup brown sugar
2 eggs
1 tbsp instant coffee powder
  dissolved in 1 tbsp hot
  water, cooled
scant 2/3 cup all-purpose flour
1/2 tsp baking powder
1/3 cup coarsely chopped
  pecans

method

1 Preheat the oven to 350°F/180°C. Grease and line the bottom of an 8-inch/20-cm square cake pan. Place the chocolate and butter in a heavy-bottom saucepan over low heat until melted. Stir and let cool.

2 Place the sugar and eggs in a large bowl and cream together until light and fluffy. Fold in the chocolate mixture and cooled coffee and mix thoroughly. Sift in the flour and baking powder and lightly fold into the mixture, then carefully fold in the pecans.

3 Pour the batter into the prepared pan and bake in the preheated oven for 25–30 minutes, or until firm and a skewer inserted into the center comes out clean.

4 Let cool in the pan for a few minutes, then run a knife around the edge of the cake to loosen it. Turn the cake out onto a wire rack and peel off the lining paper. Let cool completely. When cold, cut into squares.

mocha brownies with sour cream frosting

ingredients

MAKES 9

4 oz/115 g semisweet
　　chocolate, broken into
　　pieces
4 tbsp butter, plus extra
　　for greasing
3/4 cup dark brown sugar
2 eggs
2 tbsp strong coffee, cooled
generous 1/2 cup all-purpose
　　flour
1/2 tsp baking powder
pinch of salt
1/4 cup shelled walnuts,
　　chopped

frosting

4 oz/115 g semisweet
　　chocolate, broken into
　　pieces
2/3 cup sour cream

method

1 Preheat the oven to 350°F/180°C. Grease an 8-inch/20-cm square cake pan with butter and line with parchment paper.

2 Place the chocolate and butter in a small heatproof bowl and set over a saucepan of gently simmering water until melted. Stir until smooth. Remove from the heat and let cool.

3 Beat the sugar and eggs together until pale and thick. Fold in the chocolate mixture and coffee. Mix well. Sift the flour, baking powder, and salt into the cake batter and fold in. Fold in the walnuts. Pour the cake batter into the pan and bake in the preheated oven for 20–25 minutes, or until set. Let cool in the pan.

4 To make the frosting, melt the chocolate. Stir in the sour cream and beat until evenly blended. Spoon the topping over the brownies and make a swirling pattern with a spatula. Let set in a cool place. Cut into squares, then remove from the pan and serve.

cappuccino squares

ingredients

MAKES 15

generous 1¹/₂ cups self-rising
 flour

1 tsp baking powder

1 tsp unsweetened cocoa,
 plus extra for dusting

1 cup butter, softened, plus
 extra for greasing

generous 1 cup golden
 superfine sugar

4 eggs, beaten

3 tbsp instant coffee powder,
 dissolved in 2 tbsp
 hot water

frosting

4 oz/115 g white chocolate,
 broken into pieces

4 tbsp butter, softened

3 tbsp milk

1³/₄ cups confectioners' sugar

method

1 Preheat the oven to 350°F/180°C. Grease and line the bottom of a shallow 11 x 7-inch/ 28 x 18-cm cake pan.

2 Sift the flour, baking powder, and cocoa into a bowl and add the butter, sugar, eggs, and coffee. Beat well, by hand or with an electric mixer, until smooth, then spoon into the pan and smooth the top.

3 Bake in the preheated oven for 35–40 minutes, or until risen and firm. Let cool in the pan for 10 minutes, then turn out onto a wire rack and peel off the lining paper. Let cool completely.

4 To make the frosting, place the chocolate, butter, and milk in a bowl set over a saucepan of simmering water and stir until the chocolate has melted.

5 Remove the bowl from the pan and sift in the confectioners' sugar. Beat until smooth, then spread over the cake. Dust the top of the cake with sifted cocoa, then cut into squares.

chocolate coconut layers

ingredients

MAKES 9

8 oz/225 g chocolate graham
   crackers

6 tbsp unsalted butter or
   margarine, plus extra
   for greasing

scant 1 cup canned
   evaporated milk

1 egg, beaten

1 tsp vanilla extract

2 tbsp superfine sugar

$1/3$ cup self-rising flour, sifted

$1^1/3$ cups dry unsweetened
   coconut

$1^3/4$ oz/50 g semisweet
   chocolate (optional)

method

1 Preheat the oven to 375°F/190°C. Crush the crackers in a plastic bag with a rolling pin or process them in a food processor. Melt the butter in a pan and stir in the crushed crackers thoroughly. Remove from the heat and press the mixture into the bottom of a shallow 8-inch/20-cm square cake pan lined with parchment paper.

2 In a separate bowl, beat together the evaporated milk, egg, vanilla extract, and sugar until smooth. Stir in the flour and coconut. Pour over the cracker layer and use a spatula to smooth the top.

3 Bake in a preheated oven for 30 minutes, or until the coconut topping has become firm and just golden. Remove from the oven and let cool in the pan for about 5 minutes, then cut into squares. Let cool completely in the pan.

4 Carefully remove the squares from the pan and place them on a cutting board. Melt the semisweet chocolate, if using, and drizzle it over the squares to decorate them. Let the chocolate set before serving.

chocolate chip & walnut slices

ingredients

MAKES 18

1 cup walnut pieces

1 cup butter, plus extra for greasing

1 cup superfine sugar

few drops vanilla extract

2 cups all-purpose flour

1 cup semisweet chocolate chips

method

1 Preheat the oven to 350°F/180°C. Grease an 8 x 12-inch/20 x 30-cm jelly roll pan. Coarsely chop the walnut pieces to about the same size as the chocolate chips.

2 Beat the butter and sugar together until pale and fluffy. Add the vanilla extract, then stir in the flour. Stir in the walnuts and chocolate chips. Press the mixture into the prepared pan.

3 Bake in the preheated oven for 20–25 minutes, until golden brown. Let cool in the pan, then cut into slices.

coconut bars

ingredients

MAKES 10

generous 1/2 cup butter, plus
    extra for greasing
generous 1 cup superfine
    sugar
2 eggs, beaten
finely grated rind of 1 orange
3 tbsp orange juice
2/3 cup sour cream
1 1/4 cups self-rising flour
1 cup dry unsweetened
    coconut
toasted long shred coconut,
    to decorate

frosting

1 egg white
1 3/4 cups confectioners' sugar
1 cup dry unsweetened
    coconut
about 1 tbsp orange juice

method

1 Preheat the oven to 350°F/180°C. Grease a 9-inch/23-cm square cake pan and line the bottom with nonstick parchment paper.

2 Cream together the butter and sugar until pale and fluffy, then gradually beat in the eggs. Stir in the orange rind, orange juice, and sour cream. Fold in the flour and dry unsweetened coconut evenly using a metal spoon.

3 Spoon the batter into the prepared cake pan and level the surface. Bake in the preheated oven for 35–40 minutes, or until risen and firm to the touch.

4 Let cool for 10 minutes in the pan, then turn out and finish cooling on a wire rack.

5 For the frosting, lightly beat the egg white, just enough to break it up, and stir in the sugar and dry unsweetened coconut, adding enough orange juice to mix to a thick paste. Spread over the top of the cake, sprinkle with long shred coconut, then let set before slicing into bars.

coconut oat bars

ingredients

MAKES 16

generous ³/₄ cup unsalted
    butter, plus extra for
    greasing
1 cup raw sugar
2 tbsp corn syrup
scant 2 cups oats
generous 1 cup dry
    unsweetened coconut
generous ¹/₃ cup candied
    cherries, chopped

method

1 Preheat the oven to 325°F/160°C. Grease a 12 x 9-inch/30 x 23-cm baking sheet.

2 Put the butter, sugar, and syrup in a large saucepan and set over low heat until just melted. Stir in the oats, coconut, and cherries and mix until evenly combined.

3 Spread the mixture evenly onto the prepared baking sheet and press down with a spatula to make a smooth surface.

4 Bake in the preheated oven for 30 minutes. Remove from the oven and let cool on the baking sheet for 10 minutes. Using a sharp knife, cut the cookies into rectangles. Carefully transfer the pieces to a wire rack and let cool completely.

chocolate éclairs

ingredients

MAKES 10

dough

2/3 cup water

5 tbsp butter, cut into small
     pieces, plus extra
     for greasing

3/4 cup all-purpose flour, sifted

2 eggs

pastry cream

2 eggs, beaten lightly

1/4 cup superfine sugar

2 tbsp cornstarch

1 1/4 cups milk

1/4 tsp vanilla extract

frosting

2 tbsp butter

1 tbsp milk

1 tbsp unsweetened cocoa

1/2 cup confectioners' sugar

white chocolate, broken
     into pieces

method

1 Preheat the oven to 400°F/200°C. Lightly grease a cookie sheet. Place the water in a saucepan, add the butter, and heat gently until the butter melts. Bring to a rolling boil, then remove the pan from the heat and add the flour all at once, beating well until the mixture leaves the sides of the pan and forms a ball. Let cool slightly, then gradually beat in the eggs to form a smooth, glossy mixture. Spoon into a large pastry bag fitted with a 1/2-inch/1-cm plain tip.

2 Sprinkle the cookie sheet with a little water. Pipe éclairs 3 inches/7.5 cm long, spaced well apart. Bake in the preheated oven for 30–35 minutes, until crisp and golden. Make a small slit in the side of each éclair to let the steam escape. Let cool on a wire rack.

3 Meanwhile, make the pastry cream. Beat the eggs and sugar until thick and creamy, then fold in the cornstarch. Heat the milk until almost boiling and pour onto the eggs, beating. Transfer to the pan and cook over low heat, stirring until thick. Remove from the heat, stir in the vanilla extract, cover with parchment paper, and let cool.

4 For the frosting, melt the butter with the milk in a saucepan, remove from the heat, and stir in the cocoa and sugar. Split the éclairs lengthwise, pipe in the pastry cream, and spread the frosting over the tops. Melt the white chocolate in a heatproof bowl set over a saucepan of simmering water, then spoon it over the chocolate frosting, swirl in, and let set.

carrot bars

ingredients

MAKES 14–16

corn oil, for oiling

3/4 cup unsalted butter

generous 3/8 cup firmly packed
   brown sugar

2 eggs, beaten

scant 1/2 cup self-rising whole
   wheat flour, sifted

1 tsp baking powder, sifted

1 tsp ground cinnamon, sifted

scant 1 1/4 cups ground
   almonds

2 carrots, coarsely grated

1/2 cup golden raisins

1/2 cup plumped dried
   apricots, finely chopped

generous 1/4 cup toasted
   chopped hazelnuts

1 tbsp slivered almonds

method

1 Preheat the oven to 350°F/180°C. Lightly oil a 10 x 8-inch/25 x 20-cm shallow, rectangular baking pan and line with parchment paper.

2 Cream the butter and sugar together in a bowl until light and fluffy, then gradually beat in the eggs, adding a little flour after each addition.

3 Add all the remaining ingredients, except the slivered almonds. Spoon the mixture into the prepared pan and smooth the top. Sprinkle with the slivered almonds.

4 Bake in the preheated oven for 35–45 minutes, or until the mixture is cooked and a skewer inserted into the center comes out clean.

5 Remove from the oven and let cool in the pan. Remove from the pan, discard the lining paper, and cut into bars.

fruity crumble bars

ingredients

MAKES 12

1 1/3 cups ready-prepared
    mincemeat
confectioners' sugar,
    for dusting

bottom layer

2/3 cup butter, plus
extra for greasing
scant 1/2 cup golden superfine
    sugar
1 cup all-purpose flour
scant 2/3 cup cornstarch

topping

generous 3/4 cup self-rising
    flour
6 tbsp butter, cut into pieces
scant 1/2 cup golden superfine
    sugar
1/4 cup slivered almonds

method

1 Grease a shallow 11 x 8-inch/28 x 20-cm cake pan. To make the bottom layer, place the butter and sugar in a bowl and cream together until light and fluffy. Sift in the flour and cornstarch and, with your hands, bring the mixture together to form a ball. Push the dough into the cake pan, pressing it out and into the corners, then chill in the refrigerator for 20 minutes.

2 Meanwhile, preheat the oven to 400°F/200°C. Bake the bottom layer in the preheated oven for 12–15 minutes, or until puffed and golden.

3 To make the crumble topping, place the flour, butter, and sugar in a bowl and rub together into coarse crumbs. Stir in the almonds.

4 Spread the mincemeat over the bottom layer and scatter the crumbs on top. Bake in the oven for an additional 20 minutes, or until golden. Let cool slightly, then cut into 12 pieces and let cool completely. Dust with sifted confectioners' sugar, then serve.

cinnamon squares

ingredients

MAKES 16

1 cup butter, softened, plus extra for greasing

1 1/4 cups superfine sugar

3 eggs, lightly beaten

1 3/4 cups self-rising flour

1/2 tsp baking soda

1 tbsp ground cinnamon

2/3 cup sour cream

1/2 cup sunflower seeds

method

1 Preheat the oven to 350°F/180°C. Grease a 9-inch/23-cm square cake pan and line the bottom with parchment paper.

2 In a large mixing bowl, cream together the butter and superfine sugar until light and fluffy.

3 Gradually add the eggs, beating thoroughly after each addition.

4 Sift the flour, baking soda, and cinnamon together into the creamed mixture and fold in evenly using a metal spoon. Spoon in the sour cream and sunflower seeds and mix gently until well combined.

5 Spoon the batter into the prepared cake pan and smooth the surface.

6 Bake in the preheated oven for about 45 minutes, until firm to the touch. Loosen the edges with a knife, then turn out onto a wire rack to cool completely. Slice into squares before serving.

ginger-topped bars

ingredients

MAKES 16

1 1/2 cups all-purpose flour
1 tsp ground ginger
scant 1/2 cup golden superfine
sugar
3/4 cup unsalted butter, plus
extra for greasing

ginger topping
1 tbsp corn syrup
4 tbsp unsalted butter
2 tbsp confectioners' sugar
1 tsp ground ginger

white frosting
(optional)
1 1/4 cups confectioners' sugar
1 tbsp milk

method

1 Preheat the oven to 350°F/180°C. Grease an 11 x 7-inch/28 x 18-cm rectangular cake pan. Sift the flour and ginger into a bowl and stir in the sugar. Rub in the butter until the mixture resembles a dough.

2 Press the mixture into the prepared pan and smooth the top with a spatula. Bake in the preheated oven for 40 minutes, or until very lightly browned.

3 To make the ginger topping, place the syrup and butter in a small saucepan over low heat and stir until melted. Stir in the confectioners' sugar and ginger. Remove the cake from the oven and pour over the topping while hot. Let cool slightly in the pan, then cut into 16 fingers. Transfer to wire racks to cool completely.

4 To make the frosting, if using, mix the confectioners' sugar with the milk until smooth. Pour it into a pastry bag fitted with a thin tip, and pipe thin parallel lines lengthwise on top of each bar. Drag a toothpick or the tip of a knife crosswise through the lines, alternately toward you and then away from you, about 1/2 inch/1 cm apart, to create a wavy effect.

gingerbread squares

ingredients

MAKES 24

1/2 apple, peeled, cored, and
   cooked

3/4 cup unsalted butter, plus
   extra for greasing

1/4 cup soft brown sugar

5 tbsp molasses

1 egg white

1 tsp almond extract

1 1/3 cups all-purpose flour

1/4 tsp baking soda

1/4 tsp baking powder

pinch of salt

1/2 tsp allspice

1/2 tsp ground ginger

method

1 Preheat the oven to 350°F/180°C. Grease a large cake pan and line it with parchment paper. Chop the apple and set aside. Put the butter, sugar, molasses, egg white, and almond extract in a food processor and process until the mixture is smooth.

2 Sift the flour, baking soda, baking powder, salt, allspice, and ginger together into another bowl. Add to the creamed mixture and beat together well until combined. Stir the apple into the mixture, then pour the mixture into the prepared cake pan.

3 Transfer to the preheated oven and bake for 10 minutes, or until golden brown. Remove from the oven and cut into 24 pieces. Transfer the gingerbread to a wire rack and let cool completely before serving.

ginger chocolate chip squares

ingredients

MAKES 15

4 pieces preserved ginger in syrup
1 1/2 cups all-purpose flour
1 1/2 tsp ground ginger
1 tsp ground cinnamon
1/4 tsp ground cloves
1/4 tsp grated nutmeg
1/2 cup brown sugar
1/2 cup butter
1/3 cup corn syrup
1/2 cup semisweet chocolate chips

method

1 Preheat the oven to 300°F/150°C. Finely chop the preserved ginger. Sift the flour, ground ginger, cinnamon, cloves, and nutmeg into a large bowl. Stir in the chopped preserved ginger and sugar.

2 Put the butter and the syrup in a saucepan and heat gently until melted. Bring to a boil, then pour the mixture into the flour mixture, stirring all the time. Beat until the mixture is cool enough to handle.

3 Add the chocolate chips to the mixture. Press evenly into an 8 x 12-inch/20 x 30-cm jelly roll pan.

4 Bake in the preheated oven for 30 minutes. Cut into squares, then let cool in the pan.

buttermilk biscuits

ingredients

MAKES 8

generous 2 cups self-rising
   flour, plus extra for dusting
1 tsp baking powder
pinch of salt
4 tbsp cold butter, cut
   into pieces, plus extra
   for greasing
scant 1/4 cup golden superfine
   sugar
1 1/4 cups buttermilk
2 tbsp milk
whipped cream and
   strawberry jelly, to serve

method

1 Preheat the oven to 425°F/220°C, then grease a cookie sheet. Sift the flour, baking powder, and salt into a bowl. Add the butter and rub in until the mixture resembles fine bread crumbs. Add the sugar and buttermilk and quickly mix together.

2 Turn out the mixture onto a floured counter and knead lightly. Roll out to 1-inch/2.5-cm thick. Using a 2 1/2-inch/6-cm plain or fluted cutter, stamp out biscuits and place on the prepared cookie sheet. Gather the trimmings, reroll, and stamp out more biscuits until all the dough is used up.

3 Brush the tops of the biscuits with milk. Bake in the preheated oven for 12–15 minutes, or until well risen and golden. Transfer to a wire rack to cool. Split and serve with whipped cream and strawberry jelly.

rock drops

ingredients

MAKES 8

scant 1 1/2 cups all-purpose
    flour
2 tsp baking powder
1/2 cup butter, cut into small
    pieces, plus extra
    for greasing
1/3 cup raw sugar
generous 1/2 cup golden
    raisins
2 tbsp finely chopped candied
    cherries
1 egg, beaten
2 tbsp milk

method

1 Preheat the oven to 400°F/200°C. Lightly grease a cookie sheet large enough for eight big rock drops.

2 Sift the flour and baking powder into a mixing bowl. Rub in the butter with your fingertips until the mixture resembles fine bread crumbs. Stir in the sugar, golden raisins, and cherries, mixing well. Add the beaten egg and the milk to the mixture and mix to form a soft dough.

3 Spoon eight mounds of the mixture onto the prepared cookie sheet, spacing them well apart because they will spread while they are cooking. Bake in the preheated oven for 15–20 minutes, until firm to the touch.

4 Remove the rock drops from the cookie sheet. Either serve hot from the oven or transfer to a wire rack and let cool before serving.

strawberry & chocolate slices

ingredients

MAKES 16

1½ cups all-purpose flour

1 tsp baking powder

½ cup superfine sugar

scant ½ cup soft brown sugar

1 cup unsalted butter

1 cup oats

⅔ cup strawberry jelly

scant ⅔ cup semisweet
    chocolate chips

scant ¼ cup almonds,
    chopped

method

1 Preheat the oven to 375°F/190°C. Line a 12 x 8-inch/30 x 20-cm deep-sided jelly roll pan with parchment paper. Sift the flour and baking powder into a large bowl.

2 Add the superfine sugar and brown sugar to the flour and mix well. Add the butter and rub in until the mixture resembles bread crumbs. Stir in the oats.

3 Press three quarters of the mixture into the bottom of the prepared cake pan. Bake in the preheated oven for 10 minutes.

4 Spread the jelly over the cooked base, then sprinkle over the chocolate chips. Mix the remaining flour mixture with the almonds. Sprinkle evenly over the chocolate chips and press down gently.

5 Return to the oven and bake for an additional 20–25 minutes, or until golden brown. Remove from the oven and let cool in the pan, then cut into slices.

summer fruit tartlets

ingredients

MAKES 12

pie dough

scant 1½ cups all-purpose
  flour, plus extra for dusting
generous ¾ cup
  confectioners' sugar
⅔ cup ground almonds
½ cup butter
1 egg yolk
1 tbsp milk

filling

1 cup cream cheese
confectioners' sugar, to taste,
  plus extra for dusting
12 oz/350 g fresh summer
  fruits, such as blueberries,
  raspberries, and small
  strawberries

method

1 Preheat the oven to 400°F/200°C. To make the dough, sift the flour and confectioners' sugar into a bowl. Stir in the ground almonds. Add the butter and rub in until the mixture resembles bread crumbs. Add the egg yolk and milk and work in with a palette knife, then mix with your fingers until the dough binds together. Wrap the dough in plastic wrap and let chill in the refrigerator for 30 minutes.

2 On a floured counter, roll out the dough and use to line 12 deep tartlet or individual brioche pans. Prick the bottoms. Press a piece of foil into each tartlet, covering the edges, and bake in the preheated oven for 10–15 minutes, or until light golden brown. Remove the foil and bake for an additional 2–3 minutes. Transfer to a wire rack to cool.

3 To make the filling, place the cream cheese and confectioners' sugar in a bowl and mix together. Place a spoonful of filling in each tart shell and arrange the fruit on top. Dust with sifted confectioners' sugar and serve.

strawberry tartlets

ingredients

MAKES 4

pie dough

generous 1 cup all-purpose
   flour
2 tbsp confectioners' sugar
5 tbsp unsalted butter, at room
   temperature
1 egg yolk
1–2 tbsp water

filling

1 vanilla bean, split
scant 1 cup milk
2 egg yolks
3 tbsp superfine sugar
1 tbsp all-purpose flour
1 tbsp cornstarch
1/2 cup heavy cream, whipped
3 cups strawberries, hulled
4 tbsp grape jelly, melted

method

1 To make the pie dough, sift the flour and confectioners' sugar into a bowl. Chop the butter into small pieces and add to the flour mixture with the egg yolk, mixing with your fingertips and adding a little water, if necessary, to mix to a soft dough. Cover and place in the refrigerator to rest for 15 minutes.

2 Preheat the oven to 400°F/200°C. Roll out the dough and use to line four 3 1/2-inch/9-cm round tartlet pans. Prick the bottoms with a fork, line with parchment paper, and fill with dried beans, then bake in the preheated oven for 10 minutes. Remove the paper and beans and bake for an additional 5 minutes, until golden brown. Remove from the oven and let cool.

3 For the filling, place the vanilla bean in a saucepan with the milk and set over low heat to steep, without boiling, for 10 minutes. Beat the egg yolks, sugar, flour, and cornstarch together in a mixing bowl until smooth. Strain the milk into the bowl and whisk until smooth.

4 Pour the mixture back into the pan and stir over medium heat until boiling. Cook, stirring continuously, for about 2 minutes, until thickened and smooth. Remove from the heat and fold in the whipped cream. Spoon the mixture into the pie shells.

5 Let cool and set. When the filling has set slightly, top with strawberries, sliced if large, then spoon over a little grape jelly to glaze.

raspberry éclairs

ingredients

MAKES 8

choux pastry

4 tbsp butter

2/3 cup water

1/2 cup all-purpose flour, sifted

2 eggs, beaten

filling

1 1/3 cups heavy cream

1 tbsp confectioners' sugar

3/4 cup fresh raspberries

frosting

generous 1 cup confectioners'
    sugar

2 tsp lemon juice

pink food coloring (optional)

method

1 Preheat the oven to 400°F/200°C. To make the choux pastry, place the butter and water in a large, heavy-bottom saucepan and bring to a boil. Add the flour, all at once, and beat thoroughly until the mixture leaves the sides of the pan. Let cool slightly, then vigorously beat in the eggs, one at a time.

2 Spoon the mixture into a pastry bag fitted with a 1/2-inch/1-cm nozzle and make eight 3-inch/7.5-cm lengths on several dampened cookie sheets. Bake in the preheated oven for 30 minutes, or until crisp and golden. Remove from the oven and make a small hole in each éclair with the tip of a knife to let out the steam, then return to the oven for an additional 5 minutes, to dry out the insides. Transfer to a wire rack to cool.

3 To make the filling, place the cream and confectioners' sugar in a bowl and whisk until thick. Split the éclairs and fill with the cream and raspberries. To make the frosting, sift the confectioners' sugar into a bowl and stir in the lemon juice and enough water to make a smooth paste. Add pink food coloring, if desired. Drizzle the frosting generously over the éclairs, and let set before serving.

cherry & golden raisin rock cakes

ingredients

MAKES 10

1³/4 cups self-rising flour

1 tsp ground allspice

6 tbsp butter, plus extra
    for greasing

scant 1³/4 cup golden
    superfine sugar

¹/4 cup candied cherries,
    quartered

¹/3 cup golden raisins

1 egg

2 tbsp milk

raw sugar, for sprinkling

method

1 Preheat the oven to 400°F/200°C, then grease a cookie sheet. Sift the flour and allspice into a bowl. Add the butter and rub it in until the mixture resembles bread crumbs. Stir in the sugar, cherries, and golden raisins.

2 Break the egg into a bowl and whisk in the milk. Pour most of the egg mixture into the dry ingredients and mix with a fork to make a stiff, coarse dough, adding the rest of the egg and milk, if necessary.

3 Using two forks, pile the mixture into 10 rocky heaps on the prepared cookie sheet. Sprinkle with raw sugar. Bake in the preheated oven for 10–15 minutes, or until golden and firm to the touch. Let cool on the cookie sheet for 2 minutes, then transfer to a wire rack to cool completely.

orange & raisin brioches

ingredients

MAKES 12

generous 1¹/₂ cups strong
    white bread flour, plus
    extra for dusting

¹/₂ tsp salt

2 tsp active dry yeast

1 tbsp golden superfine sugar

¹/₃ cup raisins

grated rind of 1 orange

2 tbsp tepid water

2 eggs, beaten

4 tbsp butter, melted, plus
    extra for greasing

vegetable oil, for brushing

1 beaten egg, for glazing

method

1 Grease 12 individual brioche molds. Sift the flour and salt into a warmed bowl and stir in the yeast, sugar, raisins, and orange rind. Make a well in the center. In a separate bowl, mix together the water, eggs, and melted butter and pour into the dry ingredients. Beat vigorously to make a soft dough. Turn out onto a lightly floured counter and knead for 5 minutes, or until smooth and elastic. Brush a clean bowl with oil. Place the dough in the bowl, cover with plastic wrap, and let stand in a warm place for 1 hour, or until doubled in size.

2 Turn out onto a floured counter, knead lightly for 1 minute, then roll into a rope shape. Cut into 12 equal pieces. Shape three quarters of each piece into a ball and place in the prepared molds. With a floured finger, press a hole in the center of each. Shape the remaining pieces of dough into little plugs and press into the holes, flattening the top slightly.

3 Place the molds on a cookie sheet, cover lightly with oiled plastic wrap, and let stand in a warm place for 1 hour, until the dough comes almost to the top.

4 Meanwhile, preheat the oven to 425°F/220°C. Brush the brioches with beaten egg and bake in the preheated oven for 15 minutes, or until golden brown. Serve warm, with butter.

lemon drizzle bars

ingredients

MAKES 12

2 eggs

generous 3/4 cup superfine
    sugar

2/3 cup soft margarine, plus
    extra for greasing

finely grated rind of 1 lemon

1 1/2 cups self-rising flour

1/2 cup milk

confectioners' sugar,
    for dusting

syrup

1 1/4 cups confectioners' sugar

1/4 cup fresh lemon juice

method

1 Preheat the oven to 350°F/180°C. Grease a 7-inch/18-cm square cake pan and line with nonstick parchment paper.

2 Place the eggs, superfine sugar, and margarine in a bowl and beat hard until smooth and fluffy. Stir in the lemon rind, then fold in the flour lightly and evenly. Stir in the milk, mixing evenly, then spoon into the prepared cake pan, smoothing level.

3 Bake in the preheated oven for 45–50 minutes, or until golden brown and firm to the touch. Remove from the oven and place the pan on a wire rack.

4 To make the syrup, place the confectioners' sugar and lemon juice in a small saucepan and heat gently, stirring until the sugar dissolves. Do not boil.

5 Prick the warm cake all over with a skewer and spoon the hot syrup evenly over the top.

6 Let cool completely in the pan, then turn out the cake, cut into 12 pieces, and dust with a little confectioners' sugar before serving.

lemon butterfly cakes

ingredients

MAKES 12

generous 3/4 cup self-rising
    white flour
1/2 tsp baking powder
1/2 cup soft margarine
generous 1/2 cup superfine
    sugar
2 eggs, lightly beaten
finely grated rind of 1/2 lemon
2 tbsp milk
confectioners' sugar,
    for dusting

lemon filling
6 tbsp butter, softened
1 1/2 cups confectioners' sugar
1 tbsp lemon juice

method

1 Preheat the oven to 375°F/190°C. Put 12 paper baking liners in a muffin pan, or put 12 double-layer paper liners on a baking sheet.

2 Sift the flour and baking powder into a large bowl. Add the margarine, sugar, eggs, lemon rind, and milk and, using an electric handheld mixer, beat together until smooth. Spoon the batter into the paper liners.

3 Bake the cupcakes in the preheated oven for 15–20 minutes, or until well risen and golden brown. Transfer to a wire rack and let cool.

4 To make the filling, put the butter in a bowl and beat until fluffy. Sift in the confectioners' sugar, add the lemon juice, and beat together until smooth and creamy.

5 When the cupcakes are cold, use a serrated knife to cut a circle from the top of each cupcake and then cut each circle in half. Spread or pipe a little of the buttercream filling into the center of each cupcake, then press the two semicircular halves into it at an angle to resemble butterfly wings. Dust with sifted confectioners' sugar before serving.

apple shortcakes

ingredients

MAKES 4

generous 1 cup all-purpose
    flour, plus extra for dusting
1/2 tsp salt
1 tsp baking powder
1 tbsp superfine sugar
2 tbsp butter, cut into small
    pieces, plus extra
    for greasing
1/4 cup milk
confectioners' sugar,
    for dusting

filling

3 dessert apples, peeled,
    cored, and sliced
1/2 cup superfine sugar
1 tbsp lemon juice
1 tsp ground cinnamon
1 1/4 cups water
2/3 cup heavy cream, lightly
    whipped

method

1 Preheat the oven to 425°F/220°C. Lightly grease a cookie sheet. Sift the flour, salt, and baking powder into a large bowl. Stir in the sugar, then add the butter and rub it in with your fingertips until the mixture resembles fine bread crumbs. Pour in the milk and mix to a soft dough.

2 On a lightly floured counter, knead the dough lightly, then roll out to 1/2-inch/1-cm thick. Stamp out 4 circles, using a 2-inch/5-cm cutter. Transfer the circles to the prepared cookie sheet.

3 Bake in the oven for 15 minutes, until the shortcakes are well risen and lightly browned. Let cool.

4 To make the filling, place the apple, sugar, lemon juice, and cinnamon in a saucepan. Add the water, bring to a boil, and let simmer, uncovered, for 5–10 minutes, or until the apples are tender. Cool slightly, then remove the apples from the pan.

5 To serve, split the shortcakes in half. Place each bottom half on an individual serving plate and spoon on a quarter of the apple slices, then the cream. Place the other half of the shortcake on top. Serve dusted with confectioners' sugar.

apricot slices

ingredients

MAKES 12

pie dough

2 cups whole wheat flour

1/2 cup finely ground mixed
    nuts

5 tbsp margarine,
    cut into small pieces,
    plus extra for greasing

4 tbsp water

milk, for glazing

filling

1 cup dried apricots

grated rind of 1 orange

1 1/2 cups apple juice

1 tsp ground cinnamon

generous 1/3 cup raisins

method

1 To make the dough, place the flour and nuts in a mixing bowl and rub in the margarine with your fingers until the mixture resembles bread crumbs. Stir in the water and bring together to form a dough. Wrap and let chill for 30 minutes.

2 To make the filling, place the apricots, orange rind, and apple juice in a saucepan and bring to a boil. Simmer for 30 minutes, until the apricots are mushy. Cool slightly, then process in a food processor or blender to a puree. Alternatively, press the mixture through a fine strainer. Stir in the cinnamon and raisins.

3 Preheat the oven to 400°F/200°C. Lightly grease a 9-inch/23-cm square cake pan. Divide the dough in half, roll out one half, and use to line the bottom of the pan. Spread the apricot puree over the top and brush the edges of the dough with water. Roll out the rest of the dough to fit over the top of the apricot puree. Press down and seal the edges.

4 Prick the top of the dough with a fork and brush with milk. Bake in the oven for 20–25 minutes, until golden. Let cool slightly before cutting into 12 bars. Serve the slices either warm or cold.

chocolate & apricot squares

ingredients

MAKES 12

generous 1/2 cup butter, plus
extra for greasing

6 oz/175 g white chocolate,
chopped

4 eggs

1/2 cup superfine sugar

1 3/4 cups all-purpose flour,
sifted

1 tsp baking powder

pinch of salt

generous 1/2 cup plumped
dried apricots, chopped

method

1 Preheat the oven to 350°F/180°C. Lightly grease a 20-cm/8-inch square cake pan and line the bottom with parchment paper.

2 Melt the butter and chocolate in a heatproof bowl set over a saucepan of gently simmering water. Stir frequently with a wooden spoon until the mixture is smooth and glossy. Let the mixture cool slightly.

3 Beat the eggs and superfine sugar into the butter and chocolate mixture until well combined.

4 Fold in the flour, baking powder, salt, and apricots and mix thoroughly.

5 Pour the mixture into the pan and bake in the preheated oven for about 25–30 minutes.

6 The center of the cake may not be completely firm, but it will set as it cools. Let stand in the pan to cool.

7 When the cake is completely cold, turn it out carefully and slice into bars or small squares.

macadamia nut caramel bars

ingredients

MAKES 16

base

2 cups all-purpose flour

1 cup brown sugar

1/2 cup butter

1 cup macadamia nuts,
   coarsely chopped

topping

1/2 cup butter

1/2 cup brown sugar

1 cup milk chocolate chips

method

1 Preheat the oven to 350°F/180°C. To make the base, beat together the flour, sugar, and butter until the mixture resembles fine bread crumbs. Press the mixture into the bottom of a 12 x 8-inch/30 x 20-cm jelly roll pan. Sprinkle over the nuts.

2 To make the topping, put the butter and sugar in a saucepan and, stirring continuously, slowly bring the mixture to a boil. Boil for 1 minute, stirring continuously, then carefully pour the mixture over the nuts.

3 Bake in the preheated oven for about 20 minutes, until the caramel topping is bubbling. Remove from the oven and immediately sprinkle the chocolate chips evenly on top. Let stand for 2–3 minutes, until the chocolate chips start to melt then, using the blade of a knife, swirl the chocolate over the top. Let cool in the pan, then cut into bars.

hazelnut squares

ingredients

MAKES 16

generous 1 cup all-purpose
    flour
pinch of salt
1 tsp baking powder
6 tbsp butter, cut into small
    pieces, plus extra
    for greasing
3/4 cup brown sugar
1 egg, beaten lightly
4 tbsp milk
1 cup halved hazelnuts
raw sugar, for sprinkling
    (optional)

method

1 Preheat the oven to 350°F/180°C. Grease a 9-inch/23-cm square cake pan and line with parchment paper.

2 Sift the flour, salt, and baking powder into a large bowl.

3 Rub in the butter with your fingertips until the mixture resembles fine bread crumbs. Stir in the brown sugar.

4 Add the egg, milk, and nuts to the mixture and stir well, until thoroughly combined.

5 Spoon the mixture into the prepared pan, spreading it out evenly, and smooth the surface. Sprinkle with raw sugar, if using.

6 Bake in the preheated oven for about 25 minutes, or until the mixture is firm to the touch when pressed gently with a finger.

7 Let cool for 10 minutes in the pan, then loosen the edges with a round-bladed knife and turn out onto a wire rack. Cut into squares and let cool completely before serving.

hazelnut chocolate crunch

ingredients

MAKES 12

generous 2 cups rolled oats

1/3 cup hazelnuts, lightly
    toasted and chopped

1/3 cup all-purpose flour

1/2 cup unsalted butter, plus
    extra for greasing

1/2 cup light brown sugar

2 tbsp corn syrup

1/3 cup bittersweet chocolate
    chips

method

1 Preheat the oven to 350°F/180°C. Grease a 9-inch/23-cm shallow, square cake pan.

2 Mix the oats, nuts, and flour in a large bowl. Place the butter, sugar, and syrup in a large saucepan and heat gently until the sugar has dissolved. Pour in the dry ingredients and mix well. Stir in the chocolate chips.

3 Turn the mixture into the prepared pan and bake in the preheated oven for 20–25 minutes, or until golden brown and firm to the touch.

4 Using a knife, mark into 12 rectangles and let cool in the pan. Cut the hazelnut chocolate crunch bars with a sharp knife before carefully removing them from the pan.

nutty oat bars

ingredients

MAKES 16

scant 2³/4 cups rolled oats

³/4 cup chopped hazelnuts

6 tbsp all-purpose flour

¹/2 cup butter, plus extra
    for greasing

2 tbsp dark corn syrup

scant ¹/2 cup light brown sugar

method

1 Preheat the oven to 350°F/180°C. Grease a 9-inch/23-cm square cake pan.

2 Place the rolled oats, hazelnuts, and flour in a large mixing bowl and stir together.

3 Place the butter, corn syrup, and sugar in a saucepan over low heat and stir until melted. Pour onto the dry ingredients and mix well. Spoon into the prepared cake pan and smooth the surface with the back of a spoon.

4 Bake in the preheated oven for 20–25 minutes, or until golden and firm to the touch. Mark into 16 pieces and let cool in the pan. When completely cooled, cut through with a sharp knife and remove from the pan.

almond & raspberry slices

ingredients

MAKES 12

pie dough

1¹/₂ cups all-purpose flour

generous ¹/₂ cup butter

2 tbsp superfine sugar

1 egg yolk

about 1 tbsp cold water

filling

¹/₂ cup butter

generous ¹/₂ cup superfine
    sugar

1 cup ground almonds

3 eggs, beaten

¹/₂ tsp almond extract

4 tbsp raspberry jelly

2 tbsp slivered almonds

method

1 For the dough, sift the flour into a bowl and rub in the butter with your fingertips until the mixture resembles fine bread crumbs. Stir in the sugar, then combine the egg yolk and water and stir in to make a firm dough, adding a little more water if necessary. Wrap in plastic wrap and chill in the refrigerator for about 15 minutes, until firm enough to roll out.

2 Preheat the oven to 400°F/200°C. Roll out the dough and use to line a 9-inch/23-cm square tart pan or shallow cake pan. Prick the bottom and chill for 15 minutes.

3 For the filling, cream the butter and sugar together until pale and fluffy, then beat in the ground almonds, eggs, and almond extract.

4 Spread the jelly over the bottom of the pastry shell, then top with the almond filling, spreading it evenly. Sprinkle with the slivered almonds.

5 Bake in the preheated oven for 10 minutes, then reduce the temperature to 350°F/180°C and bake for an additional 25–30 minutes, or until the filling is golden brown and firm to the touch. Cool in the pan, then cut into bars.

maple pecan tartlets

ingredients

MAKES 12

pie dough

1 cup all-purpose flour, plus
    extra for dusting
6 tbsp butter
1/4 cup golden superfine sugar
2 egg yolks
12 pecan halves,
    to decorate

filling

2 tbsp maple syrup
2/3 cup heavy cream
generous 1/2 cup golden
    superfine sugar
pinch of cream of tartar
scant 1/3 cup water
1 cup pecans

method

1 Sift the flour into a large bowl, then cut the butter into pieces and rub it into the flour with your fingertips until the mixture resembles bread crumbs. Stir in the sugar, then stir in the egg yolks to make a smooth dough. Wrap in plastic wrap and chill in the refrigerator for 30 minutes.

2 Preheat the oven to 400°F/200°C. On a floured counter, roll out the pastry thinly, cut out circles, and use to line 12 tartlet pans. Prick the bottoms and press a piece of foil into each tart shell. Bake in the oven for 10–15 minutes, or until light golden. Remove the foil and bake for an additional 2–3 minutes. Let cool on a wire rack.

3 To make the filling, place half the maple syrup and half the cream in a bowl and mix together. Place the sugar, cream of tartar, and water in a saucepan over low heat and stir until the sugar dissolves. Bring to a boil and continue boiling until light golden. Remove from the heat and stir in the maple syrup and cream mixture.

4 Return to the heat and cook to the "soft ball" stage (240°F/116°C), when a little of the mixture forms a soft ball when dropped into cold water. Stir in the remaining cream and let stand until warm. Brush the remaining syrup over the edges of the tarts. Place the pecans in the shells, spoon in the filling and top with a pecan half. Let cool.

almond slices

ingredients

MAKES 8

3 eggs
²/₃ cup ground almonds
scant 1¹/₂ cups milk powder
1 cup granulated sugar
¹/₂ tsp saffron threads
¹/₂ cup unsalted butter
1 tbsp slivered almonds,
    to decorate

method

1 Preheat the oven to 325°F/160°C. Lightly beat the eggs together in a mixing bowl and set aside.

2 Place the ground almonds, milk powder, sugar, and saffron in a large mixing bowl and stir to mix well.

3 Melt the butter in a small saucepan over low heat. Pour the melted butter over the dry ingredients and mix well with a wooden spoon until thoroughly combined.

4 Add the beaten eggs to the mixture in the pan and stir to blend well.

5 Spread the mixture evenly in a shallow 8-inch/20-cm ovenproof dish and bake in the preheated oven for 45 minutes, or until a toothpick inserted into the center comes out clean.

6 Remove from the oven and cut into slices. Decorate the slices with slivered almonds and transfer to serving plates. Serve hot or cold.

moist walnut cupcakes

ingredients

MAKES 12

3/4 cup walnuts
4 tbsp butter, softened, and
    cut into small pieces
1/2 cup superfine sugar
grated rind of 1/2 lemon
1/2 cup self-rising white flour
2 eggs
12 walnut halves, to decorate

frosting
4 tbsp butter, softened
3/4 cup confectioners' sugar
grated rind of 1/2 lemon
1 tsp lemon juice

method

1 Preheat the oven to 375°F/190°C. Put 12 paper baking liners in a muffin pan, or put 12 double-layer paper liners on a baking sheet.

2 Put the walnuts in a food processor and, using a pulsating action, blend until finely ground, being careful not to overgrind, which will turn them to oil. Add the butter, sugar, lemon rind, flour, and eggs and blend until evenly mixed. Spoon into the paper liners.

3 Bake the cupcakes in the preheated oven for 20 minutes, or until well risen and golden brown. Transfer to a wire rack and let cool.

4 To make the frosting, put the butter in a bowl and beat until fluffy. Sift in the confectioners' sugar, add the lemon rind and juice, and mix well together.

5 When the cupcakes are cold, spread the frosting on top of each cupcake and top with a walnut half to decorate.

walnut & cinnamon blondies

ingredients

MAKES 8

1/2 cup unsalted butter, plus extra for greasing

scant 1 1/4 cups soft brown sugar

1 egg

1 egg yolk

1 cup self-rising flour

1 tsp ground cinnamon

3/4 cup walnuts, coarsely chopped

method

1 Preheat the oven to 350°F/180°C. Grease the bottom and sides of a 7-inch/18-cm square cake pan and line with parchment paper.

2 Place the butter and sugar in a pan over low heat and stir until the sugar has dissolved. Cook, stirring, for 1 minute more. The mixture will bubble slightly, but do not let it boil. Let cool for 10 minutes.

3 Stir the egg and egg yolk into the mixture. Sift in the flour and cinnamon, then add the nuts and stir until just blended. Pour the cake mixture into the prepared pan and bake in the preheated oven for 20–25 minutes, or until springy in the middle and a toothpick inserted into the center comes out clean.

4 Let cool in the pan for a few minutes, then run a knife around the edge of the pan to loosen. Turn out onto a wire rack and peel off the paper. Let cool completely. When cold, cut into squares.

walnut & chocolate chip slices

ingredients

MAKES 18

1 cup walnut pieces

1 cup unsalted butter, plus
  extra for greasing

1 cup superfine sugar

few drops vanilla extract

1$\frac{1}{2}$ cups all-purpose flour

1$\frac{1}{4}$ cups bittersweet chocolate
  chips

method

1 Preheat the oven to 350°F/180°C. Coarsely chop the walnut pieces to about the same size as the chocolate chips.

2 Beat the butter and sugar together until pale and fluffy. Add the vanilla extract, then stir in the flour. Stir in the walnuts and chocolate chips. Press the mixture into a greased 8 x 12-inch/20 x 30-cm jelly roll pan.

3 Bake in the preheated oven for 20–25 minutes, or until golden brown. Remove from the oven. Let cool in the pan and cut into slices.

fruit & nut squares

ingredients

MAKES 9

1/2 cup unsalted butter, plus
    extra for greasing
2 tbsp honey
1 egg, beaten
scant 1 cup ground almonds
2/3 cup plumped dried
    apricots, finely chopped
1/3 cup dried cherries
1/3 cup toasted hazelnuts
2 tbsp sesame seeds
1 cup jumbo oats

method

1 Preheat the oven to 350°F/180°C. Lightly grease a 7-inch/18-cm shallow, square cake pan with butter. Beat the remaining butter with the honey in a bowl until creamy, then beat in the egg with the almonds.

2 Add the remaining ingredients and mix together well. Press into the prepared pan, ensuring that the mixture is firmly packed. Smooth the top.

3 Transfer to the preheated oven and bake for 20–25 minutes, or until firm to the touch and golden brown.

4 Remove from the oven and let stand for 10 minutes before marking into squares.

5 Let stand until cold before removing from the pan. Cut into squares and store in an airtight container and consume within 2–3 days.

candy apple cakes

ingredients

MAKES 12

2 apples

1 tbsp lemon juice

$2^{1}/_{4}$ cups all-purpose flour

2 tsp baking powder

$1^{1}/_{2}$ tsp ground cinnamon

generous $1/_{4}$ cup light brown
    sugar

4 tbsp butter, plus extra
    for greasing

scant $1/_{2}$ cup milk

scant $1/_{2}$ cup apple juice

1 egg, beaten

topping

2 tbsp light cream

3 tbsp light brown sugar

1 tbsp butter

method

1 Preheat the oven to 400°F/200°C. Grease a 12-cup muffin pan (preferably nonstick).

2 Core and coarsely grate 1 apple. Slice the second apple into $1/_{4}$-inch/5-mm wedges and toss in the lemon juice. Sift together the flour, baking powder, and cinnamon, then stir in the sugar and grated apple.

3 Melt the butter and mix with the milk, apple juice, and egg. Stir the liquid mixture into the dry ingredients, mixing lightly until just combined.

4 Spoon the batter into the prepared muffin pan. Put two apple slices on top of each cake.

5 Bake in the preheated oven for 20–25 minutes, or until risen, firm, and golden brown. Run a knife around the edge of each cake to loosen, then turn out onto a wire rack to cool.

6 For the caramel topping, place all the ingredients in a small saucepan and heat, stirring, until the sugar has dissolved. Increase the heat and boil rapidly for 2 minutes, or until slightly thickened and syrupy. Cool slightly, then drizzle over the cakes and let set.

cookies

Keeping the cookie jar topped up has never been easier with this fabulous collection of scrumptious recipes for all the family. As well as all the kids' favorites such as chocolate chip and classics like florentines, there are fragrant herb-flavored biscuits to serve with cold desserts, creamy sandwich cookies, and novelty shapes for parties and festivals. There are even cookies you can hang on the Christmas tree.

Making cookies is probably even easier and quicker than any other type of baking and they not only taste more delicious than the ones you can buy, but they also cost less. Like all home-baking, cookies are a special treat and can be served with tea, coffee, milk, and fruit juice or, Italian-style, with a glass of wine. They're popular at children's parties, delicious with ice cream at the end of a family supper, and the perfect self-indulgent treat on a well-deserved coffee break.

Most of the equipment required is the same as for other types of baking. It is worth buying good-quality, nonstick cookie sheets that disperse the heat evenly and won't wobble when you take them out of the oven. A couple of wire racks are useful as cookies take up quite a lot of room and it is important that the air can circulate

properly so that the cookies end up beautifully crisp. Most cooks already have plain and/or fluted round cookie cutters, but it's great fun to use some of the other shapes available—shooting stars, diamonds, hearts, flowers, and even Santa Claus.

chocolate chip oaties

ingredients

MAKES 20

1/2 cup unsalted butter,
   softened, plus extra
   for greasing
generous 1/2 cup dark brown
   sugar
1 egg
2/3 cup oatmeal
1 tbsp milk
1 tsp vanilla extract
scant 1 cup all-purpose flour
1 tbsp unsweetened cocoa
1/2 tsp baking powder
6 squares bittersweet
   chocolate, broken into
   pieces
6 squares milk chocolate,
   broken into pieces

method

1 Preheat the oven to 350°F/180°C. Grease two large cookie sheets. Place the butter and sugar in a bowl and beat together with a wooden spoon until light and fluffy.

2 Beat in the egg, then add the oatmeal, milk, and vanilla. Beat together until well blended. Sift the flour, cocoa, and baking powder into the mixture and stir. Stir in the chocolate pieces.

3 Place tablespoonfuls of the mixture on the prepared cookie sheets and flatten slightly with a fork. Bake in the preheated oven for 15 minutes, or until slightly risen and firm. Remove from the oven, let cool on the cookie sheets for 2 minutes, then transfer to wire racks to cool completely.

double chocolate chip cookies

ingredients

MAKES 24

1/2 cup unsalted butter, softened, plus extra for greasing
1/4 cup golden granulated sugar
1/4 cup light brown sugar
1 egg, beaten
1/2 tsp vanilla extract
3/4 cup all-purpose flour
2 tbsp unsweetened cocoa
1/2 tsp baking soda
2/3 cup milk chocolate chips
1/2 cup walnuts, coarsely chopped

method

1 Preheat the oven to 350°F/180°C. Grease three cookie sheets.

2 Place the butter, granulated sugar, and light brown sugar in a bowl and beat until light and fluffy. Gradually beat in the egg and vanilla extract.

3 Sift the flour, cocoa, and baking soda into the mixture and stir in carefully. Stir in the chocolate chips and walnuts. Drop dessertspoonfuls of the mixture onto the prepared sheets, spaced well apart to allow for spreading.

4 Bake in the preheated oven, for 10–15 minutes, or until the mixture has spread and the cookies are beginning to feel firm. Remove from the oven and let cool on the cookie sheets for 2 minutes, before transferring to wire racks.

chocolate viennese cookies

ingredients

MAKES ABOUT 30

1/2 cup butter, softened, plus extra for greasing

1/2 cup golden confectioners' sugar, sifted

generous 3/4 cup all-purpose flour

1 tbsp unsweetened cocoa

31/2 oz/100 g semisweet chocolate, melted and cooled

method

1 Preheat the oven to 350°F/180°C. Grease two baking sheets. Beat the butter and sugar together until light and fluffy. Sift the flour and cocoa into the bowl and work the mixture until it is a smooth, piping consistency.

2 Spoon into a large pastry bag fitted with a 1-inch/2.5-cm fluted tip. Pipe 21/2-inch/6-cm lengths of the mixture onto the prepared baking sheets, allowing room for expansion during cooking. Bake in the preheated oven for 15 minutes, or until firm.

3 Let cool on the baking sheets for 2 minutes, then transfer to a wire rack to cool completely. Dip the ends of the cookies into the melted chocolate and let set before serving.

cookie & cream sandwiches

ingredients

MAKES 12

generous 1/2 cup unsalted
butter, softened
3/4 cup golden confectioners'
sugar
1 cup all-purpose flour
1/2 cup unsweetened cocoa
1/2 tsp ground cinnamon

filling

41/2 oz/130 g bittersweet
chocolate, broken
into pieces
4 tbsp heavy cream

method

1 Preheat the oven to 325°F/160°C. Line a cookie sheet with nonstick parchment paper. Place the butter and sugar in a large bowl and beat together until light and fluffy. Sift the flour, cocoa, and cinnamon into the bowl and mix until a smooth dough forms.

2 Place the dough between two sheets of nonstick parchment paper and roll out to 1/8 inch/3 mm thick. Stamp out 21/2-inch/6-cm circles and place on the prepared sheet. Bake in the preheated oven for 15 minutes, until firm to the touch. Let cool for 2 minutes, then transfer to wire racks to cool completely.

3 To make the filling, place the chocolate and cream in a saucepan and heat gently until the chocolate has melted. Stir until smooth. Let cool, then let chill in the refrigerator for 2 hours, or until firm. Sandwich the cookies together in pairs with a spoonful of chocolate cream and serve.

chocolate-dipped cookies

ingredients

MAKES 20

6 tbsp unsalted butter, plus
extra for greasing

1/2 cup raw brown sugar

1 egg

1/4 cup wheat germ

3/4 cup whole wheat self-rising
flour

6 tbsp white self-rising flour,
sifted

41/2 oz/130 g semisweet
chocolate, broken
into pieces

method

1 Preheat the oven to 350°F/180°C. Grease 1–2 cookie sheets. Beat the butter and sugar together in a bowl until fluffy. Add the egg and beat well. Stir in the wheatgerm and flours. Bring the mixture together with your hands.

2 Roll rounded teaspoons of the mixture into balls and place on the prepared sheets, spaced well apart to allow for spreading. Flatten the cookies slightly with a fork, then bake in the preheated oven for 15–20 minutes, until golden.

3 Remove from the oven and let cool on the sheets for a few minutes before transferring to a wire rack to cool completely.

4 Melt the chocolate in a heatproof bowl set over a saucepan of gently simmering water, then dip each cookie in the chocolate to cover the base and a little way up the sides. Let the excess chocolate drip back into the bowl. Place the cookies on a sheet of parchment paper and let set in a cool place before serving.

button cookies

ingredients

MAKES 18–20

2 oz/55 g bittersweet
chocolate, broken into
pieces

1 cup all-purpose flour

1 tsp baking powder ·

1 egg

3/4 cup superfine sugar

4 tbsp corn oil, plus extra
for oiling

1/2 tsp vanilla extract

2 tbsp confectioners' sugar

30 milk chocolate buttons

30 white chocolate buttons

method

1 Melt the bittersweet chocolate in a heatproof bowl set over a saucepan of gently simmering water. Remove from the heat and let cool. Sift the flour and baking powder together.

2 Meanwhile, in a large bowl, whisk the egg, sugar, oil, and vanilla extract together. Whisk in the cooled, melted chocolate until well blended, then gradually stir in the flour. Cover the bowl with plastic wrap and chill in the refrigerator for at least 3 hours.

3 Preheat the oven to 375°F/190°C. Oil 1–2 large cookie sheets. Shape tablespoonfuls of the mixture into log shapes using your hands, each measuring about 2 inches/5 cm. Roll the logs generously in the confectioners' sugar, then place on the prepared sheets, leaving room for the cookies to spread during cooking.

4 Bake the cookies in the preheated oven for 15 minutes, or until firm. Remove from the oven and place three chocolate buttons down the center of each cookie, alternating the colors. Transfer to a wire rack and let cool.

chocolate dominoes

ingredients

MAKES 28

1 cup butter, softened

scant 3/4 cup superfine sugar

1 egg yolk, lightly beaten

2 tsp vanilla extract

2 1/4 cups all-purpose flour

1/4 cup unsweetened cocoa
    pinch of salt

1/3 cup dry unsweetened
    coconut

scant 1/3 cup white chocolate
    chips

method

1 Put the butter and sugar into a bowl and mix well with a wooden spoon, then beat in the egg yolk and vanilla extract. Sift the flour, cocoa, and a pinch of salt together into the mixture, add the coconut, and stir until thoroughly combined. Halve the dough, shape into balls, wrap in plastic wrap, and chill in the refrigerator for 30–60 minutes.

2 Preheat the oven to 375°F/190°C. Line two cookie sheets with parchment paper.

3 Unwrap the dough and roll out between two sheets of parchment paper. Stamp out cookies with a 3 1/2-inch/9-cm plain square cutter, then cut them in half to make rectangles. Place them on the prepared cookie sheets and, using a knife, make a line across the center of each without cutting through. Arrange the chocolate chips on top of the cookies to look like dominoes, pressing them in gently.

4 Bake in the preheated oven for 10–15 minutes, until golden brown. Let cool on the cookie sheets for 5–10 minutes, then, using a metal spatula, carefully transfer to wire racks to cool completely.

chocolate fudge squares

ingredients

MAKES ABOUT 30

1 cup butter, softened

scant 3/4 cup golden superfine
   sugar

1 egg yolk, lightly beaten

2 tsp vanilla extract

2 cups all-purpose flour

1/2 cup unsweetened cocoa

pinch of salt

topping

8 chocolate-coated fudge
   fingers, broken into pieces

4 tbsp heavy cream

method

1 Put the butter and sugar into a bowl and mix well with a wooden spoon, then beat in the egg yolk and vanilla extract. Sift the flour, cocoa, and salt together into the mixture and stir until thoroughly combined. Halve the dough, shape into balls, wrap in plastic wrap, and chill in the refrigerator for 30–60 minutes.

2 Preheat the oven to 375°F/190°C. Line 2 cookie sheets with parchment paper.

3 Unwrap the dough and roll out between two sheets of parchment paper to about 1/8 inch/3 mm thick. Stamp out cookies with a 2 1/2-inch/6-cm square cutter and put them on the prepared sheets, spaced well apart.

4 Bake in the preheated oven for 10–15 minutes, until golden brown. Let cool on the cookie sheets for 5–10 minutes, then using a metal spatula, carefully transfer the cookies to wire racks to cool completely.

5 For the topping, put the fudge fingers into a heatproof bowl and melt over a saucepan of gently simmering water. Remove the bowl from the heat and gradually beat in the cream. Let cool, then chill until spreadable. Spread the fudge topping over the cookies before serving.

chocolate, date & pecan pinwheels

ingredients

MAKES ABOUT 10

1 cup butter, softened

1 cup superfine sugar

1 egg yolk, lightly beaten

2 cups all-purpose flour

$^1/_2$ cup unsweetened cocoa

pinch of salt

scant 1 cup pecans,
   finely ground

1$^2/_3$ cups coarsely chopped
   dried dates

finely grated rind of 1 orange

$^3/_4$ cup orange flower water

method

1 Put the butter and scant $^3/_4$ cup of the sugar into a bowl and mix well with a wooden spoon, then beat in the egg yolk. Sift the flour, cocoa, and salt together into the mixture, add the nuts, and stir until thoroughly combined. Halve the dough, shape into balls, wrap in plastic wrap, and let chill for 30–60 minutes.

2 Meanwhile, put the dates, orange rind, orange flower water, and remaining sugar into a saucepan and cook over low heat, stirring continuously, until the sugar has dissolved. Bring to a boil, then reduce the heat, and simmer, stirring occasionally, for 5 minutes. Remove the saucepan from the heat, pour the mixture into a bowl, and let cool, then chill in the refrigerator.

3 Unwrap the dough and roll out between two pieces of parchment paper to rectangles 5 mm/$^1/_4$ inch thick. Spread the filling over the rectangles. Roll up the dough from a short side, wrap in the paper, and chill for 30 minutes.

4 Preheat the oven to 375°F/190°C. Line two cookie sheets with parchment paper. Unwrap the rolls and cut into $^1/_2$-inch/1-cm slices. Place on the prepared sheets and bake in the preheated oven for 15–20 minutes. Let cool on the cookie sheets for 5–10 minutes, then transfer to wire racks to cool completely.

chocolate sprinkle cookies

ingredients

MAKES ABOUT 30

1 cup butter, softened

scant 3/4 cup superfine sugar

1 egg yolk, lightly beaten

2 tsp vanilla extract

2 cups all-purpose flour,
    plus extra for dusting

1/2 cup unsweetened cocoa

pinch of salt

7 oz/200 g white chocolate,
    broken into pieces

1/3 cup chocolate sprinkles

method

1 Put the butter and sugar into a bowl and mix well with a wooden spoon, then beat in the egg yolk and vanilla extract. Sift the flour, cocoa, and salt together into the mixture and stir until thoroughly combined. Halve the dough, roll each piece into a ball, wrap in plastic wrap, and let chill in the refrigerator for 30–60 minutes.

2 Preheat the oven to 375°F/190°C. Line two cookie sheets with parchment paper.

3 Unwrap the dough and roll out between two pieces of parchment paper to about 1/4 inch/5 mm thick and stamp out 30 cookies with a 2 1/2–2 3/4-inch/6–7-cm fluted round cutter. Place them on the prepared cookie sheets, spaced well apart.

4 Bake in the preheated oven for 10–12 minutes. Let cool on the cookie sheets for 5–10 minutes, then, using a metal spatula, carefully transfer to wire racks to cool completely.

5 Put the pieces of white chocolate into a heatproof bowl and melt over a saucepan of gently simmering water, then immediately remove from the heat. Spread the melted chocolate over the cookies, let cool slightly, and then sprinkle with the chocolate sprinkles. Let cool and set.

chocolate & hazelnut drops

ingredients

MAKES ABOUT 30

1 cup butter, softened

scant 3/4 cup superfine sugar

1 egg yolk, lightly beaten

2 tsp vanilla extract

2 cups all-purpose flour

1/2 cup unsweetened cocoa

pinch of salt

1/2 cup ground hazelnuts

1/3 cup semisweet chocolate
   chips

4 tbsp chocolate and hazelnut
   spread

method

1 Preheat the oven to 375°F/190°C. Line two cookie sheets with parchment paper.

2 Put the butter and sugar into a bowl and mix well with a wooden spoon, then beat in the egg yolk and vanilla extract. Sift the flour, cocoa, and salt together into the mixture, add the hazelnuts and chocolate chips, and stir until thoroughly combined.

3 Scoop out tablespoons of the mixture and shape into balls with your hands, then put them on the prepared cookie sheets, spaced well apart. Use the dampened handle of a wooden spoon to make a hollow in the center of each cookie.

4 Bake in the preheated oven for 12–15 minutes. Let cool on the cookie sheets for 5–10 minutes, then using a metal spatula, carefully transfer the cookies to wire racks to cool completely. When cool, fill the hollows in the center with chocolate and hazelnut spread.

chocolate buttons

ingredients

MAKES ABOUT 30

2 envelopes instant chocolate
   or fudge chocolate drink
1 tbsp hot water
1 cup butter, softened
scant ¾ cup superfine sugar,
   plus extra for sprinkling
1 egg yolk, lightly beaten
2½ cups all-purpose flour
pinch of salt

method

1 Empty the chocolate drink envelopes into a bowl and stir in the hot water to make a paste. Put the butter and sugar into a bowl and mix well with a wooden spoon, then beat in the egg yolk and chocolate paste. Sift together the flour and salt into the mixture and stir until thoroughly combined. Halve the dough, shape into circles, wrap in plastic wrap, and chill in the refrigerator for 30–60 minutes.

2 Preheat the oven to 375°F/190°C. Line two cookie sheets with parchment paper.

3 Unwrap the dough and roll out between two sheets of parchment paper to ⅛ inch/ 3 mm thick. Stamp out cookies with a plain 2-inch/5-cm cutter. Using a 1¼-inch/3-cm cap from a soda or mineral water bottle, make an indentation in the center of each button. Using a wooden toothpick, make four holes in the center of each button, then put them on the prepared cookie sheets, spaced well apart. Sprinkle with sugar.

4 Bake in the preheated oven for 10–15 minutes, until firm. Let cool on the cookie sheets for 5–10 minutes, then transfer to wire racks to cool completely.

mocha walnut cookies

ingredients

MAKES ABOUT 16

1/2 cup unsalted butter, softened, plus extra for greasing
1/2 cup light brown sugar
1/2 cup golden granulated sugar
1 tsp vanilla extract
1 tbsp instant coffee granules, dissolved in 1 tbsp hot water
1 egg
1 1/4 cups all-purpose flour
1/2 tsp baking powder
1/4 tsp baking soda
1/3 cup milk chocolate chips
1/2 cup shelled walnuts, coarsely chopped

method

1 Preheat the oven to 350°F/180°C. Place the butter, brown sugar, and granulated sugar in a large bowl and beat together thoroughly until light and fluffy. Place the vanilla extract, coffee, and egg in a separate large bowl and whisk together.

2 Gradually add the coffee mixture to the butter and sugar, beating until fluffy. Sift the flour, baking powder, and baking soda into the mixture and fold in carefully. Fold in the chocolate chips and walnuts.

3 Drop tablespoonfuls of the mixture onto two large cookie sheets, spacing well apart to allow room for spreading. Bake in the preheated oven for 10–15 minutes, or until crisp on the outside but still soft inside. Remove from the oven. Cool on the cookie sheets for 2 minutes, then transfer to wire racks to cool completely.

chocolate & coffee whole wheat cookies

ingredients

MAKES 24

6 tbsp unsalted butter or
   margarine, plus extra
   for greasing

1 cup soft brown sugar

1 egg

1/2 cup all-purpose flour

1 tsp baking soda

pinch of salt

1/2 cup whole wheat flour

1 tbsp bran

1/3 cup semisweet chocolate
   chips

generous 2 cups rolled oats

1 tbsp strong coffee

2/3 cup hazelnuts, toasted and
   chopped coarsely

method

1 Preheat the oven to 375°F/190°C. Grease two large cookie sheets. Beat the butter and sugar together in a bowl. Add the egg and beat well, using an electric mixer if preferred.

2 Sift the all-purpose flour, baking soda, and salt together into a bowl, then add the whole wheat flour and bran. Mix in the egg mixture, then stir in the chocolate chips, oats, coffee, and hazelnuts. Mix well, with an electric mixer if preferred.

3 Put 24 rounded tablespoonfuls of the mixture onto the prepared sheets, leaving room for the cookies to spread during cooking. Transfer to the preheated oven and bake for 16–18 minutes, or until golden brown.

4 Remove from the oven, then transfer to a wire rack and let cool before serving.

oatmeal & pecan cookies

ingredients

MAKES 15

1/2 cup unsalted butter,
    softened, plus extra
    for greasing
1/2 cup light brown sugar
1 egg, beaten
1/3 cup pecans, chopped
1/2 cup all-purpose flour
1/2 tsp baking powder
1/3 cup oatmeal

method

1 Preheat the oven to 350°F/180°C. Grease two cookie sheets. Place the butter and sugar in a bowl and beat until light and fluffy. Gradually beat in the egg, then stir in the nuts.

2 Sift the flour and baking powder into the mixture and add the oatmeal. Stir together until well combined. Drop tablespoonfuls of the mixture onto the prepared cookie sheets, spaced well apart to leave room for spreading.

3 Bake in the preheated oven for 15 minutes, or until pale golden. Remove from the oven and let cool on the cookie sheets for 2 minutes, then transfer to wire racks to cool completely.

peanut butter cookies

ingredients

MAKES 26

1/2 cup butter, softened,
    plus extra for greasing
scant 1/2 cup crunchy peanut
    butter
generous 1/2 cup superfine
    sugar
generous 1/2 cup light brown
    sugar
1 egg, beaten
1/2 tsp vanilla extract
2/3 cup all-purpose flour
1/2 tsp baking soda
1/2 tsp baking powder
pinch of salt
1 1/2 cups rolled oats

method

1 Preheat the oven to 350°F/180°C, then grease three cookie sheets.

2 Place the butter and peanut butter in a bowl and beat together. Beat in the superfine sugar and brown sugar, then gradually beat in the egg and vanilla extract.

3 Sift the flour, baking soda, baking powder, and salt into the bowl and stir in the oats.

4 Place spoonfuls of the mixture on the prepared cookie sheets, spaced well apart. Flatten slightly with a fork.

5 Bake in the preheated oven for 12 minutes, or until lightly browned. Let cool on the cookie sheets for 2 minutes, then transfer to wire racks to cool completely.

pistachio & almond tuiles

ingredients

MAKES 12

1 egg white

generous 1/4 cup superfine sugar

1/4 cup all-purpose flour

1/4 cup pistachios, finely chopped

1/4 cup ground almonds

1/2 tsp almond extract

3 tbsp unsalted butter, melted and cooled

method

1 Preheat the oven to 325°F/160°C. Line two cookie sheets with parchment paper.

2 Whisk the egg white lightly with the sugar, then stir in the flour, pistachios, ground almonds, almond extract, and butter, mixing to a soft paste.

3 Place walnut-size spoonfuls of the mixture on the prepared cookie sheets and use the back of the spoon to spread as thinly as possible. Bake in the preheated oven for 10–15 minutes, until pale golden.

4 Quickly lift each cookie with a spatula and place over the side of a rolling pin to shape into a curve. When set, transfer to a wire rack to cool.

fig & walnut cookies

ingredients

MAKES 20

scant 1/2 cup dried figs, plus
    extra fig pieces, to decorate
1 cup unsalted butter or
    margarine, plus extra
    for greasing
1/3 cup honey
4 tbsp raw sugar
2 eggs, beaten
pinch of salt
1 tsp allspice
1 tsp baking soda
1/2 tsp vanilla extract
2 tbsp dried dates, finely
    chopped
1 1/2 cups all-purpose flour
2 cups oatmeal
3/8 cup walnuts, finely
    chopped

method

1 Preheat the oven to 350°F/180°C. Grease two large cookie sheets.

2 Finely chop the figs. Mix the butter, honey, figs, and sugar together in a large bowl. Beat the eggs into the mixture and mix thoroughly.

3 In a separate bowl, combine the salt, allspice, baking soda, vanilla extract, and dates. Gradually stir them into the creamed mixture. Sift the flour into the mixture and stir well. Finally, mix in the oatmeal and walnuts.

4 Drop 20 rounded tablespoonfuls of the mixture onto the prepared cookie sheets, spaced well apart to leave room for spreading. Decorate with fig pieces. Bake in the preheated oven for 10–15 minutes, or until the cookies are golden brown.

5 Remove the cookies from the oven. Transfer to a wire rack and let cool before serving.

oat & hazelnut cookies

ingredients

MAKES 30

3/4 cup unsalted butter or
    margarine, plus extra
    for greasing
scant 1 1/4 cups raw sugar
1 egg, beaten
4 tbsp milk
1 tsp vanilla extract
1/2 tsp almond extract
generous 2/3 cup hazelnuts
1 cup all-purpose flour
1 1/2 tsp ground allspice
1/4 tsp baking soda
pinch of salt
2 cups oatmeal
scant 1 cup golden raisins

method

1 Preheat the oven to 375°F/190°C. Grease two large cookie sheets.

2 Cream the butter and sugar together in a mixing bowl. Blend in the egg, milk, vanilla extract, and almond extract until thoroughly combined. Finely chop the hazelnuts.

3 In a mixing bowl, sift the flour, allspice, baking soda, and salt together. Add to the creamed mixture slowly, stirring continuously. Mix in the oatmeal, golden raisins, and hazelnuts.

4 Put 30 rounded tablespoonfuls of the mixture onto the prepared cookie sheets, spaced well apart to leave room for spreading. Transfer to the preheated oven and bake for 12–15 minutes, or until the cookies are golden brown.

5 Remove the cookies from the oven and place on a wire rack to cool before serving.

almond biscotti

ingredients

MAKES 20–24

1³/₄ cups all-purpose flour,
   plus extra for dusting

1 tsp baking powder

pinch of salt

³/₄ cup golden superfine sugar

2 eggs, beaten

finely grated rind of 1 unwaxed
   orange

²/₃ cup whole blanched
   almonds, lightly toasted

method

1 Preheat the oven to 350°F/180°C, then lightly dust a cookie sheet with flour. Sift the flour, baking powder, and salt into a bowl. Add the sugar, eggs, and orange rind and mix to a dough, then knead in the toasted almonds.

2 Using your hands, roll the dough into a ball, cut in half, and roll each portion into a log about 1¹/₂ inches/4 cm in diameter. Place on the prepared cookie sheet and bake in the preheated oven for 10 minutes. Remove from the oven and let cool for 5 minutes.

3 Using a serrated knife, cut the logs into ¹/₂-inch/1-cm thick diagonal slices. Arrange the slices on the cookie sheet and return to the oven for 15 minutes, or until slightly golden. Transfer to a wire rack to cool and crispen.

nutty drizzles

ingredients

MAKES 24

scant 1 cup unsalted butter,
    plus extra for greasing

1¼ cups raw sugar

1 egg

1 cup all-purpose flour, sifted

1 tsp baking powder

1 tsp baking soda

1 cup oatmeal

1 tbsp bran

1 tbsp wheatgerm

4 oz/115 g mixed nuts, toasted
    and coarsely chopped

1 cup bittersweet chocolate
    chips

1 cup mixed raisins and
    golden raisins

6 oz/175 g semisweet
    chocolate, coarsely
    chopped

method

1 Preheat the oven to 350°F/180°C. Grease two large cookie sheets. In a large bowl, beat together the butter, sugar, and egg. Add the flour, baking powder, baking soda, oatmeal, bran, and wheatgerm and mix together until well combined. Stir in the nuts, chocolate chips, and dried fruit.

2 Put 24 rounded tablespoonfuls of the mixture onto the prepared sheets. Transfer to the preheated oven and bake for 12 minutes, or until golden.

3 Remove the cookies from the oven, then transfer to a wire rack and let cool. Meanwhile, heat the chocolate pieces in a heatproof bowl set over a saucepan of simmering water until melted. Stir the chocolate, then let cool slightly.

4 Use a spoon to drizzle the chocolate in waves over the cookies, or spoon it into a pastry bag and pipe zigzag lines over the cookies. When the chocolate has set, store the cookies in an airtight container in the refrigerator until ready to serve.

almond crunchies

ingredients

MAKES ABOUT 50

1 cup butter, softened

scant 3/4 cup superfine sugar

1 egg yolk, lightly beaten

1/2 tsp almond extract

2 cups all-purpose flour

pinch of salt

2 cups blanched almonds,
    chopped

method

1 Put the butter and sugar into a bowl and mix well with a wooden spoon, then beat in the egg yolk and almond extract. Sift the flour and salt together into the mixture, add the almonds, and stir until thoroughly combined. Halve the dough, shape it into balls, wrap in plastic wrap, and chill in the refrigerator for 30–60 minutes.

2 Preheat the oven to 375°F/190°C. Line 2–3 cookie sheets with parchment paper. Shape the dough into about 50 small balls and flatten them slightly between the palms of your hands. Put on the prepared cookie sheets, spaced well apart.

3 Bake for 15–20 minutes, until golden brown. Let cool on the cookie sheets for 5–10 minutes, then, using a metal spatula, carefully transfer to wire racks to cool completely.

snickerdoodles

ingredients

MAKES ABOUT 40

1 cup butter, softened
scant ³/₄ cup superfine sugar
2 extra-large eggs, lightly
 beaten
1 tsp vanilla extract
3¹/₂ cups all-purpose flour
1 tsp baking soda
¹/₂ tsp freshly grated nutmeg
pinch of salt
¹/₂ cup finely chopped pecans

cinnamon coating
1 tbsp superfine sugar
2 tsp ground cinnamon

method

1 Put the butter and sugar into a bowl and mix well with a wooden spoon, then beat in the eggs and vanilla extract. Sift the flour, baking soda, nutmeg, and salt together into the mixture, add the pecans, and stir until thoroughly combined. Shape the dough into a ball, wrap in plastic wrap, and chill in the refrigerator for 30–60 minutes.

2 Preheat the oven to 375°F/190°C. Line two cookie sheets with parchment paper.

3 For the coating, mix together the sugar and cinnamon in a shallow dish. Scoop up tablespoons of the cookie dough and roll into balls. Roll each ball in the cinnamon mixture to coat and put on the prepared cookie sheets, spaced well apart.

4 Bake in the preheated oven for 10–12 minutes, until golden brown. Let cool on the cookie sheets for 5–10 minutes, then, using a metal spatula, carefully transfer to wire racks to cool completely.

cashew & poppy seed cookies

ingredients

MAKES ABOUT 20

1 cup butter, softened

scant 3/4 cup superfine sugar

1 egg yolk, lightly beaten

2 1/2 cups all-purpose flour

1 tsp ground cinnamon

pinch of salt

1 cup cashews, chopped

2–3 tbsp poppy seeds

method

1 Put the butter and sugar into a bowl and mix well with a wooden spoon, then beat in the egg yolk. Sift together the flour, cinnamon, and salt into the mixture, add the nuts, and stir until thoroughly combined. Shape the dough into a log. Spread out the poppy seeds in a shallow dish and roll the log in them until well coated. Wrap in plastic wrap and chill in the refrigerator for 30–60 minutes.

2 Preheat the oven to 375°F/190°C. Line two cookie sheets with parchment paper.

3 Unwrap the dough and cut into 1/2-inch/1-cm slices with a sharp serrated knife. Put the slices on the prepared sheets and bake for 12 minutes, until golden brown. Let cool on the cookie sheets for 5–10 minutes, then, using a metal spatula, carefully transfer to wire racks to cool completely.

walnut & coffee cookies

ingredients

MAKES ABOUT 30

2 envelopes instant latte

1 tbsp hot water

1 cup butter, softened

scant 3/4 cup superfine sugar

1 egg yolk, lightly beaten

2 1/2 cups all-purpose flour

scant 1 cup finely chopped
    walnuts

salt

coffee sugar crystals,
    for sprinkling

method

1 Put the instant latte into a bowl and stir in the hot water to make a paste. Put the butter and sugar into a bowl and mix well with a wooden spoon, then beat in the egg yolk and coffee paste. Sift the flour and a pinch of salt together into the mixture, add the walnuts, and stir until thoroughly combined. Halve the dough, shape into balls, wrap in plastic wrap, and chill in the refrigerator for 30–60 minutes.

2 Preheat the oven to 375°F/190°C. Line two cookie sheets with parchment paper.

3 Unwrap the dough and roll out between two sheets of parchment paper to about 1/8 inch/3 mm thick. Stamp out cookies with a 2 1/2-inch/6-cm round cutter and put them on the prepared cookie sheets, spaced well apart.

4 Lightly brush the cookies with water, sprinkle with the coffee sugar crystals, and bake for 10–12 minutes. Let cool on the cookie sheets for 5–10 minutes, then, using a metal spatula, carefully transfer to wire racks to cool completely.

pineapple & cherry florentines

ingredients

MAKES ABOUT 14

4 tbsp unsalted butter

scant 1/4 cup raw sugar

1 tbsp corn syrup

1/3 cup all-purpose flour, sifted

1/8 cup angelica, coarsely chopped

1/8 cup candied cherries, coarsely chopped

1/2 cup slivered almonds, coarsely chopped

1/3 cup candied pineapple, coarsely chopped

1 tsp lemon juice

4 oz/115 g bittersweet chocolate, melted and cooled

method

1 Preheat the oven to 350°F/180°C. Line two large cookie sheets with nonstick parchment paper. Place the butter, sugar, and syrup in a saucepan and heat gently until melted, then stir in the flour, angelica, cherries, almonds, pineapple, and lemon juice.

2 Place walnut-size mounds of the mixture, spaced well apart, on the prepared sheets and flatten gently with a fork. Bake in the preheated oven for 8–10 minutes, or until golden brown. Use a spatula to neaten the ragged edges. Let cool for 1 minute, then transfer to a wire rack to cool completely.

3 Spread the melted chocolate over the bottom of each florentine, then place, chocolate-side up, on a wire rack. Use a fork to mark the chocolate with wavy lines. Let stand until set.

apricot & pecan cookies

ingredients

MAKES ABOUT 30

1 cup butter, softened
scant ³/4 cup superfine sugar
1 egg yolk, lightly beaten
2 tsp vanilla extract
2¹/2 cups all-purpose flour
pinch of salt
grated rind of 1 orange
¹/4 cup plumped dried
    apricots, chopped
scant 1 cup finely chopped
    pecans

method

1 Put the butter and sugar into a bowl and mix well with a wooden spoon, then beat in the egg yolk and vanilla extract. Sift together the flour and salt into the mixture, add the orange rind and apricots, and stir until thoroughly combined. Shape the dough into a log. Spread out the pecans in a shallow dish. Roll the log in the nuts until well coated, then wrap in plastic wrap, and chill in the refrigerator for 30–60 minutes.

2 Preheat the oven to 375°F/190°C. Line two cookie sheets with parchment paper. Unwrap the dough and cut into ¹/4-inch/5-mm slices with a sharp serrated knife. Put the slices on the prepared cookie sheets, spaced well apart.

3 Bake in the preheated oven for 10–12 minutes. Let cool on the cookie sheets for 5–10 minutes, then, using a metal spatula, carefully transfer to wire racks to cool completely.

walnut & fig pinwheels

ingredients

MAKES ABOUT 30

1 cup butter, softened

1 cup superfine sugar

1 egg yolk, lightly beaten

2 cups all-purpose flour

pinch of salt

$1/2$ cup ground walnuts

$12/3$ cups dried figs, finely
    chopped

5 tbsp freshly brewed mint tea

2 tsp finely chopped fresh
    mint

method

1 Put the butter and scant $3/4$ cup of the sugar into a bowl and mix well with a wooden spoon, then beat in the egg yolk. Sift the flour and salt together into the mixture, add the ground walnuts, and stir until thoroughly combined. Shape the dough into a ball, wrap in plastic wrap, and chill for 30–60 minutes.

2 Meanwhile, put the remaining sugar into a saucepan and stir in $1/2$ cup of water, then add the figs, mint tea, and chopped mint. Bring to a boil, stirring continuously, until the sugar has dissolved, then reduce the heat, and simmer gently, stirring occasionally, for 5 minutes. Remove from the heat and let cool.

3 Unwrap the dough and roll out between two sheets of parchment paper into a 12-inch/30-cm square. Spread the fig filling evenly over the dough, then roll up like a jelly roll. Wrap in plastic wrap and chill in the refrigerator for 30 minutes.

4 Preheat the oven to 375°F/190°C. Line two cookie sheets with parchment paper. Unwrap the roll and cut into thin slices with a sharp serrated knife. Put the slices on the prepared cookie sheets spread well apart. Bake in the preheated oven for 10–15 minutes, until golden brown. Let cool on the cookie sheets for 5–10 minutes, then transfer to wire racks to cool completely.

mixed fruit cookies

ingredients

MAKES ABOUT 30

1 cup butter, softened

scant 3/4 cup superfine sugar

1 egg yolk, lightly beaten

2 1/2 cups all-purpose flour

1/2 tsp apple pie spice

1/4 cup chopped plumped
   dried apple

1/4 cup chopped plumped
   dried pear

1/4 cup chopped plumped
   prunes

grated rind of 1 orange

salt

method

1 Put the butter and sugar into a bowl and mix well with a wooden spoon, then beat in the egg yolk. Sift the flour, apple pie spice, and a pinch of salt together into the mixture, add the apple, pear, prunes, and orange rind, and stir until thoroughly combined. Shape the dough into a log, wrap in plastic wrap, and chill in the refrigerator for 30–60 minutes.

2 Preheat the oven to 375°F/190°C. Line two cookie sheets with parchment paper.

3 Unwrap the log and cut it into 1/4-inch/ 5-mm thick slices with a sharp serrated knife. Put them on the prepared cookie sheets, spaced well apart.

4 Bake in the preheated oven for 10–15 minutes, until golden brown. Let cool on the cookie sheets for 5–10 minutes, then, using a metal spatula, carefully transfer the cookies to wire racks to cool completely.

tropical fruit & mascarpone cream cookie sandwiches

ingredients

MAKES ABOUT 15

1 cup butter, softened

scant 3/4 cup superfine sugar

1 egg yolk, lightly beaten

2 tsp passion fruit pulp

2 1/2 cups all-purpose flour

pinch of salt

1/3 cup chopped plumped
   dried mango

1/3 cup chopped plumped
   dried papaya

3 tbsp pitted and chopped
   dried dates

3–4 tbsp shredded coconut,
   toasted

mascarpone cream

1/3 cup mascarpone cheese

3 tbsp strained plain yogurt

7 tbsp prepared custard

1/2 tsp ground ginger

method

1 Put the butter and sugar into a bowl and mix well with a wooden spoon, then beat in the egg yolk and passion fruit pulp. Sift the flour and salt together into the mixture, add the mango, papaya, and dates, and stir until thoroughly combined. Shape the dough into a log, wrap in plastic wrap, and chill in the refrigerator for 30–60 minutes.

2 Meanwhile, make the mascarpone cream. Put all the ingredients in a bowl and beat with a wooden spoon until thoroughly combined and smooth. Cover the bowl with plastic wrap and chill in the refrigerator.

3 Preheat the oven to 375°F/190°C. Line two cookie sheets with parchment paper.

4 Unwrap the dough and cut into slices with a sharp serrated knife. Put them on the prepared cookie sheets spaced well apart.

5 Bake in the preheated oven for 10–15 minutes, until light golden brown. Let cool on the cookie sheets for 5–10 minutes, then, using a metal spatula, carefully transfer to wire racks to cool completely. When the cookies are cold spread the chilled mascarpone cream over half of them, sprinkle with the toasted coconut, and top with the remaining cookies.

chocolate & apricot cookies

ingredients

MAKES ABOUT 30

1 cup butter, softened

scant ³/₄ cup superfine sugar

1 egg yolk, lightly beaten

2 tsp amaretto liqueur

2¹/₂ cups all-purpose flour

¹/₃ cup bittersweet chocolate
   chips

¹/₂ cup chopped plumped
   dried apricots

scant 1 cup blanched
   almonds, chopped

salt

method

1 Put the butter and sugar into a bowl and mix well with a wooden spoon, then beat in the egg yolk and amaretto liqueur. Sift together the flour and a pinch of salt into the mixture, add the chocolate chips and apricots, and stir until thoroughly combined.

2 Shape the mixture into a log. Spread out the almonds in a shallow dish and roll the log in them to coat. Wrap in plastic wrap and chill in the refrigerator for 30–60 minutes.

3 Preheat the oven to 375°F/190°C. Line two cookie sheets with parchment paper.

4 Unwrap the dough and cut into ¹/₄-inch/5-mm slices with a sharp serrated knife. Put them on the prepared cookie sheets, spaced well apart.

5 Bake in the preheated oven for 12–15 minutes, until golden brown. Let cool on the cookie sheets for 5–10 minutes, then, using a metal spatula, carefully transfer to wire racks to cool completely.

orange & lemon cookies

ingredients

MAKES ABOUT 30

1 cup butter, softened

scant 3/4 cup superfine sugar

1 egg yolk, lightly beaten

2 1/2 cups all-purpose flour

pinch of salt

finely grated rind of 1 orange

finely grated rind of 1 lemon

to decorate

1 tbsp lightly beaten egg white

1 tbsp lemon juice

1 cup confectioners' sugar

few drops yellow food coloring

few drops orange food coloring

about 15 lemon jelly fruit
   slices

about 15 orange jelly fruit
   slices

method

1 Put the butter and sugar into a bowl and mix well with a wooden spoon, then beat in the egg yolk. Sift the flour and salt together into the mixture and stir until thoroughly combined. Halve the dough and gently knead the orange rind into one half and the lemon rind into the other. Shape into balls, wrap in plastic wrap, and chill in the refrigerator for 30–60 minutes.

2 Preheat the oven to 375°F/190°C. Line two cookie sheets with parchment paper.

3 Unwrap the orange-flavored dough and roll out between two sheets of parchment paper. Stamp out cookies with a 2 1/2-inch/6-cm cookie cutter and put them on a prepared cookie sheet, spaced well apart. Repeat with the lemon-flavored dough and stamp out crescents. Put them on the other prepared cookie sheet, spaced well apart.

4 Bake in the preheated oven for 10–15 minutes, until golden brown. Let cool for 5–10 minutes, then carefully transfer to wire racks to cool completely.

5 To decorate, combine the egg white and lemon juice. Gradually beat in the confectioners' sugar until smooth. Spoon half the frosting into another bowl. Stir yellow food coloring into one bowl and orange into the other. Spread the frosting over the cookies and decorate with the jelly slices. Let set.

grapefruit & apple mint cookies

ingredients

MAKES ABOUT 30

1 cup butter, softened

scant 3/4 cup superfine sugar, plus extra for sprinkling

1 egg yolk, lightly beaten

2 tsp grapefruit juice

2 1/2 cups all-purpose flour

grated rind of 1 grapefruit

2 tsp finely chopped fresh apple mint

salt

method

1 Put the butter and sugar into a bowl and mix well with a wooden spoon, then beat in the egg yolk and grapefruit juice. Sift together the flour and a pinch of salt into the mixture, add the grapefruit rind and chopped mint, and stir until thoroughly combined. Halve the dough, shape into balls, wrap in plastic wrap, and chill in the refrigerator for 30–60 minutes.

2 Preheat the oven to 375°F/190°C. Line two cookie sheets with parchment paper.

3 Unwrap the dough and roll out between two sheets of parchment paper to 1/8 inch/ 3 mm thick. Stamp out cookies with a 2-inch/ 5-cm flower cutter and put them on the prepared cookie sheets, spaced well apart. Sprinkle with sugar.

4 Bake in the preheated oven for 10–15 minutes, until golden brown. Let cool on the cookie sheets for 5–10 minutes, then, using a metal spatula, carefully transfer to wire racks to cool completely.

mango, coconut & ginger cookies

ingredients

MAKES ABOUT 30

1 cup butter, softened

scant 3/4 cup superfine sugar

1 egg yolk, lightly beaten

4 tbsp chopped preserved
    ginger, plus 2 tsp syrup
    from the jar

2 1/2 cups all-purpose flour

pinch of salt

1/2 cup chopped plumped
    dried mango

generous 1 cup unsweetened
    dried coconut

method

1 Put the butter and sugar into a bowl and mix well with a wooden spoon, then beat in the egg yolk and ginger syrup. Sift the flour and salt together into the mixture, add the chopped ginger and mango, and stir until thoroughly combined.

2 Spread out the coconut in a shallow dish. Shape the dough into a log and roll it in the coconut to coat. Wrap in plastic wrap and chill in the refrigerator for 30–60 minutes.

3 Preheat the oven to 375°F/190°C. Line two cookie sheets with parchment paper.

4 Unwrap the log, cut it into 1/4-inch/5-mm slices with a sharp serrated knife, and put them on the prepared cookie sheets, spaced well apart to leave room for spreading.

5 Bake in the preheated oven for 12–15 minutes. Let cool on the cookie sheets for 5–10 minutes, then, using a metal spatula, carefully transfer to wire racks to cool completely.

orange cream cheese cookies

ingredients

MAKES ABOUT 30

1 cup butter or margarine,
    plus extra for greasing
1 cup packed brown sugar
scant 1/2 cup cream cheese
1 egg, lightly beaten
generous 2 1/3 cups
    all-purpose flour
1 tsp baking soda
1 tbsp fresh orange juice
1 tsp finely grated orange rind,
    plus extra for decorating
raw sugar, for sprinkling

method

1 Preheat the oven to 375°F/190°C. Grease a large baking sheet.

2 Put the butter, sugar, and cream cheese in a large bowl and beat until light and fluffy. Beat in the egg. Sift in the flour and baking soda and add the orange juice and rind. Mix well.

3 Drop about 30 rounded tablespoonfuls of the batter onto the prepared baking sheet, making sure that they are well spaced. Sprinkle with the raw sugar.

4 Bake in the preheated oven for 10 minutes, or until the cookies are light brown at the edges.

5 Let cool on a wire rack. Decorate with orange rind before serving.

jelly rings

ingredients

MAKES ABOUT 15

1 cup butter, softened

scant 3/4 cup superfine sugar,
 plus extra for sprinkling

1 egg yolk, lightly beaten

2 tsp vanilla extract

2 1/2 cups all-purpose flour

pinch of salt

1 egg white, lightly beaten

filling

1/4 cup butter, softened

scant 1 cup confectioners'
 sugar

5 tbsp strawberry jelly or
 raspberry jelly, warmed

method

1 Put the butter and sugar into a bowl and mix well with a wooden spoon, then beat in the egg yolk and vanilla extract. Sift the flour and salt together into the mixture and stir until thoroughly combined. Halve the dough, shape into balls, wrap in plastic wrap, and chill in the refrigerator for 30–60 minutes.

2 Preheat the oven to 375°F/190°C. Line two cookie sheets with parchment paper.

3 Unwrap the dough and roll out between two sheets of parchment paper. Stamp out cookies with a 2 3/4-inch/7-cm fluted round cutter and put half of them on one of the prepared cookie sheets, spaced well apart. Using a 1 1/2-inch/ 4-cm plain round cutter, stamp out the centers of the remaining cookies and remove. Put the cookie rings on the other cookie sheet, spaced well apart.

4 Bake in the preheated oven for 7 minutes, then brush the cookie rings with beaten egg white and sprinkle with superfine sugar. Bake for 5–8 minutes more, until light golden brown. Let cool on the cookie sheets for 5–10 minutes, then, using a metal spatula, carefully transfer to wire racks to cool completely.

5 To make the filling, beat the butter and sugar together in a bowl until smooth and combined. Spread the buttercream over the whole cookies and top with a little jelly. Place the cookie rings on top and press gently together.

iced cherry rings

ingredients

MAKES ABOUT 18

1/2 cup unsalted butter, plus
  extra for greasing
scant 1/2 cup superfine sugar
1 egg yolk
finely grated rind of 1/2 lemon
13/4 cups all-purpose flour,
  plus extra for dusting
1/4 cup candied cherries, finely
  chopped

frosting
3/4 cup confectioners' sugar
11/2 tbsp lemon juice

method

1 Preheat the oven to 400°F/200°C. Lightly grease two cookie sheets.

2 Cream together the butter and sugar until pale and fluffy. Beat in the egg yolk and lemon rind. Sift in the flour, stir, then add the cherries, mixing with your hands to a soft dough.

3 Roll out the dough on a lightly floured counter to about 1/4 inch/5 mm thick. Stamp out circles with a 31/4-inch/8-cm cookie cutter. Cut out the center of each with a 1-inch/2.5-cm cutter and place the rings on the prepared cookie sheets. Reroll any trimmings and cut out more cookies.

4 Bake in the preheated oven for 12–15 minutes, until firm and golden brown.

5 Let cool on the cookie sheets for 2 minutes, then transfer to a wire rack to finish cooling.

6 For the frosting, mix the confectioners' sugar to a smooth paste with the lemon juice. Drizzle over the cookies and let set.

citrus crescents

ingredients

MAKES ABOUT 25

1/3 cup butter, softened,
   plus extra for greasing
1/3 cup superfine sugar
1 egg, separated
1 3/4 cups all-purpose flour,
   plus extra for dusting
grated rind of 1 orange
grated rind of 1 lemon
grated rind of 1 lime
2–3 tbsp orange juice

method

1 Preheat the oven to 400°F/200°C. Lightly grease two cookie sheets. In a mixing bowl, cream the butter and sugar together until light and fluffy, then gradually beat in the egg yolk.

2 Sift the flour into the creamed mixture and mix until evenly combined. Add the orange rind, lemon rind, and lime rind to the mixture with enough of the orange juice to make a soft dough.

3 Roll out the dough on a lightly floured counter. Stamp out circles using a 3-inch/7.5-cm cookie cutter. Make crescent shapes by cutting away one quarter of each circle. Reroll the trimmings to make about 25 crescents in total.

4 Place the crescents on the prepared cookie sheets. Prick the surface of each crescent with a fork. Lightly whisk the egg white in a small bowl and brush it over the cookies.

5 Bake in the preheated oven for 12–15 minutes. Let cool on a wire rack before serving.

chewy candied fruit cookies

ingredients

MAKES ABOUT 30

1 cup butter, softened
scant 3/4 cup superfine sugar
1 egg yolk, lightly beaten
2 tsp vanilla extract
2 1/2 cups all-purpose flour
pinch of salt

candied topping

4 tbsp maple syrup
1/4 cup butter
1/4 cup superfine sugar
1/2 cup chopped plumped
    dried peaches
1/4 cup chopped candied
    cherries
1/3 cup chopped candied peel
3/4 cup chopped macadamia
    nuts
1/4 cup all-purpose flour

method

1 Put the butter and sugar into a bowl and mix well with a wooden spoon, then beat in the egg yolk and vanilla extract. Sift the flour and salt together into the mixture and stir until thoroughly combined. Halve the dough, shape into balls, wrap in plastic wrap, and chill for 30–60 minutes.

2 Preheat the oven to 375°F/190°C. Line two cookie sheets with parchment paper.

3 Unwrap the dough and roll out between two sheets of parchment paper. Stamp out cookies with a 2 1/2-inch/6-cm plain round cutter and put them on the prepared cookie sheets, spaced well apart.

4 For the topping, put the syrup, butter, and sugar into a saucepan and melt over low heat, stirring occasionally. Meanwhile, put the fruit, candied peel, nuts, and flour into a bowl and mix well. When the syrup mixture is thoroughly combined, stir it into the fruit mixture. Divide the candied topping among the cookies, gently spreading it out to the edges.

5 Bake in the preheated oven for 10–15 minutes, until firm. Let cool on the cookie sheets for 5–10 minutes, then using a metal spatula, carefully transfer the cookies to wire racks to cool completely.

classic saffron cookies

ingredients

MAKES ABOUT 30

scant 1/2 cup currants
1/2 cup sweet white wine
1 cup butter, softened
scant 3/4 cup superfine sugar
1 egg yolk, lightly beaten
2 1/2 cups all-purpose flour
1/2 tsp powdered saffron
pinch of salt

method

1 Put the currants in a bowl, pour in the wine, and let soak for 1 hour. Drain the currants and reserve any remaining wine.

2 Preheat the oven to 375°F/190°C. Line two cookie sheets with parchment paper.

3 Put the butter and sugar into a bowl and mix well with a wooden spoon, then beat in the egg yolk and 2 teaspoons of the reserved wine. Sift the flour, saffron, and salt together into the mixture and stir until thoroughly combined.

4 Scoop up tablespoons of the dough and put them on the prepared cookie sheets spaced well apart. Flatten gently and smooth the tops with the back of the spoon.

5 Bake in the preheated oven for 10–15 minutes, until light golden brown. Let cool on the cookie sheets for 5–10 minutes, then, using a metal spatula, carefully transfer to wire racks to cool completely.

chamomile cookies

ingredients

MAKES ABOUT 30

1 cup butter, softened

scant ¾ cup golden superfine
      sugar, plus extra for coating

1 tbsp (3–4 tea bags)
      chamomile or chamomile
      and lime flower infusion or
      tea leaves

1 egg yolk, lightly beaten

1 tsp vanilla extract

2½ cups all-purpose flour

pinch of salt

method

1 Put the butter and sugar into a bowl and
mix well with a wooden spoon. If necessary,
remove the tea leaves from the tea bags. Stir
the tea into the butter mixture, then beat in
the egg yolk and vanilla extract. Sift the flour
and salt together into the mixture and stir until
thoroughly combined.

2 Shape the dough into a log. Spread out
3–4 tablespoons of sugar in a shallow dish and
roll the log in the sugar to coat. Wrap in plastic
wrap and chill for 30–60 minutes.

3 Preheat the oven to 375°F/190°C. Line
two cookie sheets with parchment paper.

4 Unwrap the log and cut into ¼-inch/5-mm
slices with a sharp serrated knife. Put them on
the prepared cookie sheets, spread well apart.

5 Bake in the preheated oven for about 10
minutes, until golden. Let cool on the cookie
sheets for 5–10 minutes, then, using a metal
spatula, transfer to wire racks to cool completely.

fennel & angelica cookies

ingredients

MAKES ABOUT 20

1 cup butter, softened

scant 3/4 cup superfine sugar

1 egg yolk, lightly beaten

1 tbsp finely chopped angelica

2 1/2 cups all-purpose flour

pinch of salt

1 tbsp fennel seeds

method

1 Put the butter and sugar into a bowl and mix well with a wooden spoon, then beat in the egg yolk and angelica. Sift the flour and salt together into the mixture, add the fennel seeds, and stir until thoroughly combined. Shape the dough into a log, wrap in plastic wrap, and let chill in the refrigerator for up to 1 hour.

2 Preheat the oven to 375°F/190°C. Line two cookie sheets with parchment paper.

3 Unwrap the dough and cut into 1/2-inch/1-cm slices with a sharp serrated knife. Put them on the prepared cookie sheets, spaced well apart.

4 Bake for 12–15 minutes, until golden brown. Let cool on the cookie sheets for 5–10 minutes, then, using a metal spatula, carefully transfer to wire racks to cool completely.

molasses & spice drizzles

ingredients

MAKES 25

scant 1 cup butter, softened
2 tbsp molasses
scant 3/4 cup superfine sugar
1 egg yolk, lightly beaten
2 1/2 cups all-purpose flour
1 tsp ground cinnamon
1/2 tsp grated nutmeg
1/2 tsp ground cloves
pinch of salt
2 tbsp chopped walnuts

frosting

1 cup confectioners' sugar
1 tbsp hot water
few drops yellow food coloring
few drops pink food coloring

method

1 Put the butter, molasses, and sugar into a bowl and mix well with a wooden spoon, then beat in the egg yolk. Sift the flour, cinnamon, nutmeg, cloves, and salt together into the mixture, add the walnuts, and stir until thoroughly combined. Halve the dough, shape into balls, wrap in plastic wrap, and chill in the refrigerator for 30–60 minutes.

2 Preheat the oven to 375°F/190°C. Line two cookie sheets with parchment paper.

3 Unwrap the dough and roll out between two sheets of parchment paper to about 1/4 inch/5 mm thick. Stamp out cookies with a 2 1/2-inch/6-cm fluted cutter and put them on the prepared cookie sheets.

4 Bake in the preheated oven for 10–15 minutes, until firm. Let cool on the cookie sheets for 5–10 minutes, then using a metal spatula, carefully transfer the cookies to wire racks to cool completely.

5 To decorate, sift the confectioners' sugar into a bowl, then gradually stir in the hot water until the frosting has the consistency of thick cream. Spoon half the frosting into another bowl, then stir a few drops of yellow food coloring into one bowl and a few drops of pink food coloring into the other. With the cookies still on the racks, using teaspoons, drizzle the yellow frosting over them in one direction and the pink frosting over them at right angles. Let set.

cinnamon & caramel cookies

ingredients

MAKES ABOUT 25

1 cup butter, softened

scant ¾ cup superfine sugar

1 egg yolk, lightly beaten

1 tsp vanilla extract

2½ cups all-purpose flour

1 tsp ground cinnamon

½ tsp allspice

pinch of salt

25–30 hard caramel candies

method

1 Preheat the oven to 375°F/190°C. Line two cookie sheets with parchment paper.

2 Put the butter and sugar into a bowl and mix well with a wooden spoon, then beat in the egg yolk and vanilla extract. Sift the flour, cinnamon, allspice, and salt together into the mixture and stir until thoroughly combined.

3 Scoop up tablespoons of the mixture, shape into balls, and put on the prepared cookie sheets spaced well apart. Bake for 8 minutes. Place a caramel candy on top of each cookie, return to the oven, and bake for an additional 6–7 minutes.

4 Remove from the oven and let cool on the cookie sheets for 5–10 minutes. Using a metal spatula, carefully transfer the cookies to wire racks to cool completely.

brandy snaps

ingredients

MAKES ABOUT 20

$1/3$ cup unsalted butter

scant $1/2$ cup superfine sugar

3 tbsp dark corn syrup

$3/4$ cup all-purpose flour

1 tsp ground ginger

1 tbsp brandy

finely grated rind of $1/2$ lemon

filling

$2/3$ cup heavy cream

1 tbsp brandy (optional)

1 tbsp confectioners' sugar

method

1 Preheat the oven to 325°F/160°C. Line three large cookie sheets with parchment paper.

2 Place the butter, sugar, and corn syrup in a saucepan and heat gently over low heat, stirring occasionally, until melted. Remove from the heat and let cool slightly. Sift the flour and ginger into the pan and beat until smooth, then stir in the brandy, and the lemon rind.

3 Drop small spoonfuls of the mixture onto the prepared cookie sheets, leaving plenty of room for spreading. Bake one cookie sheet at a time in the preheated oven for 10–12 minutes, or until golden brown.

4 Remove the first cookie sheet from the oven and let cool for about 30 seconds, then lift each round with a spatula and wrap around the handle of a wooden spoon. If the brandy snaps start to become too firm to wrap, return them to the oven for about 30 seconds to soften again. When the brandy snaps are firm, remove from the spoon handles and finish cooling on a wire rack. Repeat with the remaining cookie sheets.

5 For the filling, whip the cream with the brandy, if using, and confectioners' sugar until thick. Just before serving, pipe the cream mixture into each end of the brandy snaps.

lavender cookies

ingredients

MAKES 12

1/4 cup golden superfine sugar,
   plus extra for dusting

1 tsp chopped lavender leaves

1/2 cup unsalted butter,
   softened, plus extra
   for greasing

finely grated rind of 1 lemon

generous 1 cup all-purpose
   flour

method

1 Preheat the oven to 300°F/150°C, then grease a large cookie sheet. Place the sugar and lavender leaves in a food processor. Process until the lavender is very finely chopped, then add the butter and lemon rind and continue to process until light and fluffy. Transfer to a large bowl. Sift in the flour and beat, until the mixture forms a stiff dough.

2 Place the dough on a sheet of parchment paper and place another sheet on top. Gently press down with a rolling pin and roll out to 1/8–1/4 inch/3–5 mm thick. Remove the top sheet of paper and stamp out circles from the dough using a 2³/4-inch/7-cm round cookie cutter. Reknead and reroll the trimmings and stamp out more cookies.

3 Using a spatula, transfer the cookies to the prepared cookie sheet. Prick them with a fork and bake in the preheated oven for 12 minutes, or until pale brown. Remove from the oven and cool on the cookie sheet for 2 minutes, then transfer to a wire rack to cool completely.

vanilla hearts

ingredients

MAKES 12

1½ cups all-purpose flour,
plus extra for dusting
¾ cup butter, cut into small
pieces, plus extra
for greasing
generous 1 cup superfine
sugar, plus extra for
dusting
1 tsp vanilla extract

method

1 Preheat the oven to 350°F/180°C, then lightly grease a cookie sheet.

2 Sift the flour into a large bowl. Add the butter and rub it in with your fingertips until the mixture resembles fine bread crumbs. Stir in the sugar and vanilla extract and mix together to form a firm dough.

3 Roll out the dough on a lightly floured counter to a thickness of 1 inch/2.5 cm. Stamp out 12 hearts with a heart-shaped cookie cutter measuring 2 inches/5 cm across and 1 inch/ 2.5 cm deep. Arrange the hearts on the prepared cookie sheet.

4 Bake in the preheated oven for 15–20 minutes, or until the hearts are a light golden color. Transfer the vanilla hearts to a wire rack and let cool completely. Dust them with a little sugar just before serving.

gingerbread people

ingredients

MAKES ABOUT 20

3$\frac{1}{2}$ cups all-purpose flour,
plus extra for dusting

2 tsp ground ginger

1 tsp allspice

2 tsp baking soda

$\frac{1}{2}$ cup butter, plus extra for
greasing

generous $\frac{1}{3}$ cup corn syrup

generous $\frac{1}{2}$ cup brown sugar

1 egg, beaten

to decorate

currants

candied cherries

generous $\frac{3}{4}$ cup
confectioners' sugar

3–4 tsp water

method

1 Preheat the oven to 325°F/160°C, then grease three large cookie sheets. Sift the flour, ginger, allspice, and baking soda into a large bowl. Place the butter, syrup, and sugar in a saucepan over low heat and stir until melted. Pour onto the dry ingredients and add the egg. Mix together to form a dough. The dough will be sticky to start with, but will become firmer as it cools.

2 On a lightly floured counter, roll out the dough to about $\frac{1}{8}$ inch/3 mm thick and stamp out gingerbread people shapes. Place on the prepared cookie sheets. Reknead and reroll the trimmings and cut out more shapes until the dough is used up. Decorate with currants for eyes and pieces of cherry for mouths. Bake in the preheated oven for 15–20 minutes, or until firm and lightly browned.

3 Remove from the oven and let cool on the cookie sheets for a few minutes, then transfer to wire racks to cool completely. Mix the confectioners' sugar with the water to a thick consistency. Place the frosting in a small plastic bag and cut a tiny hole in one corner. Use the frosting to draw buttons or clothes shapes on the cooled cookies.

gingersnaps

ingredients

MAKES 30

3 cups self-rising flour

pinch of salt

1 cup superfine sugar

1 tbsp ground ginger

1 tsp baking soda

generous 1/2 cup butter, plus
    extra for greasing

1/4 cup corn syrup

1 egg, beaten

1 tsp grated orange zest

method

1 Preheat the oven to 325°F/160°C. Grease several cookie sheets lightly with a little butter. Sift the self-rising flour, salt, sugar, ginger, and baking soda into a large mixing bowl.

2 Melt the butter and corn syrup together in a saucepan over low heat. Remove the pan from the heat and let the butter and syrup mixture cool slightly, then pour it onto the dry ingredients. Add the egg and orange zest and mix thoroughly to form a dough.

3 Using your hands, carefully shape the dough into 30 even-size balls. Place the balls well apart on the prepared cookie sheets, then flatten them slightly with your fingers.

4 Bake in the preheated oven for 15–20 minutes, until golden. Carefully transfer the cookies to a wire rack to cool.

party cookies

ingredients

MAKES 16

1/2 cup butter, softened, plus
   extra for greasing
generous 1/2 cup brown sugar
1 tbsp corn syrup
1/2 tsp vanilla extract
11/4 cups self-rising flour
3 oz/85 g sugar-coated
   chocolate beans

method

1 Preheat the oven to 350°F/180°C, then grease two cookie sheets. Place the butter and sugar in a bowl and beat together with an electric mixer until light and fluffy, then beat in the syrup and vanilla extract.

2 Sift in half the flour and work it into the mixture. Stir in the chocolate beans and the remaining flour and work the dough together using a spatula.

3 Roll the dough into 16 balls and place them on the prepared cookie sheets, spaced well apart to allow for spreading. Do not flatten them. Bake in the preheated oven for 10–12 minutes, or until pale golden at the edges. Remove from the oven and let cool on the cookie sheets for 2 minutes, then transfer to wire racks to cool completely.

traditional easter cookies

ingredients

MAKES ABOUT 30

1 cup butter, softened

scant 3/4 cup superfine sugar,
    plus extra for sprinkling

1 egg yolk, lightly beaten

2 1/2 cups all-purpose flour

1 tsp apple pie spice

pinch of salt

1 tbsp chopped candied peel

1/4 cup currants

1 egg white, lightly beaten

method

1 Put the butter and sugar into a bowl and mix well with a wooden spoon, then beat in the egg yolk. Sift the flour, apple pie spice, and salt together into the mixture, add the candied peel and currants, and stir until thoroughly combined. Halve the dough, shape into balls, wrap in plastic wrap, and chill in the refrigerator for 30–60 minutes.

2 Preheat the oven to 375°F/190°C. Line two cookie sheets with parchment paper.

3 Unwrap the dough and roll out between two sheets of parchment paper. Stamp out circles with a 2 1/2-inch/6-cm fluted cookie cutter and put them on the prepared cookie sheets, spaced well apart.

4 Bake in the preheated oven for 7 minutes, then brush with the egg white and sprinkle with sugar. Return to the oven and bake for an additional 5–8 minutes, until light golden brown. Let cool on the cookie sheets for 5–10 minutes, then, using a metal spatula, carefully transfer to wire racks to cool completely.

easter nest cookies

ingredients

MAKES ABOUT 20–25

1 cup butter, softened, plus
    extra for greasing
scant 3/4 cup superfine sugar
1 egg yolk, lightly beaten
2 tsp lemon juice
2 1/2 cups all-purpose flour
pinch of salt
1 tbsp chopped candied peel
1/4 cup finely chopped candied
    cherries

to decorate

1 3/4 cups confectioners' sugar
few drops of edible yellow food
    coloring
mini sugar-coated Easter eggs
yellow sugar sprinkles

method

1 Put the butter and sugar into a bowl and mix well with a wooden spoon, then beat in the egg yolk and lemon juice. Sift together the flour and salt into the mixture, add the candied peel and cherries and stir until thoroughly combined. Halve the dough, shape into balls, wrap in plastic wrap, and chill in the refrigerator for 30–60 minutes.

2 Preheat the oven to 375°F/190°C. Generously grease several muffin pans with butter.

3 Unwrap the dough and roll out between two sheets of parchment paper. Stamp out cookies with a 7–8-cm/2 3/4–3 1/4-inch sun-shaped cutter and put them in the prepared muffin pans.

4 Bake in the preheated oven for 10–15 minutes, until light golden brown. Let cool in the pans.

5 For the frosting, sift the confectioners' sugar into a bowl, add the food coloring, and stir in just enough water to give it the consistency of thick cream. Put the cookies on wire racks and gently spread the frosting on them. When it is just beginning to set, gently press 3–4 eggs into it and sprinkle the sugar sprinkles around them. Let set completely.

easter bunny cookies

ingredients

MAKES ABOUT 15

1 cup butter, softened

scant ¾ cup superfine sugar,
    plus extra for sprinkling

1 egg yolk, lightly beaten

2 tsp vanilla extract

2¼ cups all-purpose flour

¼ cup unsweetened cocoa

pinch of salt

2 tbsp finely chopped
    preserved ginger

1 egg white, lightly beaten

15 white mini marshmallows

1¼ cups confectioners' sugar

few drops of edible food
    coloring

method

1 Put the butter and sugar into a bowl and mix well with a wooden spoon, then beat in the egg yolk and vanilla extract. Sift the flour, cocoa, and salt together into the mixture, add the ginger, and stir until thoroughly combined. Halve the dough, shape into balls, wrap in plastic wrap, and chill in the refrigerator for 30–60 minutes. Preheat the oven to 375°F/190°C. Line two cookie sheets with parchment paper.

2 Unwrap the dough and roll out between two sheets of parchment paper. Stamp out 15 cookies with a 2-inch/5-cm plain cutter (bodies), 15 cookies with a 1¼-inch/3-cm plain cutter (heads), 30 cookies with a ¾-inch/ 2-cm plain cutter (ears), and 15 cookies with a ½-inch/1-cm plain cutter (tails). Make up the bunnies on the cookie sheets spaced well apart. Piece together.

3 Bake in the preheated oven for 7 minutes, then brush the bunnies with egg white and sprinkle with superfine sugar. Return to the oven and bake for 5–8 minutes. Remove from the oven and put a mini marshmallow in the center of each tail. Return to the oven for 1 minute. Let cool for 5–10 minutes, then transfer to wire racks to cool completely.

4 Sift the confectioners' sugar into a bowl and stir in enough water to give the frosting the consistency of thick cream. Add the food coloring and decorate. Let set.

halloween spiderweb cookies

ingredients

MAKES ABOUT 30

1 cup butter, softened

scant 3/4 cup superfine sugar

1 egg yolk, lightly beaten

1 tsp peppermint extract

2 1/4 cups all-purpose flour

1/4 cup unsweetened cocoa

pinch of salt

to decorate

1 1/2 cups confectioners' sugar

few drops vanilla extract

1–1 1/2 tbsp hot water

few drops of edible black food
  coloring

method

1 Put the butter and sugar into a bowl and mix, then beat in the egg yolk and peppermint extract. Sift the flour, cocoa, and salt together into the mixture and stir until thoroughly combined. Halve the dough, shape into balls, wrap in plastic wrap, and chill in the refrigerator for 30–60 minutes. Preheat the oven to 375°F/190°C. Line two cookie sheets with parchment paper.

2 Unwrap the dough and roll out between two sheets of parchment paper. Stamp out cookies with a 2 1/2-inch/6-cm plain round cutter and put them on the prepared cookie sheets spaced well apart. Bake in the preheated oven for 10–15 minutes. Let cool for 5–10 minutes, then transfer to wire racks to cool completely.

3 Sift the confectioners' sugar into a bowl, add the vanilla extract, and stir in the hot water until the frosting is smooth and has the consistency of thick cream. With the cookies still on the racks, spread most of the white frosting over them. Add a few drops of black food coloring to the remaining frosting and spoon it into a pastry bag fitted with a fine tip. Starting from the middle, pipe a series of concentric circles on the cookies. Carefully draw a toothpick through the frosting from the middle to the outside edge to divide the cookies into quarters and then eighths. Let set.

christmas angels

ingredients

MAKES ABOUT 25

1 cup butter, softened

scant $3/4$ cup superfine sugar

1 egg yolk, lightly beaten

2 tsp passion fruit pulp

$2^1/2$ cups all-purpose flour

pinch of salt

$2/3$ cup unsweetened dried
    coconut

to decorate

$1^1/2$ cups confectioners' sugar

$1-1^1/2$ tbsp passion fruit pulp

edible silver glitter,
    for sprinkling

method

1 Put the butter and sugar into a bowl and mix well with a wooden spoon, then beat in the egg yolk and passion fruit pulp. Sift together the flour and salt into the mixture, add the coconut, and stir until thoroughly combined. Halve the dough, shape into balls, wrap in plastic wrap, and chill in the refrigerator for 30–60 minutes.

2 Preheat the oven to 375°F/190°C. Line two cookie sheets with parchment paper.

3 Unwrap the dough and roll out between two sheets of parchment paper. Stamp out cookies with a $2^3/4$-inch/7-cm angel-shaped cutter and put them on the prepared cookie sheets, spaced well apart.

4 Bake in the preheated oven for 10–15 minutes, until light golden brown. Let cool on the cookie sheets for 5–10 minutes, then, using a metal spatula, carefully transfer to wire racks to cool completely.

5 Sift the confectioners' sugar into a bowl and stir in the passion fruit pulp until the frosting has the consistency of thick cream. With the cookies still on the racks, spread the frosting over them. Sprinkle with the edible glitter and let set.

christmas bells

ingredients

MAKES ABOUT 30

1 cup butter, softened

scant 3/4 cup superfine sugar

finely grated rind of 1 lemon

1 egg yolk, lightly beaten

2 1/2 cups all-purpose flour

1/2 tsp ground cinnamon

pinch of salt

generous 1/2 cup semisweet
  chocolate chips

to decorate

2 tbsp lightly beaten egg white

2 tbsp lemon juice

2 cups confectioners' sugar

30 silver dragées

food coloring pens

method

1 Put the butter, sugar, and lemon rind into a bowl and mix well with a wooden spoon, then beat in the egg yolk. Sift the flour, cinnamon, and salt together into the mixture, add the chocolate chips, and stir until thoroughly combined. Halve the dough, shape into balls, wrap in plastic wrap, and chill in the refrigerator for 30–60 minutes.

2 Preheat the oven to 375°F/190°C. Line two cookie sheets with parchment paper.

3 Unwrap the dough and roll out between two sheets of parchment paper. Stamp out cookies with a 2-in/5-cm bell-shaped cutter and put them on the prepared cookie sheets, spaced well apart.

4 Bake in the preheated oven for 10–15 minutes, until light golden brown. Let cool on the cookie sheets for 5–10 minutes, then using a metal spatula, carefully transfer to wire racks to cool completely.

5 Combine the egg white and lemon juice in a bowl, then gradually beat in the confectioners' sugar, until smooth. With the cookies still on the racks, spread the frosting over them. Place a silver ball on the clapper shape at the bottom of the cookie and let set completely. When the frosting is dry, use the food coloring pens to draw patterns on the cookies.

christmas tree decorations

ingredients

MAKES 20–25

1 cup butter, softened

scant 3/4 cup superfine sugar

1 egg yolk, lightly beaten

2 tsp vanilla extract

2 1/2 cups all-purpose flour

pinch of salt

1 egg white, lightly beaten

2 tbsp colored sprinkles

14 oz/400 g fruit-flavored hard
      candies in different colors

method

1 Put the butter and sugar into a bowl and mix, then beat in the egg yolk and vanilla extract. Sift the flour and salt together into the mixture and stir until thoroughly combined. Halve the dough, shape into balls, wrap in plastic wrap, and chill for 30–60 minutes. Preheat the oven to 375°F/190°C. Line two cookie sheets with parchment paper.

2 Unwrap the dough and roll out between two sheets of parchment paper. Stamp out cookies with Christmas-themed cutters and put them on the prepared cookie sheets, spaced well apart. Using the end of a large plain piping tip, stamp out circles from each shape and remove. Make a small hole in the top of each cookie with a skewer so they can be threaded with ribbon.

3 Meanwhile, lightly crush the candies by tapping them with a rolling pin. Unwrap and sort into separate bowls by color.

4 Remove the cookies from the oven and fill the holes with the crushed candies. Return to the oven and bake for 5–8 minutes more, until the cookies are light golden brown and the candies have melted and filled the holes. If the holes for hanging the cookies have closed up, pierce them again with the skewer while the cookies are still warm. Sprinkle with the colored sprinkles and let cool completely on the cookie sheets. Thread thin ribbon through the holes in the top and hang from the tree.

pastries & desserts

Today's hectic lifestyle, combined with concerns about healthy eating and the availability of convenience foods, mean that we have lost our grandmothers' habit of routinely baking tarts, pies, strudels, and other desserts. However, this doesn't mean that we've lost our taste for them. While most of us are just too busy to make dough and peel fruit or whisk egg whites and chop nuts in the middle of the week, there is something very rewarding about preparing a traditional baked dessert for family meals when there's a little more time at the weekend.

Of course, baked desserts include much more than classic apple pie, popular though this is. Many cold desserts—from pavlovas to cheesecakes—must be baked first. The range of pastries is extensive from a simple pie dough to paper-thin layers of strudel, light-as-air puff pastry, and mouthwatering choux puffs—and that's without even mentioning the huge choice of fillings. Besides fresh fruit, these include nuts, honey, syrup, meringue, chocolate, caramel, cream, cheese, and custard. Then, in addition to pastries there are numerous other sweet treats from meringue to fruit cobbler. Some are perfect for family meals, especially a traditional Sunday lunch, while others would make an impressive ending to a formal dinner party.

Here are a few useful tips for pastry making. Keep everything, including your hands and the mixing bowl, cool. If the mixture feels greasy when you are rubbing the fat into the flour, put the bowl into the refrigerator for 30 minutes. Handle the dough as little as possible. Easy as pie!

chocolate fudge tart

ingredients

SERVES 6

flour, for sprinkling

12 oz/350 g ready-made
shortcrust pastry

confectioners' sugar, for
dusting

generous 3/4 cup whipping
cream, whipped and mixed
with ground cinnamon,
to decorate

filling

5 oz/140 g plain chocolate,
finely chopped

3/4 cup butter, diced

1 1/3 cup granulated sugar

2/3 cup all-purpose flour

1/2 tsp vanilla extract

6 eggs, beaten

method

1 Preheat the oven to 400°F/200°C. Roll out the pastry on a lightly floured counter and use to line an 8-inch/20-cm deep loose-bottom tart pan. Prick the pastry lightly with a fork, then line with foil and fill with dried beans. Bake in the preheated oven for 12–15 minutes, or until the dough no longer looks raw. Remove the beans and foil and bake for an additional 10 minutes, or until the dough is firm. Let cool. Reduce the oven temperature to 350°F/180°C.

2 To make the filling, place the chocolate and butter in a heatproof bowl set over a saucepan of gently simmering water, until melted. Stir until smooth, then remove from the heat and let cool. Place the sugar, flour, vanilla extract, and eggs in a separate bowl and whisk until well blended. Stir in the butter and chocolate mixture.

3 Pour the filling into the tart shell and bake in the preheated oven for 50 minutes, or until the filling is just set. Transfer to a wire rack to cool completely. Dust with confectioners' sugar before serving with whipped cream.

fine chocolate tart

ingredients

SERVES 6

pie dough

generous 3/4 cup all-purpose
flour, plus extra for dusting

2 tsp unsweetened cocoa,
plus extra for dusting

2 tsp confectioners' sugar

pinch of salt

4 tbsp cold butter, cut into
pieces, plus extra for
greasing

1 egg yolk

ice-cold water

plain and white chocolate
curls, to decorate

ganache filling

7 oz/200 g semisweet
chocolate with 70% cocoa
solids

2 tbsp unsalted butter,
softened

1 cup heavy cream

1 tsp dark rum (optional)

method

1 Lightly grease a 9-inch/23-cm loose-bottom fluted tart pan. Sift the flour, cocoa, confectioners' sugar, and salt into a food processor, add the butter, and process until the mixture resembles fine bread crumbs. Tip the mixture into a large bowl, add the egg yolk and a little ice-cold water, just enough to bring the dough together. Turn out onto a counter dusted with more flour and cocoa and roll out the dough 31/4 inches/8 cm larger than the pan. Carefully lift the dough into the pan and press to fit. Roll the rolling pin over the pan to neaten the edges and trim the excess dough. Fit a piece of parchment paper into the tart shell, fill with dried beans, and let chill in the refrigerator for 30 minutes. Meanwhile, preheat the oven to 375°F/190°C.

2 Remove the pastry shell from the refrigerator and bake in the preheated oven for 15 minutes, then remove the beans and paper and bake for an additional 5 minutes.

3 To make the ganache filling, chop the chocolate and put in a bowl with the softened butter. Bring the cream to a boil, then pour onto the chocolate, stirring well. Add the rum, if using, and continue stirring to make sure the chocolate is melted completely. Pour into the pastry shell and let chill for 3 hours.

white chocolate & cardamom tart

ingredients

SERVES 6

pie dough

generous 3/4 cup all-purpose
    flour, plus extra for dusting
pinch of salt
6 tbsp cold butter,
    cut into pieces, plus extra
    for greasing
cold water

filling

2 pieces or 1/4 oz/6 g fine leaf
    gelatin
cold water
seeds of 8 cardamom pods
12 oz/350 g white chocolate,
    chopped into small pieces
generous 11/2 cups whipping
    cream

method

1 Preheat the oven to 375°F/190°C. Lightly grease a 9-inch/23-cm loose-bottom tart pan. Sift the flour and salt into a food processor, add the butter, and process until the mixture resembles fine bread crumbs. Tip the mixture into a large bowl and add a little cold water, just enough to bring the dough together. Turn out onto a counter dusted with more flour and roll out the dough 31/4 inches/8 cm larger than the pan. Carefully lift the dough into the pan and press to fit. Roll the rolling pin over the pan to neaten the edges and trim the excess dough. Fit a piece of parchment paper into the tart shell, fill with dried beans, and let chill for 30 minutes.

2 Bake the pastry shell for 15 minutes in the preheated oven, remove the beans and paper, and bake for an additional 10 minutes. Let cool completely.

3 Soak the gelatin in a little cold water in a small heatproof bowl for 5 minutes. Heat a saucepan of water to simmering point. Crush the cardamom seeds and put in a large bowl with the chocolate. Place the bowl of gelatin over the pan of water and stir until dissolved. In a separate saucepan heat the cream until just boiling, then pour over the chocolate, using a whisk to stir the chocolate until it has melted. Add the gelatin and stir until smooth. Let cool and pour into the shell, then let chill for 3 hours.

baked chocolate alaska

ingredients

SERVES 4

butter, for greasing

2 eggs

generous ¾ cup superfine
sugar, plus 4 tbsp

4 tbsp all-purpose flour

2 tbsp unsweetened cocoa

3 egg whites

4 cups good-quality chocolate
ice cream

method

1 Preheat the oven to 425°F/220°C. Grease a 7-inch/18-cm round cake pan and line the base with parchment paper.

2 Beat the eggs and the 4 tablespoons of sugar in a mixing bowl until very thick and pale. Sift the flour and cocoa together and carefully fold in.

3 Pour into the prepared pan and bake in the preheated oven for 7 minutes, or until springy to the touch. Turn out and transfer to a wire rack to cool completely.

4 Whisk the egg whites in a clean, greasefree bowl until soft peaks form. Gradually add the remaining sugar, whisking until you have a thick, glossy meringue. Place the sponge on a baking sheet. Soften the ice cream in the refrigerator and pile it onto the center to form a dome.

5 Pipe or spread the meringue over the ice cream, making sure it is completely enclosed. (At this point the dessert can be frozen, if wished.)

6 Return to the oven for 5 minutes, until the meringue is just golden. Serve at once.

mississippi mud pie

ingredients

SERVES 8

pie dough

generous 1 1/2 cups all-purpose
    flour, plus extra for dusting
2 tbsp unsweetened cocoa
2/3 cup butter
2 tbsp superfine sugar
1–2 tbsp cold water

filling

3/4 cup butter
scant 1 3/4 cups firmly packed
    brown sugar
4 eggs, lightly beaten
4 tbsp unsweetened cocoa,
    sifted
5 1/2 oz/150 g semisweet
    chocolate
1 1/4 cups light cream
1 tsp chocolate extract

to decorate

scant 2 cups heavy cream,
    whipped
chocolate flakes and curls

method

1 To make the pie dough, sift the flour and cocoa into a mixing bowl. Rub in the butter with your fingertips until the mixture resembles fine bread crumbs. Stir in the sugar and enough cold water to mix to a soft dough. Wrap the dough and let chill in the refrigerator for 15 minutes.

2 Preheat the oven to 375°F/190°C. Roll out the dough on a lightly floured counter and use to line a 9-inch/23-cm loose-bottom tart pan or ceramic pie plate. Line with parchment paper and fill with dried beans. Bake in the preheated oven for 15 minutes. Remove from the oven and take out the paper and beans. Bake the pastry shell for an additional 10 minutes.

3 To make the filling, beat the butter and sugar together in a bowl and gradually beat in the eggs with the cocoa. Melt the chocolate and beat it into the mixture with the cream and the chocolate extract.

4 Reduce the oven temperature to 325°F/ 160°C. Pour the mixture into the pastry shell and bake for 45 minutes, or until the filling has set gently.

5 Let the mud pie cool completely, then transfer it to a serving plate, if you like. Cover with the whipped cream.

6 Decorate the pie with chocolate flakes and curls and let chill until ready to serve.

chocolate nut strudel

ingredients

SERVES 6

generous 1¹/₄ cups mixed chopped nuts

4 oz/115 g semisweet chocolate, chopped

4 oz/115 g milk chocolate, chopped

4 oz/115 g white chocolate, chopped

7 oz/200 g filo dough, thawed if frozen

²/₃ cup butter, preferably unsalted, plus extra for greasing

3 tbsp corn syrup

¹/₂ cup confectioners' sugar

ice cream, to serve

method

1 Preheat the oven to 375°F/190°C. Lightly grease a baking sheet with butter. Set aside 1 tablespoon of the nuts. Mix the three types of chocolate together.

2 Place a sheet of filo on a clean dish towel. Melt the butter and brush the sheet of filo with the butter, drizzle with a little syrup, and sprinkle with some nuts and chocolate. Place another sheet of filo on top and repeat until you have used all the nuts and chocolate.

3 Use the dish towel to help you carefully roll up the strudel and place on the baking sheet, drizzle with a little more syrup, and sprinkle with the reserved nuts. Bake in the preheated oven for 20–25 minutes. If the nuts start to brown too much, cover the strudel with a sheet of foil.

4 Sprinkle the strudel with confectioners' sugar, slice, and eat warm with ice cream.

cream puffs & chocolate sauce

ingredients

SERVES 4

choux pastry

generous 3/4 cup water

5 tbsp butter, plus extra
    for greasing

3/4 cup all-purpose flour, sifted

3 eggs, beaten

cream filling

1 1/4 cups heavy cream

3 tbsp superfine sugar

1 tsp vanilla extract

chocolate sauce

4 1/2 oz/125 g semisweet
    chocolate, broken into
    small pieces

2 1/2 tbsp butter

6 tbsp water

2 tbsp brandy

method

1 Preheat the oven to 400°F/200°C. Grease a large cookie sheet.

2 To make the pastry, put the water and butter into a saucepan and bring to a boil. Immediately add all the flour, remove the pan from the heat, and stir the mixture into a paste that leaves the sides of the pan clean. Let cool slightly. Beat in enough of the eggs to give the mixture a soft dropping consistency.

3 Put the mixture into a pastry bag fitted with a 1/2-inch/1-cm plain tip. Pipe small balls onto the prepared cookie sheet. Bake in the preheated oven for 25 minutes. Remove from the oven. Pierce each ball with a skewer to let the steam escape.

4 To make the filling, whip the cream, sugar, and vanilla extract together. Cut the pastry balls almost in half, then fill with cream.

5 To make the sauce, gently melt the chocolate and butter with the water in a heatproof bowl set over a saucepan of gently simmering water, stirring, until smooth. Stir in the brandy. Pile the cream puffs into individual serving dishes or into a pyramid on a raised cake stand. Pour over the sauce and serve.

pains au chocolat

ingredients

MAKES 4

scant 2 cups white bread flour,
    plus extra for dusting

1 tsp salt

2 tsp active dry yeast

3/4 cup milk

2 tbsp golden superfine sugar

1 tbsp oil, plus extra for
    brushing

scant 1/2 cup butter, plus extra
    for greasing

4 oz/115 g semisweet
    chocolate, coarsely
    chopped

glaze

1 egg yolk

2 tbsp milk

method

1 Grease a baking sheet. Sift the flour and salt into a bowl and stir in the yeast. Make a well in the center. Heat the milk in a saucepan until tepid. Add the sugar and oil and stir until the sugar has dissolved. Stir into the flour and mix well. Turn out the dough onto a lightly floured counter and knead until smooth, then place in an oiled bowl. Cover and let rise in a warm place for 2–3 hours, or until doubled in size.

2 Knead on a floured counter and roll into a rectangle three times as long as it is wide. Divide the butter into thirds. Dot one portion over the top two thirds of the dough, leaving a 1/2-inch/1-cm margin around the edges. Fold the lower third up and the top third down. Seal the edges. Give the dough a half-turn. Roll into a rectangle. Repeat the process twice, then fold in half. Put into an oiled plastic bag and let chill for 1 hour.

3 Preheat the oven to 425°F/220°C. Cut the dough in half and roll out into two rectangles of 12 x 6 inches/30 x 15 cm. Cut each half into four rectangles of 6 x 3 inches/15 x 7.5 cm. Sprinkle chocolate along one short end of each and roll up. Place on the baking sheet in a warm place for 2–3 hours, or until doubled in size. To glaze, mix the egg yolk and milk and brush over the rolls. Bake for 15–20 minutes, or until golden and well risen.

chocolate chiffon pie

ingredients

SERVES 8

base
2 cups shelled Brazil nuts
4 tbsp granulated sugar
4 tsp melted butter

filling
1 cup milk
2 tsp powdered gelatin
1/2 cup superfine sugar
2 eggs, separated
8 oz/225 g semisweet
    chocolate, roughly
    chopped
1 tsp vanilla extract
2/3 cup heavy cream
2 tbsp chopped Brazil nuts,
    to decorate

method

1 Preheat the oven to 400°F/200°C. To make the base, process the whole Brazil nuts in a food processor until finely ground. Add the sugar and melted butter and process briefly to combine. Tip the mixture into a 9-inch/23-cm round tart pan and press it onto the bottom and sides with a spoon. Bake in the preheated oven for 8–10 minutes, or until light golden brown. Let cool.

2 For the filling, pour the milk into a bowl and sprinkle over the gelatin. Let soften for 2 minutes, then set over a saucepan of gently simmering water. Stir in half of the sugar, then add the egg yolks and the chocolate. Stir continuously over low heat for 4–5 minutes, until the gelatin has dissolved and the chocolate has melted. Remove from the heat and beat until the mixture is smooth. Stir in the vanilla extract, cover, and let chill in the refrigerator for 45–60 minutes, until starting to set.

3 Whip the cream until stiff, then fold all but 3 tablespoons into the chocolate mixture. Whisk the egg whites in a separate, clean, greasefree bowl until soft peaks form. Add 2 teaspoons of the remaining sugar and whisk until stiff peaks form. Fold in the remaining sugar, then fold the egg whites into the chocolate mixture. Pour the filling into the pastry shell and let chill in the refrigerator for 3 hours. Decorate with the remaining whipped cream and the chopped nuts before serving.

chocolate orange pie

ingredients

SERVES 4

pie dough

scant 1¹/₂ cups all-purpose flour, plus extra for dusting
scant ¹/₂ cup butter, cut into small pieces, plus extra for greasing
scant ¹/₂ cup confectioners' sugar, sifted
finely grated rind of 1 orange
1 egg yolk, beaten
3 tbsp milk

filling

7 oz/200 g semisweet chocolate, broken into small pieces
2 eggs, separated
¹/₂ cup milk
¹/₂ cup superfine sugar
8 amaretti cookies, crushed

orange cream

1 tbsp orange-flavored liqueur, such as Cointreau
1 tbsp finely grated orange rind, plus extra to decorate
¹/₂ cup heavy cream

method

1 To make the pie dough, sift the flour into a bowl. Rub in the butter with your fingertips until the mixture resembles bread crumbs. Mix in the sugar, orange rind, egg yolk, and milk. Turn out onto a lightly floured counter and knead briefly. Wrap the dough and let chill in the refrigerator for 30 minutes.

2 Preheat the oven to 350°F/180°C. Roll out two thirds of the pie dough to a thickness of ¹/₄ inch/5 mm and use it to line a greased 9-inch/23-cm tart pan.

3 To make the filling, melt the chocolate in a heatproof bowl set over a saucepan of barely simmering water. Beat in the egg yolks, then the milk. Remove from the heat. In a separate, greasefree bowl, whisk the egg whites until stiff, then stir in the sugar. Fold the egg whites into the chocolate mixture, then stir in the cookies. Spoon into the pastry shell.

4 Roll out the remaining pie dough, cut into strips, and use to form a lattice over the pie. Bake in the preheated oven for 1 hour.

5 To make the orange cream, beat the liqueur, orange rind, and cream together. Remove the pie from the oven, decorate with orange rind, and serve with the orange cream.

candy apple tart

ingredients

SERVES 6

pie dough

generous 3/4 cup all-purpose
    flour
pinch of salt
6 tbsp cold butter, cut into
    pieces
cold water

filling

3 lb/1.3 kg Pippin or other
    firm, sweet apples, peeled
    and cored
1 tsp lemon juice
3 generous tbsp butter
1/2 cup superfine sugar
1 cup granulated sugar
1/3 cup cold water
2/3 cup heavy cream, plus
    extra for serving

method

1 Lightly grease a 9-inch/23-cm loose-bottom fluted tart pan. Sift the flour and salt into a food processor, add the butter, and process until the mixture resembles fine bread crumbs. Tip the mixture into a large bowl and add enough cold water to bring the dough together. Turn out onto a floured counter and roll out the dough 3 1/4 inches/8 cm larger than the pan. Carefully lift the dough into the pan and press to fit. Fit a piece of parchment paper into the tart shell, fill with dried beans, and chill for 30 minutes. Meanwhile, preheat the oven to 375°F/190°C. Bake the pastry shell for 10 minutes in the preheated oven, then remove the beans and paper. Return to the oven for 5 minutes.

2 Cut four of the apples into eight pieces each and toss in the lemon juice. Melt the butter in a skillet and sauté the apple pieces until just starting to caramelize and brown on the edges. Remove from the skillet and let cool. Slice the remaining apples thinly, put them in a saucepan with the superfine sugar, and cook for 20–30 minutes, until soft. Spoon the cooked apple into the pastry shell and arrange the reserved apple pieces on top in a circle. Bake for 30 minutes.

3 Put the granulated sugar and water in a saucepan and heat until the sugar dissolves. Boil, remove from the heat, and add the cream, stirring continuously to combine into toffee. Remove the tart from the oven, pour the toffee over the apples, and let chill for 1 hour. Serve with thick cream.

pear tarte tatin

ingredients

SERVES 6

6 tbsp butter

generous 1/2 cup superfine
   sugar

6 pears, peeled, halved, and
   cored

flour, for dusting

8 oz/225 g prepared puff
   pastry

heavy cream, to serve
   (optional)

method

1 Preheat the oven to 400°F/200°C. Melt the butter and sugar in an ovenproof skillet over medium heat. Stir carefully for 5 minutes, until it turns a light caramel color. Take care, because it gets very hot.

2 Remove the skillet from the heat, place on a heatproof surface, and arrange the pears, cut side up, in the caramel. Place one half in the center and surround it with the others.

3 On a lightly floured counter, roll out the dough to a circle, slightly larger than the skillet, and place it on top of the pears. Tuck the edges down into the skillet.

4 Bake near the top of the preheated oven for 20–25 minutes, until the pastry is well risen and golden brown. Remove from the oven and let cool for 2 minutes.

5 Invert the tart onto a serving dish that is larger than the skillet and has enough depth to take any juices that may run out. Remember that this is very hot so be careful with this maneuver and use a pair of thick oven mitts.

6 Serve warm, with heavy cream, if using.

sicilian marzipan tart with candied fruit

ingredients

SERVES 6

pie dough

generous 3/4 cup all-purpose
    flour
pinch of salt
6 tbsp cold butter,
    cut into pieces
cold water

filling

10 1/2 oz/300 g marzipan
generous 1 1/2 cups ground
    almonds
3/4 cup unsalted butter
1/2 cup superfine sugar
scant 1/2 cup all-purpose flour
2 eggs
1/2 cup golden raisins
scant 1/3 cup mixed candied
    peel, chopped
scant 1/2 cup natural candied
    cherries, halved
1/2 cup slivered almonds

method

1 Lightly grease a 9-inch/23-cm loose-bottom fluted tart pan. Sift the flour and salt into a food processor, add the butter, and process until the mixture resembles fine bread crumbs. Tip the mixture into a large bowl and add a little cold water to bring the dough together. Turn out onto a counter dusted with flour and roll out the dough 3 1/4 inches/8 cm larger than the pan. Carefully lift the dough into the pan and press to fit. Roll the rolling pin over the pan to neaten the edges and trim the excess dough. Fit a piece of parchment paper into the tart shell, fill with dried beans, and let chill for 30 minutes. Meanwhile, preheat the oven to 375°F/190°C.

2 Bake the pastry shell for 10 minutes in the preheated oven, then remove the beans and paper and bake for 5 minutes.

3 Reduce the oven temperature to 350°F/180°C. Grate the marzipan straight onto the bottom of the warm dough, distributing evenly. Put the ground almonds, butter, and sugar in a food processor and pulse until smooth. Add 1 tablespoon of flour and 1 egg and blend, then add another 1 tablespoon of flour and the other egg and blend. Finally, add the remaining flour. Scoop the mixture into a bowl and stir in the golden raisins, peel, and cherries. Spoon the mixture over the marzipan, sprinkle with the slivered almonds, and bake for 40 minutes.

caramelized lemon tart

ingredients

SERVES 6

pie dough

generous 1 cup all-purpose
   flour
pinch of salt
scant $1/2$ cup cold butter,
   cut into pieces
2 tbsp superfine sugar
1 egg yolk
cold water

filling

5 lemons
2 eggs
$1^1/2$ cups superfine sugar
generous $1^1/2$ cups ground
   almonds
generous $1/3$ cup whipping
   cream
generous $1/3$ cup water

method

1 Lightly grease a 9-inch/23-cm loose-bottom tart pan. Sift the flour and salt into a food processor, add the butter, and process until the mixture resembles fine bread crumbs. Tip the mixture into a large bowl, add the sugar, egg yolk, and a little cold water to bring the dough together. Turn out onto a counter dusted with flour and roll out the dough $3^1/4$ inches/ 8 cm larger than the pan. Carefully lift the dough into the pan and press to fit. Roll the rolling pin over the pan to neaten the edges and trim the excess dough. Fit a piece of parchment paper into the tart shell, fill with dried beans, and let chill in the refrigerator for 30 minutes. Meanwhile, preheat the oven to 375°F/190°C.

2 Bake the pastry shell in the preheated oven for 10 minutes, then remove the beans and paper and bake for 5 minutes.

3 Put the juice and finely grated rind of three of the lemons in a large bowl and add the eggs, $1/2$ cup of sugar, the ground almonds, and the cream, beating to combine. Pour into the pastry shell and bake for 25 minutes. Meanwhile, thinly slice the remaining lemons, discarding the seeds and ends. Put the remaining sugar and the water in a saucepan and heat until the sugar is melted. Let simmer for 5 minutes, add the lemon slices, and boil for 10 minutes.

4 Remove the tart from the oven and arrange the lemon slices over the surface. Drizzle the remaining syrup over the slices and serve.

peach & ginger tarte tatin

ingredients

SERVES 6

9 oz/250 g prepared puff
    pastry
flour, for dusting

filling

6–8 just ripe peaches
1/2 cup golden superfine sugar
31/2 tbsp unsalted butter
3 pieces preserved ginger in
    syrup, chopped
1 tbsp ginger syrup from the
    preserved ginger jar
1 egg, beaten
thick cream or ice cream,
    to serve

method

1 Preheat the oven to 375°F/190°C. For the filling, plunge the peaches into boiling water, then let drain and peel. Cut each in half. Put the sugar in a 10-inch/25-cm heavy, ovenproof skillet and heat it gently until it caramelizes. Don't stir, just shake the skillet if necessary. Once the sugar turns a dark caramel color, remove from the heat and drop in 2 tablespoons of the butter.

2 Place the peaches, cut-side up, on top of the caramel, packing them as close together as possible, and tucking the preserved ginger pieces into any gaps. Dot with the remaining butter and drizzle with the ginger syrup.

3 Return to gentle heat while, on a lightly floured counter, you roll out the dough in a circle larger than the skillet you are using. Drape the dough over the peaches and tuck it in well around the edges, brush with the beaten egg, and bake in the preheated oven for 20–25 minutes, until the pastry is browned and puffed up. Remove from the oven and let rest for 5 minutes, then invert onto a serving plate and serve.

plum & almond tart

ingredients

SERVES 8

butter, for greasing

all-purpose flour, for dusting

14 oz/400 g prepared sweet
   pie dough

filling

1 egg

1 egg yolk

scant 3/4 cup golden superfine
   sugar

4 tbsp butter, melted

generous 1 cup ground
   almonds

1 tbsp brandy

2 lb/900 g plums, halved and
   pitted

whipped cream, to serve
   (optional)

method

1 Preheat the oven to 400°F/200°C. Grease a 9-inch/23-cm tart pan. On a lightly floured counter, roll out the pastry and use it to line the tart pan, then line with parchment paper and fill with dried beans. Place a baking sheet in the oven.

2 To make the filling, place the egg, egg yolk, 1/2 cup of the sugar, the melted butter, the ground almonds, and the brandy in a bowl and mix together to form a paste. Spread the paste in the tart shell.

3 Arrange the plum halves, cut-side up, on top of the almond paste, fitting them together tightly. Sprinkle with the remaining sugar. Place the pan on the preheated cookie sheet and bake in the preheated oven for 35–40 minutes, or until the filling is set and the tart shell is brown. Serve warm with whipped cream, if using.

walnut custard tarts

ingredients

SERVES 4

2 tbsp butter

8 sheets filo dough (work with
   one sheet at a time and
   keep the remaining sheets
   covered with a damp dish
   towel)

$1/4$ cup walnut halves

$2/3$ cup Greek-style yogurt,
   plus extra to serve
   (optional)

4 tbsp honey

$2/3$ cup heavy cream

2 tbsp superfine sugar

2 eggs

1 tsp vanilla extract

confectioners' sugar,
   for dusting

method

1 Preheat the oven to 350°F/180°C. Melt the butter. Brush four deep 4-inch/10-cm tartlet pans with a little of the butter. Cut the sheets of filo in half to make 16 rough squares.

2 Take a square of filo, brush it with a little of the melted butter, and use it to line one of the pans. Repeat with three more filo squares, placing each of them at a different angle. Line the remaining three pans and place the pans on a baking sheet.

3 To make the filling, finely chop 2 tablespoons of the walnuts. Put the yogurt, honey, cream, sugar, eggs, and vanilla extract in a bowl and beat together. Stir in the chopped walnuts until well mixed.

4 Pour the yogurt filling into the pastry shells. Coarsely break the remaining walnuts and scatter over the top. Bake in the preheated oven for 25–30 minutes, until the filling is firm to the touch.

5 Let the tartlets cool, then carefully remove from the pans and dust with confectioners' sugar. Serve with a bowl of yogurt, if using.

almond & strawberry tart

ingredients

SERVES 4

pie dough

1 cup all-purpose flour, plus
extra for dusting

4 tbsp butter, cut into small
pieces, plus extra for
greasing

1/4 cup confectioners' sugar,
sifted

finely grated rind of 1/2 lemon

1/2 egg yolk, beaten

1 1/2 tbsp milk

4 tbsp strawberry jelly

filling

scant 1/2 cup butter

1/2 cup firmly packed brown
sugar

2 eggs, beaten

1 tsp almond extract

3/4 cup rice flour

3 tbsp ground almonds

3 tbsp slivered almonds,
toasted

confectioners' sugar,
to decorate

method

1 To make the pie dough, sift the flour into a bowl. Rub in the butter with your fingertips until the mixture resembles fine bread crumbs. Mix in the confectioners' sugar, lemon rind, egg yolk, and milk. Knead briefly on a lightly floured counter. Wrap the dough and let chill in the refrigerator for 30 minutes.

2 Preheat the oven to 375°F/190°C. Grease an 8-inch/20-cm ovenproof tart pan. Roll out the pie dough to a thickness of 1/4 inch/5 mm and use it to line the bottom and sides of the pan. Prick all over the bottom with a fork, then spread with the jelly.

3 To make the filling, cream the butter and brown sugar together until fluffy. Gradually beat in the eggs, followed by the almond extract, rice flour, and ground almonds. Spread the mixture evenly over the jelly-covered pie dough, then sprinkle over the slivered almonds. Bake in the preheated oven for 40 minutes, until golden. Remove from the oven, dust with confectioners' sugar, and serve warm.

honey & lemon tart

ingredients

SERVES 8–12

pie dough

1/2 cup plus 3 tbsp all-purpose
flour

pinch of salt

1 1/2 tsp superfine sugar

2/3 cup butter, cut into cubes

3-4 tbsp cold water

filling

1 1/3 cups cottage cheese,
cream cheese, or ricotta
cheese

6 tbsp Greek honey

3 eggs, beaten

1/2 tsp cinnamon

grated rind and juice of
1 lemon

lemon slices, to decorate

method

1 To make the pie dough, put the flour, salt, sugar, and butter in a food processor. Mix in short bursts, until the mixture resembles fine bread crumbs. Sprinkle over the water and mix until the mixture forms a smooth dough. Alternatively, make the pastry in a bowl and rub in with your hands. The pastry can be used right away, but is better if refrigerated, wrapped in wax paper or foil, for about 30 minutes before use.

2 Meanwhile, preheat the oven to 400°F/200°C, then make the filling. (If using cottage cheese, pass the cheese through a strainer into a bowl.) Add the honey to the cheese and beat until smooth. Add the eggs, cinnamon, and the lemon rind and juice, and mix well.

3 On a lightly floured surface, roll out the pastry and use to line a 9-inch/23-cm tart pan. Line with parchment paper, fill with dried beans, place on a baking sheet and bake in the preheated oven for 15 minutes. Remove from the oven, take out the parchment paper and beans, return to the oven, and bake for an additional 5 minutes, until the bottom is firm but not brown.

4 Reduce the oven temperature to 350°F/180°C. Pour the filling into the pastry shell and bake in the oven for about 30 minutes, until set. Serve cold, decorated with lemon slices.

fig, ricotta & honey tart

ingredients

SERVES 6

pie dough

3/4 cup all-purpose flour

pinch of salt

5 tbsp cold butter, cut into
    pieces, plus extra
    for greasing

1/3 cup ground almonds

cold water

filling

6 figs

1/2 cup superfine sugar

1/2 cup water

4 egg yolks

1/2 tsp vanilla extract

2 1/4 cups ricotta cheese,
    drained of any liquid

2 tbsp flower honey, plus 1 tsp
    for drizzling

method

1 Lightly grease a 9-inch/23-cm loose-bottom fluted tart pan. Sift the flour and salt into a food processor, add the butter, and process until the mixture resembles fine bread crumbs. Tip the mixture into a bowl, stir in the almonds, and add just enough cold water to bring the dough together. Turn out onto a floured counter and roll out the dough 3 1/4 inches/8 cm larger than the pan. Carefully lift the dough into the pan and press to fit. Roll the rolling pin over the pan to neaten the edges and trim the excess dough. Fit a piece of parchment paper into the tart shell, fill with dried beans, and let chill for 30 minutes.

2 Meanwhile, preheat the oven to 375°F/190°C. Remove the tart shell from the refrigerator and bake in the preheated oven for 15 minutes, then remove the beans and paper. Return to the oven for an additional 5 minutes.

3 Put the figs, half the superfine sugar, and the water in a saucepan and bring to a boil. Poach gently for 10 minutes, drain, and let cool. Stir the egg yolks and vanilla extract into the ricotta cheese, add the remaining sugar and the honey, and mix well. Spoon into the tart shell and bake for 30 minutes. Remove from the oven and, when you are ready to serve, cut the figs in half lengthwise and arrange on the tart, cut-side up. Drizzle with honey and serve at once.

brandied plum tart

ingredients

SERVES 6

pie dough

generous 3/4 cup all-purpose
    flour
pinch of salt
5 tbsp cold butter, cut into
    pieces
cold water

filling

2/3 cup brandy or armagnac
1/2 cup golden superfine sugar
4–5 ripe but not soft plums,
    halved
1 whole egg, plus 2 egg yolks
1 1/4 cups heavy cream

method

1 Preheat the oven to 375°F/190°C. Lightly grease a 9-inch/23-cm loose-bottom fluted tart pan. Sift the flour and salt into a food processor, add the butter, and process until the mixture resembles fine bread crumbs. Tip the mixture into a large bowl and add a little cold water to bring the dough together. Turn out onto a counter dusted with flour and roll out the dough 3 1/4 inches/8 cm larger than the pan. Carefully lift the dough into the pan and press to fit. Line with parchment paper, fill with dried beans, and let chill for 30 minutes. Bake for 10 minutes in the preheated oven, then remove the beans and paper and bake for 5 minutes.

2 Put the brandy and 2 tablespoons of the sugar in a saucepan and bring to a simmer, making sure the sugar has dissolved. Add the plum halves and let simmer for 5 minutes, then let cool. Reduce the oven temperature to 325°F/160°C. Remove the plums from the syrup, reserving the syrup. Peel the plums, slice each half plum into 3–4 slices, and arrange on the bottom of the pastry shell.

3 Beat the egg and the egg yolks with the remaining sugar and heat the cream until just boiling. Whisk the hot cream into the eggs, stirring. Spoon the filling over the plums, return the tart to the oven, and cook for 30–40 minutes, until set. Let stand in the pan until completely cold, then carefully lift onto a serving plate. Serve with the reserved syrup.

crème brûlée tarts

ingredients

SERVES 6

pie dough

1 cup all-purpose flour, plus
    extra for dusting

1–2 tbsp superfine sugar

generous $1/2$ cup butter, cut
    into pieces

1 tbsp water

filling

4 egg yolks

$3/4$ cup superfine sugar

$1^3/4$ cups heavy cream

1 tsp vanilla extract

raw sugar, for sprinkling

red currants and raspberries,
    to serve

method

1 To make the pie dough, place the flour and sugar in a large bowl. Rub in the butter with your fingertips until the mixture resembles bread crumbs. Add the water and mix to form a soft dough. Wrap and chill for 30 minutes.

2 Divide the dough into 6 pieces. Roll out each piece on a lightly floured counter to line 6 tart pans 4 inches/10 cm wide. Prick the bottom of the pastry with a fork and chill for 20 minutes.

3 Meanwhile, preheat the oven to 375°F/190°C. Line the tart shells with parchment paper and dried beans and bake in the preheated oven for 15 minutes. Remove the paper and beans and cook the tart shells for an additional 10 minutes, or until crisp. Let cool.

4 To make the filling, beat the egg yolks and sugar together in a bowl until pale. Heat the cream and vanilla extract in a saucepan until just below boiling point, then pour it onto the egg mixture, whisking continuously. Transfer the mixture to a clean saucepan and bring to just below a boil, stirring, until thick. Do not let the mixture boil or it will curdle. Let cool slightly, then pour it into the tart shells. Let cool, then chill overnight.

5 Preheat the broiler. Sprinkle the tarts with the sugar. Cook under the hot broiler for a few minutes. Let cool, then let chill for 2 hours before serving with red currants and raspberries.

blackberry tart with cassis cream

ingredients

SERVES 6

pie dough

2¼ cups all-purpose flour
pinch of salt
¾ cup unsalted butter
¼ cup superfine sugar
cold water

filling

1 lb 10 oz/750 g blackberries
6 tbsp golden superfine sugar
1 tbsp cassis
5 tsp semolina
1 egg white

to serve

generous 1 cup heavy cream
1 tbsp cassis
fresh mint leaves

method

1 To make the pie dough, sift the flour and salt into a large bowl and rub in the butter. Stir in the sugar and add enough cold water to bring the dough together, then wrap in plastic wrap and let chill for 30 minutes.

2 Meanwhile, put the blackberries in a bowl with 4 tablespoons of the sugar and the cassis, stirring to coat. Preheat the oven to 400°F/200°C.

3 Roll out the dough to a large circle, handling carefully because it is a soft dough. Leave the edges ragged and place on a baking sheet. Sprinkle the dough with the semolina, leaving a good 2½-inch/6-cm edge. Pile the fruit into the center and brush the edges of the dough with the egg white. Fold in the edges of the dough to overlap and enclose the fruit, making sure to press together the dough in order to close any gaps. Brush with the remaining egg white, sprinkle with the remaining sugar, and bake for 25 minutes.

4 Whip the cream until it starts to thicken and stir in the cassis. Serve the tart hot, straight from the oven, with a good spoonful of the cassis cream and decorated with mint leaves.

banana & chocolate pie

ingredients

SERVES 4

filling

scant 1/2 cup canned
    sweetened condensed milk
4 ripe bananas
juice of 1/2 lemon
1 tsp vanilla extract
2 3/4 oz/75 g semisweet
    chocolate, grated
2 cups heavy cream, whipped

crust

6 tbsp butter, melted, plus
    extra for greasing
5 1/2 oz/150 g graham
    crackers, crushed into
    crumbs
scant 1/2 cup shelled almonds,
    toasted and ground
scant 1/3 cup shelled
    hazelnuts, toasted and
    ground

method

1 Place the unopened cans of milk in a large saucepan and add enough water to cover them. Bring to a boil, then reduce the heat and let simmer for 2 hours, topping up the water level to keep the cans covered. Carefully lift out the hot cans from the pan and let cool.

2 Preheat the oven to 350°F/180°C. Grease a 9-inch/23-cm tart pan with butter. To make the crust, place the remaining butter in a bowl and add the crushed graham crackers and ground nuts. Mix together well, then press the mixture evenly into the bottom and sides of the tart pan. Bake for 10–12 minutes, then remove from the oven and let cool.

3 Peel and slice the bananas and place in a bowl. Squeeze over the juice from the lemon, add the vanilla extract, and mix together. Spread the banana mixture over the cookie crust in the pan, then spoon the contents of the cooled cans of condensed milk over the bananas. Sprinkle over 1 3/4 oz/50 g of the chocolate, then top with a layer of whipped cream. Sprinkle over the remaining grated chocolate and serve the pie at room temperature.

mixed berry fruit pie

ingredients

SERVES 4

9 oz/250 g blueberries

9 oz/250 g raspberries

9 oz/250 g blackberries

1/2 cup superfine sugar

scant 1 1/2 cups all-purpose
    flour, plus extra for dusting

scant 1/4 cup ground hazelnuts

scant 1/2 cup butter, diced,
    plus extra for greasing

finely grated zest of 1 lemon

1 egg yolk, beaten

4 tbsp milk

2 tsp confectioner's sugar,
    for dusting

whipped cream, to serve

method

1 Put the fruit into a saucepan with 3 tablespoons of the superfine sugar and simmer, stirring, for 5 minutes. Remove from the heat.

2 Sift the flour into a bowl, then add the hazelnuts. Rub in the butter, then sift in the remaining sugar. Add the lemon zest, egg yolk, and 3 tablespoons of milk, and mix. Turn out onto a lightly floured counter and knead briefly. Let rest for 30 minutes.

3 Preheat the oven to 375°F/190°C. Grease an 8-inch/20-cm ovenproof pie plate with butter. Roll out half the dough to a thickness of 1/4 inch/5 mm and use it to line the plate. Spoon the fruit into the pie shell. Brush the rim with water, then roll out the remaining dough and use it to cover the pie. Trim and crimp the edges, make two small slits in the top, and decorate with two leaf shapes cut from the dough trimmings. Brush all over with the remaining milk. Bake for 40 minutes. Remove from the oven, sprinkle over the confectioner's sugar, and serve with whipped cream.

lemon meringue pie

ingredients

SERVES 8–10

all-purpose flour, for dusting

9 oz/250 g prepared pastry,
 thawed if frozen

3 tbsp cornstarch

scant $1/2$ cup superfine sugar

grated rind of 3 lemons

$1^1/4$ cups cold water

$2/3$ cup lemon juice

3 egg yolks

4 tbsp unsalted butter, cut into
 small cubes, plus extra for
 greasing

topping

3 egg whites

$3/4$ cup superfine sugar

1 tsp golden granulated sugar

method

1 Grease a 10-inch/25-cm fluted tart pan. On a lightly floured counter, roll out the pastry into a circle 2 inches/5 cm larger than the pan. Press the pastry into the pan. Prick the bottom and chill, uncovered, for 20–30 minutes.

2 Preheat the oven to 400°F/200°C and put in a baking sheet to heat. Line the tart shell with parchment paper and fill with dried beans. Place on the heated baking sheet and bake in the preheated oven for 15 minutes. Remove the beans and paper and return to the oven for 10 minutes. Remove from the oven and reduce the temperature to 300°F/150°C.

3 Put the cornstarch, sugar, and lemon rind into a saucepan. Pour in a little water and blend to a smooth paste. Gradually add the remaining water and the lemon juice. Place the pan over medium heat and bring to a boil, stirring. Simmer for 1 minute, until smooth and glossy. Remove from the heat and beat in the egg yolks, one at a time, then the butter. Place the pan in a bowl of cold water to cool the filling. Spoon the mixture into the tart shell.

4 To make the topping, whisk the egg whites until soft peaks form. Add the superfine sugar gradually, whisking well with each addition. Spoon the meringue over the filling to cover it completely, making a seal with the tart shell and swirling the meringue into peaks. Sprinkle with the granulated sugar and bake for 20–30 minutes. Serve warm.

traditional apple pie

ingredients

SERVES 6

pie dough

scant 2 1/2 cups all-purpose
    flour
pinch of salt
6 tbsp butter or margarine, cut
    into small pieces
6 tbsp lard or vegetable
    shortening, cut into small
    pieces
about 6 tbsp cold water
beaten egg or milk, for glazing
whipped heavy cream,
    to serve

filling

1 lb 10 oz–2 lb 4 oz/
    750 g–1 kg cooking
    apples, peeled, cored, and
    sliced
2/3 cup firmly packed brown or
    superfine sugar, plus extra
    for sprinkling
1/2–1 tsp ground cinnamon,
    allspice, or ground ginger
1–2 tbsp water (optional)

method

1 To make the pie dough, sift the flour and salt into a large bowl. Add the butter and fat and rub in with your fingertips until the mixture resembles fine bread crumbs. Add the water and gather the mixture together into a dough. Wrap the dough and let chill in the refrigerator for 30 minutes.

2 Preheat the oven to 425°F/220°C. Roll out almost two thirds of the pie dough thinly and use to line a deep 9-inch/23-cm pie plate.

3 Mix the apples with the sugar and spice and pack into the pastry shell; the filling can come up above the rim. Add the water if needed, particularly if the apples are a dry variety.

4 Roll out the remaining pie dough to form a lid. Dampen the edges of the pie rim with water and position the lid, pressing the edges firmly together. Trim and crimp the edges.

5 Use the trimmings to cut out leaves or other shapes to decorate the top of the pie, dampen, and attach. Glaze the top of the pie with beaten egg or milk, make 1–2 slits in the top, and place the pie on a baking sheet.

6 Bake in the preheated oven for 20 minutes, then reduce the temperature to 350°F/180°C and bake for an additional 30 minutes, or until the pastry is a light golden brown. Serve hot or cold, sprinkled with sugar, with whipped cream.

apple lattice pie

ingredients

SERVES 4

pie dough

2 cups all-purpose flour, plus
    extra for dusting

pinch of salt

1/4 cup superfine sugar

1 cup plus 2 tbsp butter, cut
    into small pieces

1 egg

1 egg yolk

1 tbsp water

confectioners' sugar,
    for dusting

cream, to serve

filling

3 tbsp black currant or plum
    jelly

scant 1/2 cup chopped toasted
    mixed nuts

2 lb 2 oz/950 g cooking apples

1 tbsp lemon juice

1 tsp apple pie spice

scant 1/2 cup golden raisins

1/4 cup grapes, halved and
    seeded

1/3 cup firmly packed brown
    sugar

method

1 To make the pie dough, sift the flour and salt into a bowl. Make a well in the center and add the sugar, butter, egg, egg yolk, and water. Mix together to form a smooth dough, adding more water if necessary. Wrap the dough and let chill in the refrigerator for 1 hour.

2 Preheat the oven to 400°F/200°C. Shape about three-quarters of the dough into a ball and roll out on a lightly floured counter into a circle large enough to line a shallow 10-inch/25-cm tart pan. Fit it into the pan and trim the edge. Roll out the remaining pie dough and cut into long strips, about 1/2 inch/ 1 cm wide.

3 To make the filling, spread the jelly evenly over the bottom of the pastry shell, then sprinkle over the toasted nuts. Peel and core the apples, then cut them into thin slices. Place them in a bowl with the lemon juice, apple pie spice, golden raisins, grapes, and brown sugar. Mix together gently. Spoon the mixture into the pastry shell, spreading it out evenly.

4 Arrange the pie dough strips in a lattice over the top of the pie. Moisten with a little water, seal, and trim the edges. Bake in the preheated oven for 50 minutes, until golden. Dust with confectioners' sugar. Serve at once with cream.

one roll fruit pie

ingredients

SERVES 8

generous 1 cup all-purpose
flour, plus extra for dusting
scant 1/2 cup butter, cut into
small pieces, plus extra
for greasing
1 tbsp water
1 egg, separated
crushed sugar cubes,
for sprinkling

filling

1 lb 5 oz/600 g prepared
fruit, such as rhubarb,
gooseberries, or plums
generous 1/3 cup light brown
sugar
1 tbsp ground ginger

method

1 Place the flour in a large bowl, add the butter, and rub it in with your fingertips until the mixture resembles bread crumbs. Add the water and mix together to form a soft dough. Cover and let chill in the refrigerator for 30 minutes.

2 Preheat the oven to 400°F/200°C. Grease a large cookie sheet. Roll out the dough on a lightly floured counter to a 14-inch/35-cm circle. Transfer to the prepared cookie sheet and brush with the egg yolk.

3 To make the filling, mix the fruit with the sugar and ground ginger and pile it into the center of the pie dough. Turn in the edges of the dough all the way around. Brush the surface of the dough with the egg white and sprinkle with the crushed sugar cubes.

4 Bake in the preheated oven for 35 minutes, or until golden brown. Transfer to a serving plate and serve warm.

pumpkin pie

ingredients

SERVES 6

4 lb/1.8 kg sweet pumpkin, halved and the stem, seeds, and stringy insides removed and discarded

1 cup all-purpose flour, plus extra for dusting

1/4 tsp baking powder

1 tsp salt

1 1/2 tsp ground cinnamon

3/4 tsp ground nutmeg

3/4 tsp ground cloves

1/4 cup superfine sugar

4 tbsp unsalted butter, diced, plus extra for greasing

3 eggs

1 3/4 cups sweetened condensed milk

1/2 tsp vanilla extract

1 tbsp raw sugar

streusel topping

2 tbsp all-purpose flour

4 tbsp raw sugar

1 tsp ground cinnamon

2 tbsp cold unsalted butter, in small pieces

2/3 cup shelled pecans, chopped

2/3 cup shelled walnuts, chopped

method

1 Preheat the oven to 375°F/190°C. Place the pumpkin halves, face down, in a baking pan and cover with foil. Bake in the preheated oven for 1 1/2 hours, then remove and let cool. Switch off the oven. Puree the pumpkin flesh in a food processor, drain away any excess liquid, then cover with plastic wrap and let chill.

2 To make the pie dough, sift the flour and baking powder into a bowl with 1/2 teaspoon each of salt and cinnamon and 1/4 teaspoon each of nutmeg and cloves. Add the superfine sugar and rub in the butter until the mixture resembles fine bread crumbs. Add 1 egg, lightly beaten, and mix to a soft dough. Roll out the dough on a lightly floured counter, use to line a greased 9-inch/23-cm round pie plate, then trim the edge. Cover with plastic wrap and let chill for 30 minutes.

3 Preheat the oven to 425°F/220°C. To make the filling, place the pumpkin puree in a bowl, then stir in the condensed milk and remaining eggs. Add the remaining spices and salt, then stir in the vanilla extract and raw sugar. Pour into the pastry shell and bake in the preheated oven for 15 minutes.

4 Meanwhile, make the topping. Combine the flour, sugar, and cinnamon in a bowl, rub in the butter until crumbly, then stir in the nuts. Remove the pie from the oven and reduce the heat to 350°F/180°C. Sprinkle over the topping, bake for 35 minutes, and serve hot or cold.

sweet potato pie

ingredients

SERVES 8

pie dough

1¹/₄ cups all-purpose flour,
    plus extra for dusting

¹/₂ tsp salt

¹/₄ tsp superfine sugar

1¹/₂ tbsp butter, diced

3 tbsp shortening, diced

2–2¹/₂ tbsp cold water

filling

1 lb 2 oz/500 g orange-fleshed
    sweet potatoes, peeled

3 extra-large eggs, beaten

¹/₂ cup firmly packed light
    brown sugar

1¹/₂ cups canned condensed
    milk

3 tbsp butter, melted

2 tsp vanilla extract

1 tsp ground cinnamon

1 tsp ground nutmeg

¹/₂ tsp salt

method

1 Sift the flour, salt, and superfine sugar into a bowl. Add the butter and shortening to the bowl and rub in until the mixture resembles fine bread crumbs. Sprinkle over 2 tablespoons of water and mix with a fork to make a soft dough. If the dough is too dry, sprinkle in the extra ¹/₂ tablespoon of water. Wrap in plastic wrap and chill in the refrigerator for at least 1 hour.

2 Meanwhile, bring a large saucepan of water to a boil over high heat. Add the sweet potatoes and cook for 15 minutes. Drain, then cool under cold running water. When cool, cut each into eight wedges. Place in a bowl and beat in the eggs and brown sugar until very smooth. Beat in the remaining ingredients and set aside.

3 Preheat the oven to 425°F/220°C. Roll out the pie dough on a lightly floured counter into a thin 11-inch/28-cm circle and use to line a 9-inch/23-cm round tart pan, about 1¹/₂ inches/ 4 cm deep. Trim off the excess and press a floured fork around the edge. Prick the bottom all over with the fork. Line with parchment paper and fill with dried beans. Bake in the preheated oven for 12 minutes, until lightly golden. Remove from the oven and take out the paper and beans.

4 Pour the filling into the pastry shell and return to the oven for 10 minutes. Reduce the temperature to 325°F/160°C and bake for 35 minutes, until a knife inserted into the center comes out clean. Let cool on a wire rack.

peach cobbler

ingredients

SERVES 4–6

filling

6 peaches, peeled and sliced

4 tbsp superfine sugar

$1/2$ tbsp lemon juice

$1^{1}/2$ tsp cornstarch

$1/2$ tsp almond or vanilla
    extract

pie topping

scant $1^{1}/4$ cups all-purpose
    flour

generous $1/2$ cup superfine
    sugar

$1^{1}/2$ tsp baking powder

$1/2$ tsp salt

6 tbsp butter, diced

1 egg

5–6 tbsp milk

vanilla or pecan ice cream,
    to serve

method

1 Preheat the oven to 425°F/220°C. Place the peaches in a 9-inch/23-cm square ovenproof dish that is also suitable for serving. Add the sugar, lemon juice, cornstarch, and almond extract and toss together. Bake the peaches in the oven for 20 minutes.

2 Meanwhile, to make the topping, sift the flour, all but 2 tablespoons of the sugar, the baking powder, and the salt into a bowl. Rub in the butter with your fingertips until the mixture resembles bread crumbs. Mix the egg and 5 tablespoons of the milk in a pitcher, then mix into the dry ingredients with a fork until a soft, sticky dough forms. If the dough seems too dry, stir in the remaining milk.

3 Reduce the oven temperature to 400°F/200°C. Remove the peaches from the oven and drop spoonfuls of the topping over the surface, without smoothing. Sprinkle with the remaining sugar, return to the oven, and bake for an additional 15 minutes, or until the topping is golden brown and firm—the topping will spread as it cooks. Serve hot or at room temperature with ice cream.

cherry clafoutis

ingredients

SERVES 6

1 lb/450 g ripe fresh cherries, pitted

1/2 cup superfine sugar

2 large eggs

1 egg yolk

2/3 cup all-purpose flour

pinch of salt

1 3/4 cups milk

4 tbsp heavy cream

1 tsp vanilla extract or almond extract

method

1 Preheat the oven to 400°F/200°C. Lightly grease a 5-cup ovenproof serving dish or a 10-inch/25-cm quiche pan. Scatter the cherries over the bottom of the prepared pan, then place the dish on a baking sheet.

2 Using an electric mixer, beat the sugar, eggs, and egg yolk together, until blended and a pale yellow color, scraping down the sides of the bowl as necessary.

3 Beat in the flour and salt, then slowly beat in the milk, cream, and vanilla extract until a light, smooth batter forms. Pour into the dish.

4 Transfer the filled dish on the baking sheet to the oven and bake for 45 minutes, or until the top is golden brown and the batter is set.

5 Remove from the oven and let stand for at least 5 minutes, then serve hot, lukewarm, or at room temperature.

pear & pecan strudel

ingredients

SERVES 4

2 ripe pears

4 tbsp butter

1 cup fresh white bread
   crumbs

generous 1/3 cup shelled
   pecans, chopped

2 tbsp light brown sugar

finely grated rind of 1 orange

3 1/2 oz/100 g filo dough,
   thawed if frozen

6 tbsp orange blossom honey

2 tbsp orange juice

sifted confectioners' sugar,
   for dusting

strained plain yogurt, to serve
   (optional)

method

1 Preheat the oven to 400°F/200°C. Peel, core, and chop the pears. Melt 1 tablespoon of the butter in a skillet and gently sauté the bread crumbs until golden. Transfer to a bowl and add the pears, nuts, brown sugar, and orange rind. Place the remaining butter in a small saucepan and heat until melted.

2 Set aside a sheet of filo, keeping it well wrapped, and brush the remaining sheets with a little melted butter. Spoon the nut filling onto the first sheet, leaving a 1-inch/2.5-cm margin around the edge. Build up the strudel by placing buttered filo sheets on top of the first, spreading each one with the nut filling as you build up the layers. Drizzle the honey and orange juice over the top.

3 Fold the short ends over the filling, then roll up, starting at a long side. Carefully lift onto a baking sheet, with the seam uppermost. Brush with any remaining melted butter and crumple the reserved sheet of filo around the strudel. Bake in the preheated oven for 25 minutes, or until golden and crisp. Dust with confectioners' sugar and serve warm with the yogurt, if using.

pear pie

ingredients

SERVES 6

pie dough

2 cups all-purpose flour

pinch of salt

2/3 cup superfine sugar

1/2 cup butter, cut into small
    pieces

1 egg

1 egg yolk

few drops vanilla extract

2–3 tsp water

filling

4 tbsp apricot jelly

2 oz/55 g amaretti or ratafia
    cookies, crumbled

4 oz/850 g–1 kg pears, peeled
    and cored

1 tsp ground cinnamon

1/2 cup raisins

1/3 cup firmly packed brown or
    raw sugar

sifted confectioners' sugar,
    for sprinkling

method

1 To make the dough, sift the flour and salt onto a counter, make a well in the center, and add the sugar, butter, egg, egg yolk, vanilla extract, and most of the water. Using your fingers, gradually work the flour into the other ingredients to form a smooth dough, adding more water if necessary. Wrap the dough and let chill in the refrigerator for at least 1 hour.

2 Preheat the oven to 400°F/200°C. Roll out three quarters of the dough and use to line a shallow 10-inch/25-cm cake pan or deep tart pan.

3 To make the filling, spread the jelly over the bottom and sprinkle with the crushed cookies. Slice the pears very thinly. Arrange over the cookies in the pastry shell. Sprinkle with cinnamon, then with raisins, and finally with brown sugar.

4 Roll out a thin sausage shape using one third of the remaining pie dough, and place around the edge of the pie. Roll the remainder into thin sausages and arrange in a lattice over the pie, 4 or 5 strips in each direction, attaching them to the strip around the edge.

5 Cook in the preheated oven for 50 minutes, until golden brown and cooked through. Let cool, then serve warm or chilled, sprinkled with confectioners' sugar.

paper-thin fruit pies

ingredients

MAKES 4

1 apple

1 ripe pear

2 tbsp lemon juice

4 tbsp melted butter

4 sheets filo dough, thawed
  if frozen

2 tbsp apricot jelly

1 tbsp unsweetened orange
  juice

1 tbsp finely chopped
  pistachios

2 tsp confectioners' sugar,
  for dusting

method

1 Core and thinly slice the apple and pear and immediately toss them in the lemon juice to prevent them from turning brown. Melt the butter in a saucepan over low heat.

2 Preheat the oven to 400°F/200°C. Cut each sheet of filo in four and cover with a clean, damp dish towel. Brush a four-cup nonstick muffin pan (cup size 4 inches/10 cm in diameter) with a little of the butter.

3 Brush four small sheets of filo with melted butter. Press a sheet of pastry into the bottom of one cup. Arrange the other sheets of filo on top at slightly different angles. Repeat with the other sheets of filo to make another three pies. Arrange alternate slices of apple and pear in the center of each pie shell and lightly crimp the edges of the pastry.

4 Stir the jelly and orange juice together until smooth and brush over the fruit. Bake in the preheated oven for 12–15 minutes. Sprinkle with the pistachios, dust lightly with confectioners' sugar, and serve hot, straight from the oven.

mixed fruit pavlova

ingredients

SERVES 4

6 egg whites

pinch of cream of tartar

pinch of salt

1^1/$_2$ cups superfine sugar

scant 2^1/$_2$ cups heavy cream

1 tsp vanilla extract

2 kiwis, peeled and sliced

9 oz/250 g strawberries, hulled
    and sliced

3 ripe peaches, sliced

1 ripe mango, peeled and
    sliced

2 tbsp orange liqueur, such as
    Cointreau

fresh mint leaves, to decorate

method

1 Preheat the oven to 225°F/110°C. Line three cookie sheets with parchment paper, then draw an 8^1/$_2$-inch/22-cm circle in the center of each one. Beat the egg whites into stiff peaks. Mix in the cream of tartar and salt. Gradually add 1 cup of sugar. Beat for 2 minutes, until glossy. Fill a pastry bag with the mixture and use it to fill each circle, making them slightly domed in the center. Bake for 3 hours. Remove from the oven and let cool.

2 Whip together the cream and vanilla extract with all but 2 tablespoons of the remaining sugar. Put the fruit into a separate bowl and stir in the liqueur. Put one meringue circle onto a serving plate, then spread over one third of the sugared cream. Spread over one third of the fruit, then top with a meringue. Spread over another third of cream, then another third of fruit. Top with the last meringue. Spread over the remaining cream, followed by the remaining fruit. Decorate with mint leaves and serve.

chestnut, maple syrup & pecan tart

ingredients

SERVES 6

pie dough

generous 3/4 cup all-purpose
  flour, plus extra for dusting
pinch of salt
6 tbsp cold butter,
  cut into pieces
cold water

filling

2 lb 4 oz/1 kg canned
  sweetened chestnut paste
1 1/4 cups heavy cream
2 tbsp butter
2 tbsp maple syrup
1 cup pecans

method

1 Lightly grease a 9-inch/23-cm loose-bottom fluted tart pan. Sift the flour and salt into a food processor, add the butter, and process until the mixture resembles fine bread crumbs. Tip the mixture into a large bowl and add a little cold water, just enough to bring the dough together. Turn out onto a counter dusted with more flour and roll out the dough 3 1/4 inches/8 cm larger than the pan. Carefully lift the dough into the pan and press to fit. Roll the rolling pin over the pan to neaten the edges and trim the excess dough. Fit a piece of parchment paper into the tart shell, fill with dried beans, and let chill in the refrigerator for 30 minutes. Meanwhile, preheat the oven to 375°F/190°C.

2 Remove the tart shell from the refrigerator and bake in the preheated oven for 15 minutes, then remove the beans and paper and bake for an additional 10 minutes.

3 Empty the chestnut paste into a large bowl. Whip the cream until stiff and fold into the chestnut paste. Spoon into the tart shell and let chill for 2 hours. Melt the butter with the maple syrup and, when bubbling, add the pecans and stir for 1–2 minutes. Spoon onto parchment paper and let cool. When ready to serve, arrange the pecans on the chestnut cream.

florentine praline tartlets

ingredients

MAKES 6

p r a l i n e

butter, for greasing

$1/2$ cup sugar

3 tbsp water

scant $1/2$ cup slivered almonds

p i e   d o u g h

generous $3/4$ cup all-purpose flour

pinch of salt

6 tbsp cold butter, cut into pieces

1 tsp confectioners' sugar

cold water

f r a n g i p a n e

6 tbsp butter

2 eggs

generous $1/3$ cup superfine sugar

2 tbsp all-purpose flour

1 cup ground almonds

t o p p i n g

8 natural candied cherries, chopped

2 tbsp mixed candied peel, chopped

$31/2$ oz/100 g semisweet chocolate, chopped

method

1 First make the praline. Grease some foil. Put the sugar and the water in a saucepan and dissolve the sugar over low heat. Do not stir the sugar, just let it boil for 10 minutes, until it turns to caramel, then stir in the nuts and turn out onto the prepared foil. Let cool and harden, then break up and chop into smallish pieces.

2 Grease six $31/2$-inch/9-cm loose-bottom fluted tart pans. Sift the flour and salt into a food processor, add the butter, and process until the mixture resembles fine bread crumbs. Tip the mixture into a large bowl, add the sugar, and a little cold water, just enough to bring the dough together. Turn out onto a floured counter and divide into six equal-size pieces. Roll each piece to fit a tart pan. Carefully fit each piece of dough into the pan. Roll the rolling pin over the pan to neaten the edges and trim the excess dough. Put in the freezer for 30 minutes. Meanwhile, preheat the oven to 400°F/200°C.

3 While the tarts are in the freezer, make the frangipane. Melt the butter and beat the eggs and sugar together. Stir the melted butter into the egg and sugar mixture, then add the flour and almonds. Bake the tart shells, straight from the freezer, for 10 minutes in the preheated oven. Divide the frangipane between the tart shells and return to the oven for 8–10 minutes. Let cool completely, then scatter over the candied cherries, candied peel, and chocolate.

almond tart

ingredients

MAKES 1

pie dough

2 cups all-purpose flour, plus
    extra for dusting

generous 3/4 cup superfine
    sugar

1 tsp finely grated lemon rind

pinch of salt

2/3 cup unsalted butter, chilled
    and cut into small dice,
    plus extra for greasing

1 medium egg, lightly beaten

1 tbsp chilled water

filling

3/4 cup unsalted butter,
    at room temperature

3/4 cup superfine sugar

3 large eggs

generous 1 1/2 cups finely
    ground almonds

2 tsp all-purpose flour

1 tbsp finely grated orange
    rind

1/2 tsp almond extract

sifted confectioners' sugar,
    to decorate

whipped heavy cream
    (optional), to serve

method

1 Put the flour, sugar, lemon rind, and salt in a bowl. Rub or cut in the butter until the mixture resembles fine bread crumbs. Combine the egg and water, then slowly pour into the flour, stirring with a fork until a coarse mass forms. Shape into a ball and let chill for at least 1 hour.

2 Preheat the oven to 425°F/220°C. Grease a 10-inch/25-cm loose-bottom tart pan. Roll out the pie dough on a lightly floured counter until 1/8 inch/3 mm thick. Use to line the prepared pan. Place the tart pan in the refrigerator for at least 15 minutes.

3 Cover the pastry shell with foil and fill with dried beans. Bake in the preheated oven for 12 minutes. Remove the beans and foil and return the pastry shell to the oven for 4 minutes to dry the bottom. Remove from the oven and reduce the oven temperature to 400°F/200°C.

4 Meanwhile, make the filling. Beat the butter and sugar until creamy. Beat in the eggs, one at a time. Add the almonds, flour, orange rind, and almond extract, and beat until blended. Spoon the filling into the pastry shell and smooth the surface. Bake for 30–35 minutes until the top is golden and the tip of a knife inserted in the center comes out clean. Let cool completely on a wire rack, then dust with confectioners' sugar. Serve with a spoonful of whipped cream, if using.

truffled honey tart

ingredients

SERVES 6

pie dough

generous 3/4 cup all-purpose
    flour, plus extra for dusting
pinch of salt
6 tbsp cold butter, cut into
    pieces, plus extra for
    greasing
1 tsp confectioners' sugar
cold water

filling

generous 1 cup curd cheese
scant 1/2 cup cream cheese
1/2 cup heavy cream
2 egg yolks, plus 1 whole egg
2 tbsp superfine sugar
4 tbsp flower honey, plus extra
    for drizzling

crystallized violets or sugared
    rose petals, to decorate

method

1 Lightly grease a 9-inch/23-cm loose-bottom fluted tart pan. Sift the flour and salt into a food processor, add the butter, and process until the mixture resembles fine bread crumbs. Tip the mixture into a large bowl, add the sugar, and a little cold water, just enough to bring the dough together. Turn out onto a counter dusted with more flour and roll out the dough 31/4 inches/ 8 cm larger than the pan. Carefully lift the dough into the pan and press to fit. Roll the rolling pin over the pan to neaten the edges and trim the excess dough. Fit a piece of parchment paper into the tart shell, fill with dried beans, and let chill in the refrigerator for 30 minutes. Meanwhile, preheat the oven to 375°F/190°C.

2 Remove the pastry shell from the refrigerator and bake for 10 minutes in the preheated oven, then remove the beans and paper and bake for an additional 5 minutes.

3 Mix the curd cheese, cream cheese, and cream together until smooth, then stir in the egg yolks, whole egg, sugar, and honey until completely smooth. Pour into the pastry shell and bake for 30 minutes. Remove from the oven and let cool in the pan for 10 minutes. Drizzle with honey and decorate with violets.

custard pie

ingredients

SERVES 8

pie dough

1¼ cups all-purpose flour

2 tbsp superfine sugar

½ cup butter, cut into small
   pieces

1 tbsp water

filling

3 eggs

⅓ cup superfine sugar

⅔ cup light cream

⅔ cup milk

freshly grated nutmeg

whipped cream (optional), to
   serve

method

1 To make the pie dough, place the flour and sugar in a mixing bowl. Rub in the butter with your fingertips until the mixture resembles fine bread crumbs. Add the water and mix together until a soft dough has formed. Wrap the dough and let chill in the refrigerator for 30 minutes, then roll out to a circle slightly larger than a 9½-inch/24-cm loose-bottom tart pan.

2 Line the pan with the dough, trimming off the edge. Prick all over the bottom with a fork and let chill in the refrigerator for about 30 minutes. Meanwhile, preheat the oven to 375°F/190°C.

3 Line the pastry shell with parchment paper and fill with dried beans. Bake in the preheated oven for 15 minutes. Remove the paper and beans and bake the pastry shell for an additional 15 minutes.

4 To make the filling, whisk the eggs, sugar, cream, milk, and nutmeg together. Pour the filling into the prepared pastry shell.

5 Return the pie to the oven and cook for an additional 25–30 minutes, or until the filling is just set. Serve with whipped cream, if you like.

sticky lemon tart

ingredients

SERVES 8

9 oz/250 g prepared pie
 dough, thawed if frozen
1 cup corn syrup
scant 2 cups fresh white bread
 crumbs
1/2 cup heavy cream
finely grated rind of 1/2 lemon
 or orange
2 tbsp lemon or orange juice
light cream, to serve

method

1 Roll out the pie dough to line an 8-inch/
20-cm loose-bottom tart pan, reserving the
dough trimmings. Prick the bottom of the
pie dough with a fork and let chill in the
refrigerator for 30 minutes. Preheat the oven
to 375°F/190°C.

2 Cut out small shapes from the reserved dough
trimmings, such as hearts, leaves, or stars,
to decorate the top of the tart.

3 In a bowl, combine the corn syrup, bread
crumbs, heavy cream, grated lemon or orange
rind, and lemon or orange juice.

4 Pour the mixture into the pastry shell and
decorate the edges of the tart with the reserved
dough shapes.

5 Bake in the preheated oven for 35–40 minutes,
or until the filling is just set.

6 Let the tart cool slightly in the pan. Turn
out and serve hot or cold, with light cream.

coconut tart

ingredients

SERVES 8

butter, for greasing

all-purpose flour, for dusting

14 oz/400 g prepared sweet
    pie dough

filling

2 eggs

grated rind and juice of
    2 lemons

1 cup golden superfine sugar

$2/3$ cup heavy cream

$2^3/_4$ cups dry unsweetened
    coconut

method

1 Preheat the oven to 400°F/200°C, then grease a 9-inch/23-cm tart pan. On a lightly floured counter, roll out the pastry and use it to line the prepared pan. Line with parchment paper, fill with dried beans, then bake in the preheated oven for 15 minutes. Reduce the oven temperature to 325°F/160°C and place a baking sheet in the oven to heat.

2 To make the filling, place the eggs, lemon rind, and sugar in a bowl and beat together for 1 minute. Gently stir in the cream, then the lemon juice, and, finally, the coconut.

3 Spoon the filling into the tart shell and place the tart pan on the preheated baking sheet. Bake in the oven for 40 minutes, or until set and golden. Let cool for 1 hour to firm up. Serve at room temperature.

pecan pie

ingredients

SERVES 8

pie dough

generous 1½ cups all-purpose
flour

pinch of salt

½ cup butter, cut into small
pieces

1 tbsp lard or vegetable
shortening, cut into small
pieces

generous ¼ cup golden
superfine sugar

6 tbsp cold milk

filling

3 eggs

generous 1 cup light brown
sugar

1 tsp vanilla extract

pinch of salt

6 tbsp butter, melted

3 tbsp corn syrup

3 tbsp molasses

2 cups shelled pecans,
roughly chopped

pecan halves, to decorate

vanilla ice cream or whipped
cream, to serve

method

1 To make the pie dough, sift the flour and salt into a mixing bowl and rub in the butter and lard with your fingertips until the mixture resembles fine bread crumbs. Work in the sugar and add the milk. Work the mixture into a soft dough. Wrap the dough and let chill in the refrigerator for 30 minutes.

2 Preheat the oven to 400°F/200°C. Roll out the pie dough and use it to line a 9–10-inch/ 23–25-cm tart pan. Trim off the excess by running the rolling pin over the top of the tart pan. Line with parchment paper, and fill with dried beans. Bake in the oven for 20 minutes. Take out of the oven and remove the paper and dried beans. Reduce the oven temperature to 350°F/180°C. Place a baking sheet in the oven.

3 To make the filling, place the eggs in a bowl and beat lightly. Beat in the sugar, vanilla extract, and salt. Stir in the butter, syrup, molasses, and chopped nuts. Pour into the pastry shell and decorate with the pecan halves.

4 Place on the heated baking sheet and bake in the oven for 35–40 minutes, until the filling is set. Serve warm or at room temperature with whipped cream or vanilla ice cream.

croissants

ingredients

MAKES 12

1 lb 2 oz/500 g white bread
flour, plus extra for dusting

scant 1/4 cup superfine sugar

1 tsp salt

2 tsp active dry yeast

1 1/4 cups milk, heated until
just warm to the touch

1 1/4 cups butter, softened,
plus extra for greasing

1 egg, lightly beaten with
1 tbsp milk, to glaze

jelly, to serve

method

1 Stir the dry ingredients into a large bowl, make a well in the center, and add the milk. Mix to a soft dough, adding more milk if too dry. Knead on a lightly floured counter for 5–10 minutes, until smooth and elastic. Let rise in a large, greased bowl, covered, in a warm place until doubled in size. Meanwhile, flatten the butter with a rolling pin between two sheets of wax paper to form a rectangle 1/4 inch/5 mm thick, then let chill. Knead for a minute. Remove the butter from the refrigerator and let soften slightly.

2 Roll out the dough on a well-floured counter to 18 x 6 inches/46 x 15 cm. Place the butter in the center, folding up the sides, and squeezing the edges together gently. With the short end of the dough toward you, fold the top third down toward the center, then fold the bottom third up. Rotate 45° clockwise so that the fold is to your left and the top flap toward your right. Roll out to a rectangle and fold again. If the butter feels soft, wrap the dough in plastic wrap, and let chill. Repeat twice. Cut the dough in half. Roll out each half into a triangle 1/4 inch/5 mm thick. Use a cardboard triangular template, bottom 7 inches/18 cm and sides 8 inches/20 cm, to cut out the croissants.

3 Preheat the oven to 400°F/200°C. Brush lightly with the glaze. Roll into croissant shapes, starting at the base and tucking the point underneath. Brush again with the glaze. Place on a baking sheet and let double in size. Bake for 15–20 minutes, until golden brown. Serve with jelly.

new york cheesecake

ingredients

SERVES 9–10

sunflower oil or corn oil, for
   brushing
6 tbsp butter
7 oz/200 g graham crackers,
   crushed
1^3/$_4$ cups cream cheese
2 large eggs
scant ^{3}/$_4$ cup superfine sugar
1^1/$_2$ tsp vanilla extract
scant 2 cups sour cream

blueberry topping
^{1}/$_4$ cup superfine sugar
4 tbsp water
9 oz/250 g fresh blueberries
1 tsp arrowroot

method

1 Preheat the oven to 375°F/190°C. Brush an 8-inch/20-cm springform pan with oil. Melt the butter in a saucepan over low heat. Stir in the crackers, then spread in the bottom of the prepared pan. Place the cream cheese, eggs, ^{1}/$_2$ cup of the sugar, and ^{1}/$_2$ teaspoon of the vanilla extract in a food processor. Process until smooth. Pour over the cracker layer and smooth the top. Place on a baking sheet and bake in the preheated oven for 20 minutes, or until set. Remove from the oven and let stand for 20 minutes. Leave the oven turned on.

2 Mix the cream with the remaining sugar and vanilla extract in a bowl. Spoon over the cheesecake. Return it to the oven for 10 minutes, let cool, then chill in the refrigerator for 8 hours, or overnight.

3 To make the topping, put the sugar in a saucepan with half of the water over low heat and stir until the sugar has dissolved. Increase the heat, add the blueberries, cover, and cook for a few minutes, or until they start to soften.

4 Remove from the heat. Mix the arrowroot and remaining water in a bowl, add to the fruit, and stir until smooth. Return to low heat. Cook until the juice thickens and turns translucent. Let cool. Remove the cheesecake from the pan 1 hour before serving. Spoon the fruit on top and chill until ready to serve.

hot chocolate cheesecake

ingredients

SERVES 8–10

pie dough

scant 1 1/2 cups all-purpose
　　flour, plus extra for dusting
2 tbsp unsweetened cocoa
4 tbsp butter, plus extra
　　for greasing
2 tbsp golden superfine sugar
1/4 cup ground almonds
1 egg yolk

filling

2 eggs, separated
scant 1/2 cup golden superfine
　　sugar
1 1/2 cups cream cheese
4 tbsp ground almonds
2/3 cup heavy cream
1/4 cup unsweetened cocoa,
　　sifted
1 tsp vanilla extract
confectioners' sugar, for
　　dusting

method

1 Grease an 8-inch/20-cm loose-bottom cake pan. To make the pie dough, sift the flour and cocoa into a bowl and rub in the butter until the mixture resembles fine bread crumbs. Stir in the sugar and ground almonds. Add the egg yolk and sufficient water to make a soft dough.

2 Roll out the pie dough on a lightly floured counter and use to line the prepared pan. Let chill for 30 minutes. Preheat the oven to 325°F/160°C. To make the filling, put the egg yolks and sugar in a large bowl and beat until thick and pale. Beat in the cream cheese, ground almonds, cream, cocoa, and vanilla extract until well combined.

3 Put the egg whites in a large bowl and whisk until stiff but not dry. Stir a little of the egg white into the cheese mixture, then fold in the remainder. Pour into the pastry shell. Bake in the oven for 1 hour 30 minutes, until well risen and just firm to the touch. Carefully remove from the pan and dust with confectioners' sugar. Serve warm.

chocolate amaretto cheesecake

ingredients

SERVES 10–12

base

vegetable oil, for oiling

6 oz/175 g graham crackers

2 oz/55 g amaretti cookies

7 tbsp butter

filling

8 oz/225 g semisweet chocolate, broken into pieces

1³/4 cups cream cheese, at room temperature

generous ¹/2 cup golden superfine sugar

4 eggs

1¹/4 cups heavy cream

¹/4 cup amaretto

topping

1 tbsp amaretto

1¹/4 cups sour cream

crushed amaretti cookies

method

1 Line the bottom of a 9-inch/23-cm springform cake pan with foil and brush the sides of the pan with oil. Place the graham crackers and amaretti cookies in a plastic bag and crush with a rolling pin. Place the butter in a saucepan, heat gently until just melted, then stir in the crushed cookies. Press into the bottom of the prepared pan and chill for 1 hour.

2 Melt the chocolate in a heatproof bowl set over a saucepan of gently simmering water, then set aside to cool slightly. Preheat the oven to 325°F/160°C. To make the filling, put the cream cheese in a bowl and beat until fluffy, then add the sugar and beat until smooth. Gradually add the eggs, beating until well blended. Blend in the melted chocolate, cream, and amaretto. Pour the mixture over the chilled cookie shell and bake in the oven for 50 minutes–1 hour, until set.

3 Leave the cheesecake in the oven with the door slightly ajar, until cold. Run a knife around the inside of the pan to loosen the cheesecake. Chill for 2 hours, then remove from the pan and place on a serving plate. To make the topping, stir the amaretto into the sour cream and spread over the cheesecake. Sprinkle the crushed cookies around the edge to decorate.

irish cream cheesecake

ingredients

SERVES 12

oil, for brushing

6 oz/175 g chocolate chip
  cookies

4 tbsp butter

filling

8 oz/225 g semisweet
  chocolate

8 oz/225 g milk chocolate

3/4 cup golden superfine sugar

1 1/2 cups cream cheese

1 3/4 cups heavy cream,
  whipped

3 tbsp Irish cream liqueur

sour cream and fresh fruit, to
  serve

method

1 Line the bottom of a 20-cm/8-inch springform pan with foil and brush the sides with oil. Place the cookies in a plastic bag and crush with a rolling pin. Place the butter in a saucepan and heat gently until just melted, then stir in the crushed cookies. Press the mixture into the bottom of the pan and let chill in the refrigerator for 1 hour.

2 To make the filling, melt the semisweet chocolate and milk chocolate together, stir to combine, and let cool. Place the sugar and cream cheese in a large bowl and beat together until smooth, then fold in the whipped cream. Fold the mixture gently into the melted chocolate, then stir in the liqueur.

3 Spoon the filling over the chilled cookie base and smooth the surface. Cover and let chill in the refrigerator for 2 hours, or until quite firm. Transfer to a serving plate and cut into small slices. Serve with sour cream and fresh fruit.

chocolate cheesecake

ingredients

SERVES 12

generous 3/4 cup all-purpose flour

scant 1 cup ground almonds

scant 1 cup molasses sugar

3/4 cup margarine, plus extra for greasing

1 lb 8 oz/675 g firm tofu

3/4 cup vegetable oil

1/2 cup orange juice

1/4 cup cognac

6 tbsp unsweetened cocoa, plus extra to decorate

2 tsp almond extract

confectioners' sugar, for dusting

cape gooseberries, to decorate (optional)

method

1 Preheat the oven to 325°F/160°C. Lightly grease and line the bottom of a 9-inch/23-cm springform cake pan. Put the flour, ground almonds, and 1 tablespoon of the sugar in a bowl and mix well. Rub the margarine into the mixture to form a dough.

2 Press the dough into the bottom of the pan to cover, pushing the dough right up to the edge of the pan.

3 Coarsely chop the tofu and put in a food processor with the vegetable oil, orange juice, cognac, cocoa, almond extract, and remaining sugar and process until smooth and creamy. Pour into the pastry shell and cook in the preheated oven for about 1–11/4 hours, or until set.

4 Let cool in the pan for 5 minutes, then remove from the pan and let chill in the refrigerator. Dust with confectioners' sugar and cocoa. Decorate with cape gooseberries, if using, and serve.

ginger cheesecake

ingredients

SERVES 6–8

6 oz/175 g gingersnaps

sunflower oil, for oiling

4 tbsp butter, sweet
    for preference

14 oz/400 g good-quality
    bittersweet chocolate

1/2 cup confectioners' sugar

2 tbsp maple syrup or corn
    syrup

3 bay leaves

seeds from 1 vanilla bean,
    soaked in 4 tsp milk

scant 1 cup cream cheese

1/2 cup heavy cream, whipped

1/2 cup candied ginger pieces,
    sliced thinly, plus extra
    to decorate

to serve

whipped cream

unsweetened cocoa

method

1 To make the base, crush the gingersnaps in a food processor, or place them in a plastic bag, loosely seal the end, and pound with a rolling pin to reduce them to crumbs. Oil an 8-inch/20-cm loose-bottom cake pan, line the bottom with wax paper, and oil again.

2 Melt the butter, stir in the crushed cookies, then press the mixture over the bottom of the pan. Refrigerate to set while you make the filling.

3 Break the chocolate into pieces and place in a large heatproof bowl set over a saucepan of gently simmering water. Add the confectioners' sugar, syrup, bay leaves, vanilla seeds, and their soaking liquid, and stir until the chocolate has melted and the mixture is smooth and glossy. Remove from the heat and let cool, stirring occasionally. Remove and discard the bay leaves.

4 Beat in the cream cheese, then fold in the whipped cream and the candied ginger. Pour into the pan, cover with plastic wrap, and return to the refrigerator for about 3 hours. When firm, carefully remove the cheesecake from the pan.

5 Decorate the cheesecake with swirls of whipped cream topped with slices of ginger and dust with cocoa.

marble cheesecake

ingredients

SERVES 10

base

8 oz/225 g toasted oat cereal

$^1\!/_2$ cup toasted hazelnuts, chopped

4 tbsp butter

1 oz/25 g semisweet chocolate

filling

1$^1\!/_2$ cups cream cheese

$^1\!/_2$ cup superfine sugar

generous $^3\!/_4$ cup plain yogurt

1$^1\!/_4$ cups heavy cream

$^1\!/_4$ oz/7 g powdered gelatin

3 tbsp water

6 oz/175 g semisweet chocolate, melted

6 oz/175 g white chocolate, melted

method

1 Place the cereal in a plastic bag and crush with a rolling pin. Pour the crushed cereal into a mixing bowl and stir in the hazelnuts.

2 Melt the butter and chocolate together over low heat and stir into the cereal mixture, stirring until well coated.

3 Using the bottom of a glass, press the mixture into the bottom and up the sides of an 8-inch/20-cm springform pan.

4 Beat together the cheese and sugar with a wooden spoon until smooth. Beat in the yogurt. Whip the cream until just holding its shape and fold into the mixture. Sprinkle the gelatin over the water in a heatproof bowl and let it go spongy. Place over a pan of hot water and stir until dissolved. Stir into the mixture.

5 Divide the mixture in half and beat the semisweet chocolate into one half and the white chocolate into the other half.

6 Place alternate spoonfuls of mixture on top of the cereal base. Swirl the filling together with the tip of a knife to give a marbled effect. Decorate the top using a serrated scraper. Let chill for at least 2 hours, until set, before serving.

strawberry cheesecake

ingredients

SERVES 8

base

4 tbsp butter, sweet for
    preference
$2^2/_3$ cups crushed graham
    crackers
$1/_2$ cup chopped walnuts

filling

2 cups mascarpone cheese
2 eggs, beaten
3 tbsp superfine sugar
9 oz/250 g white chocolate,
    broken into pieces
2 cups strawberries, hulled
    and quartered

topping

$3/_4$ cup mascarpone cheese
chocolate curls
16 whole strawberries

method

1 Melt the butter over low heat and stir in the crushed crackers and the nuts. Spoon the mixture into a 9-inch/23-cm springform cake pan and press evenly over the bottom with the back of a spoon. Set aside.

2 Preheat the oven to 300°F/150°C. To make the filling, beat the cheese until smooth, then beat in the eggs and sugar. Put the chocolate in a heatproof bowl set over a saucepan of gently simmering water. Stir over low heat until melted and smooth. Remove from the heat and cool slightly, then stir into the cheese mixture. Finally, stir in the strawberries.

3 Spoon the mixture into the cake pan, spread out evenly, and smooth the surface. Bake in the preheated oven for 1 hour, until the filling is just firm. Turn off the oven and let the cheesecake cool inside with the door slightly ajar until completely cold.

4 Transfer the cheesecake to a serving plate and spread the mascarpone on top. Decorate with chocolate curls and whole strawberries.

berry cheesecake

ingredients

SERVES 8

base

6 tbsp margarine

6 oz/175 g oatmeal cookies

2/3 cup dry unsweetened
   coconut

topping

1 1/2 tsp powdered gelatin

generous 1/2 cup cold water

1/2 cup evaporated milk

1 egg

6 tbsp brown sugar

2 cups soft cream cheese

3 cups mixed berries

2 tbsp honey

method

1 Line the base of an 8-inch/20-cm springform cake pan. Melt the margarine in a saucepan. Put the cookies into a food processor and process until crushed, or crush finely with a rolling pin. Stir the crumbs into the margarine with the coconut.

2 Press the mixture evenly into the prepared pan and set aside to chill in the refrigerator.

3 To make the topping, sprinkle the gelatin over the water in a heatproof bowl and let it go spongy. Place over a saucepan of hot water and stir until dissolved. Set aside to cool slightly.

4 Beat the milk with the egg, sugar, and cream cheese until smooth. Stir in 1/2 cup of the berries. Add the gelatin in a thin stream, stirring continuously.

5 Spoon the mixture onto the cookie base and return to the refrigerator to chill for 2 hours, or until set.

6 Remove the cheesecake from the pan and transfer to a serving plate. Arrange the remaining berries on top of the cheesecake and drizzle the honey over the top. Serve.

mascarpone cheesecake

ingredients

SERVES 8

4 tbsp butter, salted for
    preference, plus extra
    for greasing

3 cups gingersnap crumbs

1 tbsp chopped preserved
    ginger

2¹/₄ cups mascarpone cheese

finely grated rind and juice of
    2 lemons

¹/₂ cup superfine sugar

2 large eggs, separated

fruit coulis, to serve

method

1 Preheat the oven to 350°F/180°C. Grease and line the bottom of a 10-inch/25-cm springform cake pan or loose-bottom cake pan.

2 Melt the butter in a saucepan and stir in the cookie crumbs and chopped ginger. Use the mixture to line the pan, pressing the mixture about ¹/₄ inch/5 mm up the sides.

3 Beat together the cheese, lemon rind and juice, sugar, and egg yolks until smooth.

4 Whisk the egg whites until stiff and fold into the cheese and lemon mixture.

5 Pour the mixture into the cake pan and bake in the preheated oven for 35–45 minutes, until just set. Don't worry if it cracks or sinks—this is normal.

6 Let cool in the pan. Serve with fruit coulis.

ricotta lemon cheesecake

ingredients

SERVES 6–8

generous 1/3 cup golden
  raisins
3 tbsp Marsala or grappa
butter, for greasing
2 tbsp semolina, plus extra
  for dusting
1 1/2 cups ricotta cheese,
  drained
3 large egg yolks, beaten
1/2 cup superfine sugar
3 tbsp lemon juice
2 tbsp candied orange peel,
  finely chopped
finely grated rind of 2 large
  lemons

to decorate
confectioners' sugar
fresh mint sprigs
red currants or berries
  (optional)

method

1 Soak the golden raisins in the Marsala in a small bowl for about 30 minutes, or until the liquid is absorbed and the fruit is swollen.

2 Preheat the oven to 350°F/180°C. Cut out a circle of parchment paper to fit the bottom of a loose-bottom 8-inch/20-cm round cake pan about 2 inches/5 cm deep. Grease the sides and bottom of the pan and line the bottom. Dust with semolina and tip out the excess.

3 Using a wooden spoon, press the ricotta cheese through a nylon strainer into a bowl. Beat in the egg yolks, sugar, semolina, and lemon juice and continue beating until blended.

4 Fold in the golden raisins, orange peel, and lemon rind. Pour into the prepared pan and smooth the surface.

5 Bake the cheesecake in the center of the preheated oven for 30–40 minutes, until firm to the touch and coming away slightly from the side of the pan.

6 Turn off the oven and open the door. Let the cheesecake cool in the oven for 2–3 hours. To serve, remove from the pan and transfer to a plate. Sift over a layer of confectioners' sugar from at least 12 inches/30 cm above the cheesecake to dust the top and sides lightly. Decorate with mint and red currants, if using.

breads & savory

You might ask why make bread yourself when supermarket shelves are packed with a huge variety of different loaves. There are several reasons, the first being that it's utterly delicious and as fresh as it's possible to be. Secondly, it's a very pleasurable and rewarding activity—and much easier than many people think. Then, given that bread is a staple, making your own is cost-saving and, finally, it's very likely to be healthier. Commercially made bread is one of the main sources of unhealthily high levels of salt in the diet and some loaves also contain large quantities of sugar, although only small amounts of both are required to ensure that yeast doughs rise successfully.

There are many recipes for all kinds of leavened bread—from a classic white loaf to Italian focaccia, including loaves made with rising agents other than yeast, such as soda bread. Some are plain, while others are flavored with cheese, nuts, seeds, olives, tomatoes, and herbs. In addition, there are flat breads, bagels, breadsticks, and other tasty treats. It's a truly international compilation of this most basic, yet infinitely varied of foods.

Finally, there is a superb collection of recipes for mouthwatering savory baking from snacks to serve with predinner drinks, party foods,

and crackers to more substantial tarts, pies, quiches, and gratins. The choice is vast with a wide range of ingredients to suit all tastes: cheese, fish, bacon, chicken, herbs, spices, nuts, and all kinds of different vegetables from artichokes to zucchini.

crusty white bread

ingredients

MAKES 1 MEDIUM LOAF

1 egg

1 egg yolk

lukewarm water, as required

generous 3 cups white bread
    flour, plus extra for dusting

1 1/2 tsp salt

2 tsp sugar

1 tsp active dry yeast

2 tbsp butter, diced

corn oil, for oiling

method

1 Place the egg and egg yolk in a pitcher and beat lightly to mix. Add enough lukewarm water to make up to 1 1/4 cups. Stir well.

2 Place the flour, salt, sugar, and yeast in a large bowl. Add the butter and rub it in with your fingertips until the mixture resembles bread crumbs. Make a well in the center, add the egg mixture, and work to a smooth dough.

3 Turn out the dough onto a lightly floured counter and knead for 10 minutes, or until the dough is smooth and elastic. Brush a bowl with oil. Place the dough in the bowl, cover with plastic wrap, and let rise in a warm place for 1 hour, or until it has doubled in size.

4 Preheat the oven to 425°F/220°C. Oil a loaf pan. Turn out the dough onto a lightly floured counter and knead for 1 minute, until smooth. Shape the dough the length of the pan and three times the width. Fold the dough in three lengthwise and place it in the pan with the seam underneath. Cover and let stand in a warm place for 30 minutes, until it has risen above the pan.

5 Bake in the oven for 30 minutes, or until firm and golden brown. Test that the loaf is cooked by tapping it on the bottom—it should sound hollow. Transfer to a wire rack to cool completely before serving.

whole wheat harvest bread

ingredients

MAKES 1 LOAF

2 cups whole wheat bread
   flour, plus extra for dusting

1 tsp salt

1 tbsp nonfat dry milk

2 tbsp light brown sugar

1 tsp active dry yeast

1½ tbsp vegetable oil, plus
   extra for brushing

¾ cup lukewarm water

method

1 Sift the flour and salt together into a bowl, add the bran from the sifter, and stir in the milk, sugar, and yeast. Make a well in the center and pour in the oil and lukewarm water. Stir well with a wooden spoon until the dough begins to come together, then knead with your hands until it leaves the side of the bowl.

2 Turn out onto a lightly floured counter and knead well for about 10 minutes, until smooth and elastic. Brush a bowl with oil. Shape the dough into a ball, put it into the bowl, and cover with a damp dish towel. Let rise in a warm place for 1 hour, until the dough has doubled in volume.

3 Brush a 6½ x 4¼ x 3¼-inch/17 x 11 x 8-cm loaf pan with oil. Turn out the dough onto a lightly floured counter, punch down with your fist, and knead for 1 minute. With lightly floured hands, shape the dough into a rectangle the same length as the pan and flatten slightly. Fold it lengthwise in three and place in the prepared pan, seam-side down. Cover with a damp dish towel and let rise in a warm place for 30 minutes, until the dough has reached the top of the pan.

4 Preheat the oven to 425°F/220°C. Bake the loaf in the preheated oven for about 30 minutes, until it has shrunk from the sides of the pan, the crust is golden brown, and it sounds hollow when tapped on the bottom. Turn out onto a wire rack to cool.

pita breads

ingredients

MAKES 6–8

3 cups white bread flour,
plus extra for dusting

1¹/₂ tsp salt

1 tsp superfine sugar

1 tsp active dry yeast

1 tbsp olive oil, plus extra
for brushing

scant 1 cup lukewarm water

method

1 Sift the flour and salt together into a bowl and stir in the sugar and yeast. Make a well in the center and pour in the oil and lukewarm water. Stir well with a wooden spoon until the dough begins to come together, then knead with your hands until it leaves the side of the bowl. Turn out onto a lightly floured counter and knead for 10 minutes, until smooth and elastic.

2 Brush a bowl with oil. Shape the dough into a ball, put it in the bowl, and put the bowl into a plastic bag or cover with a damp dish towel. Let rise in a warm place for 1 hour, until the dough has doubled in volume. Turn out onto a lightly floured counter and punch down with your fist. Divide the dough into six or eight equal pieces, shape each piece into a ball, and place on a cookie sheet. Put the sheet into a plastic bag and let rest for 10 minutes.

3 With floured hands, slightly flatten a dough ball and roll out on a lightly floured surface to an oval about 6 inches/15 cm long and about ¹/₄ inch/5 mm thick. Place on a lightly floured dish towel, sprinkle lightly with flour, and cover with a dish towel. Repeat with the remaining dough balls and let rise for 30 minutes.

4 Meanwhile, put two or three cookie sheets in the oven and preheat to 450°F/230°C. Transfer the pita breads to the heated cookie sheets, spacing them well apart, and bake for 5 minutes, until puffed up and golden brown. Transfer to wire racks to cool, then cover with a dish towel.

braided poppy seed bread

ingredients

MAKES 1 LOAF

2 cups white bread flour,
    plus extra for dusting

1 tsp salt

2 tbsp nonfat dry milk

1 1/2 tbsp superfine sugar

1 tsp active dry yeast

3/4 cup lukewarm water

2 tbsp vegetable oil, plus extra
    for brushing

5 tbsp poppy seeds

topping

1 egg yolk

1 tbsp milk

1 tbsp superfine sugar

2 tbsp poppy seeds

method

1 Sift the flour and salt together into a bowl and stir in the milk, sugar, and yeast. Make a well in the center and pour in the lukewarm water and oil. Stir well until the dough begins to come together. Add the poppy seeds and knead with your hands until they are fully incorporated and the dough leaves the side of the bowl. Turn out onto a lightly floured counter and knead well for about 10 minutes, until smooth and elastic.

2 Brush a bowl with oil. Shape the dough into a ball, put it into the bowl, and cover with a damp dish towel. Let rise in a warm place for 1 hour, until the dough has doubled in volume.

3 Brush a cookie sheet with oil. Turn out the dough onto a lightly floured surface, punch down with your fist, and knead for 1–2 minutes. Divide the dough into three equal pieces and shape each into a rope 10–12 inches/25–30 cm long. Place the ropes side by side and press them together at one end. Braid the dough, pinch the other ends together, and tuck underneath. Put the loaf on the prepared cookie sheet, cover with a damp dish towel, and let rise in a warm place for 30 minutes.

4 Preheat the oven to 400°F/200°C. To make the topping, beat the egg yolk with the milk and sugar. Brush over the top of the loaf and sprinkle with the poppy seeds. Bake in the preheated oven for 30–35 minutes, until golden brown and the loaf sounds hollow when tapped on the bottom. Transfer to a wire rack to cool.

rye bread

ingredients

MAKES 1 LARGE LOAF

4 cups rye flour

2 cups white bread flour,
    plus extra for dusting

2 tsp salt

2 tsp light brown sugar

1 1/2 tsp active dry yeast

scant 2 cups lukewarm water

2 tsp vegetable oil, plus extra
    for brushing

1 egg white

method

1 Sift the flours and salt together into a bowl. Add the sugar and yeast and stir to mix. Make a well in the center and pour in the lukewarm water and oil. Stir with a wooden spoon until the dough begins to come together, then knead with your hands until it leaves the side of the bowl. Turn out onto a lightly floured counter and knead for 10 minutes, until elastic and smooth.

2 Brush a bowl with oil. Shape the dough into a ball, put it into the bowl, and cover with a damp dish towel. Let rise in a warm place for 2 hours, until the dough has doubled in volume.

3 Brush a cookie sheet with oil. Turn out the dough onto a lightly floured counter and punch down with your fist, then knead for an additional 10 minutes. Shape the dough into a ball, put it on the prepared cookie sheet, and cover with a damp dish towel. Let rise in a warm place for an additional 40 minutes, until the dough has doubled in volume.

4 Meanwhile, preheat the oven to 375°F/190°C. Beat the egg white with 1 tablespoon of water in a bowl. Bake in the preheated oven for 20 minutes, remove from the oven, and brush the top with the egg white glaze. Return to the oven and bake for an additional 20 minutes. Brush the top of the loaf with the glaze again and return to the oven for 20–30 minutes, until the crust is a rich brown color and the loaf sounds hollow when tapped on the bottom with your knuckles. Transfer to a wire rack to cool.

walnut & seed bread

ingredients

MAKES 2 LARGE LOAVES

4 cups whole wheat flour

4 cups multigrain flour

1 cup white bread flour, plus
    extra for dusting

2 tbsp sesame seeds

2 tbsp sunflower seeds

2 tbsp poppy seeds

1 cup chopped walnuts

2 tsp salt

$1^{1}/_{2}$ tsp active dry yeast

2 tbsp olive oil or walnut oil

3 cups lukewarm water

1 tbsp melted butter or oil,
    for greasing

method

1 In a mixing bowl, combine the flours, seeds, walnuts, salt, and yeast. Add the oil and lukewarm water and stir well to form a soft dough. Turn out the dough onto a lightly floured counter and knead well for 5–7 minutes. The dough should have a smooth appearance and feel elastic.

2 Return the dough to the bowl, cover with a clean dish towel or plastic wrap, and let stand in a warm place for $1–1^{1}/_{2}$ hours to rise. When the dough has doubled in size, turn it out onto a lightly floured counter and knead again for 1 minute.

3 Grease two 9 x 5 x 3-inch/23 x 13 x 8-cm loaf pans well with melted butter or oil. Divide the dough in two. Shape one piece the length of the pan and three times the width. Fold the dough into three lengthwise and place in one of the pans with the seam underneath. Repeat with the other piece of dough.

4 Cover and let rise again in a warm place for about 30 minutes, until the bread is well risen above the pans. Meanwhile, preheat the oven to 450°F/230°C.

5 Bake in the center of the preheated oven for 25–30 minutes. If the loaves are getting too brown, reduce the temperature to 425°F/220°C. Test that the bread is cooked by tapping on the bottom with your knuckles—it should sound hollow. Transfer to a wire rack to cool.

irish soda bread

ingredients

MAKES 1 LOAF

vegetable oil, for brushing

4 cups all-purpose flour, plus
    extra for dusting

1 tsp salt

1 tsp baking soda

1³/₄ cups buttermilk

method

1 Preheat the oven to 425°F/220°C. Brush a cookie sheet with oil.

2 Sift the flour, salt, and baking soda together into a bowl. Make a well in the center and pour in most of the buttermilk. Mix well, first with a wooden spoon and then with your hands. The dough should be very soft but not too wet. If necessary, add the remaining buttermilk.

3 Turn out the dough onto a lightly floured counter and knead lightly and briefly. Shape into an 8-inch/20-cm circle. Put the loaf onto the prepared cookie sheet and cut a cross in the top with a sharp knife.

4 Bake in the preheated oven for 25–30 minutes, until golden brown and the loaf sounds hollow when tapped on the bottom with your knuckles. Transfer to a wire rack to cool slightly and serve warm.

corn bread

ingredients

MAKES 1 LOAF

vegetable oil, for brushing

1 1/2 cups all-purpose flour

1 tsp salt

4 tsp baking powder

1 tsp superfine sugar

2 1/2 cups yellow cornmeal

1/2 cup butter, softened, diced

4 eggs

1 cup milk

3 tbsp heavy cream

method

1 Preheat the oven to 400°F/200°C. Brush an 8-inch/20-cm square cake pan with oil.

2 Sift the flour, salt, and baking powder together into a bowl. Add the sugar and cornmeal and stir to mix. Add the butter, then rub in with your fingertips until the mixture resembles bread crumbs.

3 Lightly beat the eggs with the milk and cream in a bowl, then stir into the cornmeal mixture until thoroughly combined.

4 Spoon the mixture into the prepared pan and smooth the surface. Bake in the preheated oven for 30–35 minutes, until a skewer inserted into the center of the loaf comes out clean. Remove the pan from the oven and let the bread cool for 5–10 minutes, then cut into squares and serve warm.

cilantro & garlic naan

ingredients

MAKES 3

2¹/₂ cups white bread flour, plus extra for dusting

1 tsp salt

1 tbsp ground coriander

1 garlic clove, very finely chopped

1 tsp active dry yeast

2 tsp honey

scant ¹/₂ cup lukewarm water

4 tbsp plain yogurt

1 tbsp vegetable oil, plus extra for brushing

1 tsp black onion seeds

1 tbsp chopped fresh cilantro

method

1 Sift the flour, salt, and coriander together into a bowl and stir in the garlic and yeast. Make a well in the center and pour in the honey, water, yogurt, and oil. Stir well with a wooden spoon until the dough begins to come together, then knead with your hands until it leaves the side of the bowl. Turn out onto a lightly floured counter and knead well for about 10 minutes, until smooth and elastic.

2 Brush a bowl with oil. Shape the dough into a ball, put it into the bowl, and cover with a damp dish towel. Let rise in a warm place for 1–2 hours, until the dough has doubled in volume.

3 Put three cookie sheets into the oven and preheat to 475°F/240°C. Preheat the broiler. Turn out the dough onto a lightly floured counter and punch down with your fist. Divide the dough into three pieces, shape each piece into a ball, and cover two of them with oiled plastic wrap.

4 Roll out the uncovered piece of dough into a teardrop shape about ³/₈ inch/8 mm thick and cover with oiled plastic wrap. Roll out the other pieces of dough in the same way. Place the naans on the preheated cookie sheets and sprinkle with the onion seeds and chopped cilantro. Bake in the preheated oven for 5 minutes, until puffed up. Transfer the naans to the broiler pan, brush with oil, and broil for 2–3 minutes. Serve warm.

turkish flatbread

ingredients

MAKES 8

6½ cups all-purpose flour,
   plus extra for dusting

1½ tsp salt

1 tsp ground cumin

½ tsp ground coriander

1 tsp superfine sugar

2¼ tsp active dry yeast

2 tbsp olive oil, plus extra
   for brushing

1¾ cups lukewarm water

method

1 Sift together the flour, salt, cumin, and coriander into a bowl and stir in the sugar and yeast. Make a well in the center and pour in the oil and lukewarm water. Stir well with a wooden spoon until the dough begins to come together, then knead with your hands until it leaves the side of the bowl. Turn out onto a lightly floured counter and knead well for about 10 minutes, until smooth and elastic.

2 Brush a bowl with oil. Shape the dough into a ball, put it into the bowl, and cover with a damp dish towel. Let rise in a warm place for 1 hour, until the dough has doubled in volume.

3 Lightly brush a cookie sheet with oil. Turn out the dough onto a lightly floured counter, punch down, and knead for 1–2 minutes. Divide the dough into eight equal pieces, shape each piece into a ball, then roll out to an 8-inch/20-cm circles. Cover the circles with a damp dish towel and let rest for 20 minutes.

4 Heat a heavy skillet and brush the bottom with oil. Add one of the dough circles, cover, and cook for 2–3 minutes, until lightly browned on the underside. Turn over with a metal spatula, re-cover the skillet, and cook for an additional 2 minutes, until lightly browned on the second side. Remove from the skillet and cook the remaining dough circles in the same way.

vegetable & hazelnut loaf

ingredients

SERVES 4

2 tbsp sunflower oil, plus extra
for oiling

1 onion, chopped

1 garlic clove, finely chopped

2 celery stalks, chopped

1 tbsp all-purpose flour

scant 1 cup strained canned
tomatoes

2 cups fresh whole wheat
bread crumbs

2 carrots, grated

3/4 cup toasted hazelnuts,
ground

1 tbsp dark soy sauce

2 tbsp chopped fresh cilantro

1 egg, lightly beaten

salt and pepper

mixed red and green salad
leaves, to serve

method

1 Preheat the oven to 350°F/180°C. Oil and line a 8 x 4 x 2-inch/20 x 10 x 5-cm loaf pan. Heat the oil in a heavy-bottom skillet over medium heat. Add the onion and cook, stirring frequently, for 5 minutes, or until softened. Add the garlic and celery and cook, stirring frequently, for 5 minutes. Add the flour and cook, stirring continuously, for 1 minute. Gradually stir in the tomatoes and cook, stirring continuously, until thickened. Remove the skillet from the heat.

2 Put the bread crumbs, carrots, ground hazelnuts, soy sauce, and cilantro in a bowl. Add the tomato mixture and stir well. Let cool slightly, then beat in the egg and season with salt and pepper to taste.

3 Spoon the mixture into the prepared pan and smooth the surface. Cover with foil and bake in the preheated oven for 1 hour. If serving hot, turn out the loaf onto a warmed serving dish and serve immediately. Alternatively, let cool in the pan before turning out and serving with salad leaves.

focaccia with roasted cherry tomatoes, basil & crispy pancetta

ingredients

SERVES 4–6

generous 3 cups white
    bread flour, plus extra for
    kneading and rolling
1 tbsp dried basil
1/2 tsp sugar
2 tsp active dry yeast
2 tsp salt
generous 1 1/4 cups water,
    lukewarm
2 tbsp olive oil, plus extra
    for oiling

topping
14 oz/400 g cherry tomatoes
7 oz/200 g thick pancetta,
    diced
1 tbsp olive oil, plus extra for
    oiling and drizzling
4 tbsp chopped fresh basil
salt and pepper

method

1 Place the flour, dried basil, sugar, yeast, and salt in a bowl. Combine the water and oil and mix with the dry ingredients to form a soft dough, adding more water if the dough appears too dry. Turn out onto a lightly floured counter and knead for 10 minutes, or until the dough bounces back when pressed lightly with your finger. Lightly oil a bowl. Place the dough in the bowl and cover with plastic wrap. Let stand in a warm place for 1 hour, until doubled in size.

2 Meanwhile, preheat the oven to 275°F/140°C. Place the tomatoes on a baking sheet covered with parchment paper, sprinkle with oil, and season with salt and pepper to taste. Bake for 30 minutes, or until the tomatoes are soft.

3 Increase the oven temperature to 425°F/220°C. Remove the dough from the bowl and knead briefly. Shape into a rectangle and place on a lightly oiled baking sheet, turning the dough over to oil both sides. Make rough indentations in the dough using your fingers. Top with the tomatoes and pancetta. Sprinkle with salt and pepper. Let rise in a warm place for 10 minutes. Bake for 15–20 minutes, or until golden brown and cooked through. Drizzle with oil and top with fresh basil. Serve warm.

olive & sun-dried tomato bread

ingredients

MAKES 2 LOAVES

generous 2³/₄ cups
    all-purpose flour, plus
    extra for dusting

1 tsp salt

2¹/₄ tsp active dry yeast

1 tsp brown sugar

1 tbsp chopped fresh thyme

scant 1 cup warm water
    (heated to 122°F/50°C)

4 tbsp olive oil, plus extra
    for oiling

¹/₃ cup black olives, pitted and
    sliced

¹/₃ cup green olives, pitted and
    sliced

³/₈ cup sun-dried tomatoes in
    oil, drained and sliced

1 egg yolk, beaten

method

1 Place the flour, salt, and yeast in a bowl and mix together, then stir in the sugar and thyme. Make a well in the center. Slowly stir in enough water and oil to make a dough. Mix in the olives and sun-dried tomatoes. Knead the dough for 5 minutes, then form it into a ball. Brush a bowl with oil, add the dough, and cover with plastic wrap. Let rise in a warm place for about 1¹/₂ hours, or until it has doubled in size.

2 Dust a baking sheet with flour. Knead the dough lightly, then cut into two halves and shape into ovals or circles. Place them on the baking sheet, cover with plastic wrap, and let rise again in a warm place for 45 minutes, or until they have doubled in size.

3 Preheat the oven to 400°F/200°C. Make three shallow diagonal cuts on the top of each piece of dough. Brush with the egg. Bake for 40 minutes, or until cooked through—they should be golden on top and sound hollow when tapped on the bottom. Transfer to wire racks to cool. Store in an airtight container for up to 3 days.

black olive focaccia

ingredients

SERVES 12

scant 4 cups strong white
bread flour, plus extra
for dusting

1 tsp salt

2 tsp active dry yeast

1 1/2 cups lukewarm water

6 tbsp extra virgin olive oil,
plus extra for brushing

2/3 cup pitted black olives,
coarsely chopped

1 tsp rock salt

method

1 Sift the flour and salt into a warmed bowl and stir in the yeast. Pour in the water and 2 tablespoons of the olive oil and mix to a soft dough. Knead the dough on a lightly floured counter for 5–10 minutes, or until it becomes smooth and elastic. Oil a warmed bowl. Transfer the dough to the bowl and cover with plastic wrap. Let stand in a warm place for 1 hour, until the dough has doubled in size.

2 Brush two cookie sheets with oil. Punch down the dough to knock out the air, then knead on a lightly floured counter for 1 minute. Add the olives and knead until combined. Divide the dough in half and shape into two ovals 11 x 9 inches/28 x 23-cm long, and place on the prepared cookie sheets. Cover with oiled plastic wrap and let stand in a warm place for 1 hour, or until the dough is puffy.

3 Preheat the oven to 400°F/200°C. Press your fingers into the dough to make dimples, drizzle over 2 tablespoons of oil, and sprinkle with the rock salt. Bake in the preheated oven for 30–35 minutes, or until golden. Drizzle with the remaining olive oil and cover with a cloth, to give a soft crust. Slice each loaf into six pieces and serve warm.

mixed seed bread

ingredients

MAKES 1 MEDIUM LOAF

generous 2$\frac{1}{2}$ cups white
   bread flour

generous 1$\frac{1}{4}$ cups rye flour

1$\frac{1}{2}$ tbsp nonfat dry milk

1$\frac{1}{2}$ tsp salt

1 tbsp brown sugar

1 tsp active dry yeast

1$\frac{1}{2}$ tbsp sunflower oil, plus
   extra for brushing

2 tsp lemon juice

1$\frac{1}{4}$ cups lukewarm water

1 tsp caraway seeds

$\frac{1}{2}$ tsp poppy seeds

$\frac{1}{2}$ tsp sesame seeds

topping

1 egg white

1 tbsp water

1 tbsp sunflower or pumpkin
   seeds (pepitas)

method

1 Place the flours, milk, salt, sugar, and yeast in a large bowl. Pour in the oil and add the lemon juice and water. Stir in the seeds and mix well to make a smooth dough.

2 Turn out the dough onto a lightly floured counter and knead for 10 minutes, or until the dough is smooth and elastic. Oil a bowl. Place the dough in the bowl, cover with plastic wrap, and let stand in a warm place to rise for 1 hour, until it has doubled in size.

3 Oil a 9 x 5 x 3-inch/23 x 13 x 8-cm loaf pan. Turn out the dough onto a lightly floured counter and knead for 1 minute, until smooth. Shape the dough the length of the pan and three times the width. Fold the dough in three lengthwise and place it in the pan with the seam underneath. Cover and leave in a warm place for 30 minutes, until it has risen above the pan.

4 Preheat the oven to 425°F/220°C. For the topping, lightly beat the egg white with the water to make a glaze. Just before baking, brush the glaze over the loaf, then gently press the sunflower seeds all over the top.

5 Bake in the oven for 30 minutes, or until firm and golden brown. Test that the loaf is cooked by tapping it on the bottom with your knuckles—it should sound hollow. Transfer to a wire rack to cool completely before serving.

cheese & chive braid

ingredients

SERVES 10

3¹/₂ cups strong white bread
    flour, plus extra for dusting

1 tsp salt

1 tsp superfine sugar

1¹/₂ tsp active dry yeast

2 tbsp butter

generous 1 cup coarsely
    grated cheddar cheese

3 tbsp snipped fresh chives

4 scallions, chopped

²/₃ cup lukewarm milk

³/₄ cup lukewarm water

vegetable oil, for brushing

beaten egg, for glazing

method

1 Sift the flour and salt into a warmed bowl and stir in the sugar and yeast. Rub in the butter, then stir in the cheese, chives, and scallions. Make a well in the center. Mix together the milk and water and pour into the well. Mix to make a soft dough. Turn out the dough onto a lightly floured counter and knead for 10 minutes, or until it is smooth and elastic.

2 Oil a bowl. Put the dough in the bowl and cover with plastic wrap. Let stand in a warm place for 1 hour, or until doubled in size. Preheat the oven to 425°F/220°C, then brush a large cookie sheet with oil. Turn out the dough onto a floured counter and knead for 1 minute. Divide the dough into three pieces. Roll out each piece into a rope shape and braid the three pieces together, pinching the ends to seal.

3 Place on the prepared cookie sheet and cover with oiled plastic wrap. Let stand in a warm place for 45 minutes, or until doubled in size. Brush with beaten egg and bake in the preheated oven for 20 minutes.

4 Reduce the oven temperature to 350°F/180°C and bake for an additional 15 minutes, or until golden brown and the loaf sounds hollow when tapped on the bottom. Serve warm or cold.

english muffins

ingredients

MAKES 10–12

2¹/₄ tsp active dry yeast

generous 1 cup lukewarm
    water

¹/₂ cup plain yogurt

3 cups white bread flour, plus
    extra for dusting

¹/₂ tsp salt

¹/₄ cup fine semolina

oil, for greasing

butter and jelly (optional), to
    serve

method

1 Mix the yeast with half the water in a bowl until it has dissolved.

2 Add the remaining water and the yogurt and mix well.

3 Sift the flour into a large bowl and add the salt. Pour in the yeast liquid and mix well to a soft dough.

4 Turn out onto a floured counter and knead well until very smooth. Put the dough back into the bowl, cover with plastic wrap, and let rise in a warm place for 30–40 minutes, until it has doubled in size.

5 Turn out again onto the counter and knead lightly. Roll out the dough to a thickness of 3/4 inch/2 cm.

6 Using a 3-inch/7.5-cm cutter, cut into circles and scatter the semolina over each muffin. Reroll the trimmings of the dough and make additional muffins until it is all used up. Place them on a lightly floured baking sheet, cover, and let rise again for 30–40 minutes.

7 Heat a large skillet and lightly grease with a little oil. Cook half the muffins for 7–8 minutes on each side, being careful not to burn them. Repeat with the remaining muffins. Serve freshly cooked, with plenty of butter and jelly, if using.

bagels

ingredients

MAKES 10

3 cups white bread flour, plus
 extra for dusting

2 tsp salt

$2^{1}/_{4}$ tsp active dry yeast

1 tbsp lightly beaten egg

scant 1 cup lukewarm water

vegetable oil, for brushing

1 egg white

2 tsp water

2 tbsp caraway seeds

method

1 Sift the flour and salt together into a bowl and stir in the yeast. Make a well in the center, pour in the egg and lukewarm water, and mix to a dough. Turn out onto a lightly floured counter and knead well for about 10 minutes, until smooth. Brush a bowl with oil. Shape the dough into a ball, place it in the bowl, and cover with a damp dish towel. Let rise in a warm place for 1 hour, until the dough has doubled in volume.

2 Brush two cookie sheets with oil and dust a baking sheet with flour. Turn out the dough onto a lightly floured counter and punch down with your fist. Knead for 2 minutes, then divide into ten pieces. Shape each piece into a ball and let rest for 5 minutes. Flatten each ball with a lightly floured hand and make a hole in the center with the handle of a wooden spoon. Put the bagels on the floured sheet, cover with a damp dish towel, and let rise in a warm place for 20 minutes.

3 Meanwhile, preheat the oven to 425°F/220°C and bring a large saucepan of water to a boil. Reduce the heat until barely simmering, then add two bagels. Poach for 1 minute, turn over, and poach for 30 seconds more. Remove with a slotted spoon and drain on a dish towel. Poach the remaining bagels, then transfer to the oiled cookie sheets. Beat the egg white with the water in a bowl and brush it over the bagels. Sprinkle with the caraway seeds and bake in the preheated oven for 25–30 minutes, until golden brown. Let cool on a wire rack.

breadsticks

ingredients

MAKES 30

scant 2¹/₄ cups white bread
    flour, plus extra for dusting
1¹/₂ tsp salt
1¹/₂ tsp active dry yeast
scant 1 cup lukewarm water
3 tbsp olive oil, plus extra
    for brushing
sesame seeds, for coating

method

1 Lightly oil two cookie sheets. Sift the flour and salt together into a warmed bowl. Stir in the yeast. Make a well in the center. Add the water and oil to the well and mix to form a soft dough.

2 Turn out the dough onto a lightly floured counter and knead for 5–10 minutes, or until smooth and elastic. Put the dough in an oiled bowl, cover with a damp dish towel, and let rise in a warm place for 1 hour, or until doubled in size.

3 Turn out the dough again and knead lightly. Roll out to a rectangle measuring 9 x 8 inches/ 23 x 20 cm. Cut the dough into three strips, each 8 inches/20 cm long, then cut each strip across into ten equal pieces.

4 Gently roll and stretch each piece of dough into a stick about 12 inches/30 cm long, then brush with oil. Spread the sesame seeds out on a large shallow plate or tray. Roll each breadstick in the sesame seeds to coat, then place them, spaced well apart, on the prepared cookie sheets. Brush with oil, cover with a damp dish towel, and let rise in a warm place for 15 minutes. Meanwhile, preheat the oven to 400°F/200°C.

5 Bake the breadsticks in the preheated oven for 10 minutes. Turn over and bake for an additional 5–10 minutes, until golden. Transfer to a wire rack and let cool.

cheese straws

ingredients

MAKES 24

generous 3/4 cup all-purpose
   flour, plus extra for dusting
pinch of salt
1 tsp curry powder
4 tbsp butter, plus extra
   for greasing
1/2 cup grated cheddar cheese
1 egg, beaten
poppy and cumin seeds,
   for sprinkling

method

1 Sift the flour, salt, and curry powder into a bowl. Add the butter and rub in until the mixture resembles bread crumbs. Add the cheese and half the egg and mix to form a dough. Wrap in plastic wrap and let chill in the refrigerator for 30 minutes.

2 Preheat the oven to 400°F/200°C. Grease several cookie sheets. On a floured counter, roll out the dough to 1/4-inch/5-mm thick. Cut into 3 x 1/2-inch/7.5 x 1-cm strips. Pinch the strips lightly along the sides and place on the prepared cookie sheets.

3 Brush the straws with the remaining egg and sprinkle half with poppy seeds and half with cumin seeds. Bake in the preheated oven for 10–15 minutes, or until golden. Transfer to wire racks to cool.

savory oatcakes

ingredients

MAKES 12–14

scant $\frac{1}{2}$ cup unsalted butter, plus extra for greasing

scant 1 cup rolled oats

$\frac{1}{4}$ cup whole wheat flour

$\frac{1}{2}$ tsp coarse salt

1 tsp dried thyme

$\frac{1}{3}$ cup walnuts, finely chopped

1 egg, beaten

3 tbsp sesame seeds

method

1 Preheat the oven to 350°F/180°C and lightly grease two cookie sheets.

2 Rub the butter into the oats and flour using your fingertips. Stir in the salt, thyme, and walnuts, then add the egg and mix to a soft dough. Break off walnut-size pieces of dough and roll into balls, then roll in the sesame seeds to coat lightly and evenly.

3 Place the balls of dough on the prepared cookie sheets, spacing them well apart, and roll the rolling pin over them to flatten them as much as possible. Bake in the preheated oven for 12–15 minutes, or until firm and pale golden in color.

4 Let cool on the cookie sheets for 3–4 minutes, then transfer to a wire rack to finish cooling.

cheese & mustard biscuits

ingredients

MAKES 8

generous 1¹/₂ cups self-rising
    flour, plus extra for dusting
1 tsp baking powder
pinch of salt
4 tbsp butter, cut into small
    pieces, plus extra for
    greasing
1¹/₂ cups grated sharp
    cheddar cheese
1 tsp mustard powder
²/₃ cup milk, plus extra
    for brushing
pepper

method

1 Preheat the oven to 425°F/220°C. Lightly grease a cookie sheet.

2 Sift the flour, baking powder, and salt together into a mixing bowl. Rub in the butter with your fingertips until the mixture resembles bread crumbs.

3 Stir in the cheese, mustard, and enough milk to form a soft dough.

4 On a lightly floured counter, knead the dough very lightly, then flatten it out with the palm of your hand to a depth of about 1 inch/2.5 cm.

5 Cut the dough into eight wedges with a knife. Brush each one with a little milk and sprinkle with pepper to taste.

6 Bake in the preheated oven for 10–15 minutes, until golden brown. Transfer the biscuits to a wire rack and let cool slightly before serving.

blinis

ingredients

MAKES 8

3/4 cup buckwheat flour

3/4 cup white bread flour

1 1/2 tsp sachet active dry yeast

1 tsp salt

scant 1 3/4 cups lukewarm milk

2 eggs, 1 whole and
    1 separated

vegetable oil, for brushing

sour cream and smoked
    salmon, to serve

method

1 Sift both flours into a large, warmed bowl. Stir in the yeast and salt. Beat in the milk, whole egg, and egg yolk until smooth. Cover the bowl and let stand in a warm place for 1 hour.

2 Place the egg white in a clean, greasefree bowl and whisk until soft peaks form. Fold into the batter. Brush a heavy-bottom skillet with oil and set over medium–high heat. When the skillet is hot, pour enough of the batter onto the surface to make a blini about the size of a saucer.

3 When bubbles rise, turn the blini over with a spatula and cook the other side until light brown. Wrap in a clean dish towel to keep warm while cooking the remainder. Serve the warm blinis with sour cream and smoked salmon.

spiced cocktail bites

ingredients

MAKES ABOUT 20

1 cup all-purpose flour, plus
    extra for dusting

2 tsp curry powder

1/2 cup butter, plus extra for
    greasing

generous 3/4 cup grated
    cheddar cheese

2 tsp poppy seeds

1 tsp black onion seeds

1 egg yolk

cumin seeds, for sprinkling

method

1 Preheat the oven to 375°F/190°C, then grease two cookie sheets. Sift the flour and curry powder into a bowl. Cut the butter into pieces and add to the flour. Rub in until the mixture resembles bread crumbs, then stir in the cheese, poppy seeds, and black onion seeds. Stir in the egg yolk and mix to a firm dough.

2 Wrap the dough in plastic wrap and let chill in the refrigerator for 30 minutes. On a floured counter, roll out the dough to 1/8-inch/3-mm thick. Stamp out shapes with a cutter. Reroll the trimmings and stamp out more cookies until the dough is used up.

3 Place the cookies on the prepared cookie sheets and sprinkle with the cumin seeds. Let chill for an additional 15 minutes. Bake in the preheated oven for 20 minutes, or until crisp and golden. Serve warm or transfer to wire racks to cool.

curried cheese bites

ingredients

MAKES 40

3/4 cup all-purpose flour, plus extra for dusting

1 tsp salt

2 tsp curry powder

1 cup grated mellow semihard cheese

1 cup freshly grated Parmesan cheese

1/2 cup butter, softened, plus extra for greasing

method

1 Preheat the oven to 350°F/180°C. Lightly grease four cookie sheets. Sift the flour and salt into a mixing bowl.

2 Stir in the curry powder and both the grated cheeses. Rub in the softened butter with your fingertips, then bring the mixture together to form a soft dough.

3 Roll out the dough thinly on a lightly floured counter to form a rectangle.

4 Cut out 40 crackers using a 2-inch/5-cm cookie cutter. Arrange the crackers on the cookie sheets.

5 Bake in the preheated oven for 10–15 minutes, until golden brown.

6 Let the crackers cool slightly on the cookie sheets. Transfer them to a wire rack to cool completely and crispen, then serve.

pesto palmiers

ingredients

MAKES 20

butter, for greasing

all-purpose flour, for dusting

9 oz/250 g prepared puff
  pastry

3 tbsp green or red pesto

1 egg yolk, beaten with 1 tbsp
  water

1/4 cup freshly grated
  Parmesan cheese

method

1 Preheat the oven to 400°F/200°C, then grease a cookie sheet. On a floured counter, roll out the pastry to a 14 x 6-inch/35 x 15-cm rectangle and trim the edges with a sharp knife. Spread the pesto evenly over the pastry. Roll up the ends tightly to meet in the center of the pastry.

2 Wrap in plastic wrap and chill in the refrigerator for 20 minutes, until firm, then remove from the refrigerator and unwrap. Brush with the beaten egg yolk on all sides. Cut across into 1/2-inch/1-cm thick slices. Place the slices on the prepared cookie sheet.

3 Bake in the preheated oven for 10 minutes, or until crisp and golden. Remove from the oven and immediately sprinkle over the Parmesan cheese. Serve the palmiers warm or transfer to a wire rack and let cool to room temperature.

cheese & rosemary bites

ingredients

MAKES 40

1³/₄ cups all-purpose flour

1 cup cold butter, diced, plus
   extra for greasing

2¹/₂ cups grated Gruyère
   cheese

¹/₂ tsp cayenne pepper

2 tsp finely chopped fresh
   rosemary leaves

1 egg yolk, beaten with 1 tbsp
   water

method

1 Preheat the oven to 350°F/180°C, then grease two cookie sheets. Place the flour, butter, cheese, cayenne pepper, and rosemary in a food processor. Pulse until the mixture forms a dough, adding a little cold water, if necessary, to bring the mixture together.

2 On a floured counter, roll out the dough to ¹/₄-inch/5-mm thick. Stamp out shapes, such as stars and hearts, with 2¹/₂-inch/6-cm cookie cutters.

3 Place the shapes on the prepared cookie sheets, then cover with plastic wrap and let chill in the refrigerator for 30 minutes, or until firm. Brush with the beaten egg yolk and bake in the oven for 10 minutes, or until golden brown. Let cool on the cookie sheets for 2 minutes, then serve warm or transfer to wire racks to cool.

spicy chicken muffins

ingredients

MAKES 12

1/2 cup sunflower oil or peanut
    oil, plus extra for oiling

2 onions, chopped

3 scallions, chopped

1 small fresh red chile, seeded
    and finely chopped

3 skinless, boneless chicken
    thighs, chopped into small
    pieces

1 tsp paprika

scant 2 1/4 cups self-rising flour

1 tsp baking powder

2 large eggs

1 tbsp lemon juice

1 tbsp grated lemon rind

1/2 cup sour cream

1/2 cup plain yogurt

salt and pepper

method

1 Preheat the oven to 375°F/190°C. Oil a 12-cup muffin pan. Heat a little oil in a skillet, add the onions, scallions, and chile, and cook over low heat, stirring continuously, for 3 minutes. Remove from the heat, lift out the onions and chile, and set aside. Heat a little more of the remaining oil in the skillet, add the chicken and paprika, and cook, stirring, over medium heat for 5 minutes. Remove from the heat and set aside.

2 Sift the flour and baking powder into a large mixing bowl. In a separate bowl, lightly beat the eggs, then stir in the remaining oil and the lemon juice and rind. Pour in the sour cream and the yogurt and mix together. Add the egg mixture to the flour mixture, then gently stir in the onions, scallions, chile, and chicken. Season with salt and pepper to taste. Do not overstir—it is fine for it to be a little lumpy.

3 Divide the muffin batter evenly between the 12 cups in the muffin pan (they should reach the top), then transfer to the oven. Bake for 20 minutes, or until risen and golden. Remove the muffins from the oven and serve warm, or place them on a wire rack and let cool.

leek & ham muffins

ingredients

MAKES 12

2 tbsp sunflower oil or peanut oil, plus extra for oiling (if using)

1 leek, washed, trimmed, and finely chopped

2 cups all-purpose flour

2 tsp baking powder

$^1/_2$ tsp baking soda

1 large egg, lightly beaten

$1^1/_4$ cups strained plain yogurt

4 tbsp butter, melted

$^1/_4$ cup grated cheddar cheese

$^1/_2$ cup finely snipped fresh chives

$5^1/_2$ oz/150 g cooked ham, chopped

method

1 Preheat the oven to 400°F/200°C. Oil a 12-cup muffin pan or line it with 12 muffin paper liners. Heat the oil in a skillet, add the leek, and cook, stirring, over low heat for 2 minutes. Remove from the heat and let cool.

2 Sift the flour, baking powder, and baking soda into a large mixing bowl. In a separate bowl, lightly mix the egg, yogurt, and melted butter together. Add the cheese, chives, cooked leek, and half of the chopped ham, then mix together well. Add the cheese mixture to the flour mixture and then gently stir together until just combined. Do not overstir the batter—it is fine for it to be a little lumpy.

3 Divide the muffin batter evenly between the 12 cups in the muffin pan or the paper liners (they should be about two-thirds full). Sprinkle over the remaining chopped ham, then transfer to the oven. Bake for 20 minutes, or until risen and golden. Remove the muffins from the oven and serve warm, or place them on a wire rack and let cool.

potato & pancetta muffins

ingredients

MAKES 12

1 tbsp sunflower oil or peanut oil, plus extra for oiling (if using)

3 shallots, finely chopped

generous 2$\frac{1}{4}$ cups self-rising flour

1 tsp salt

1 lb/450 g potatoes, cooked and mashed

2 large eggs

1$\frac{1}{2}$ cups milk

$\frac{1}{2}$ cup sour cream

1 tbsp finely snipped fresh chives

5$\frac{1}{2}$ oz/150 g pancetta, broiled and crumbled into pieces

4 tbsp grated cheddar cheese

method

1 Preheat the oven to 400°F/200°C. Oil a 12-cup muffin pan or line it with 12 paper baking liners. Heat the oil in a skillet, add the chopped shallots, and cook, stirring, over low heat for 2 minutes. Remove from the heat and let cool.

2 Sift the flour and salt into a large mixing bowl. In a separate bowl, mix the mashed potatoes, eggs, milk, sour cream, chives, and half the pancetta together. Add the potato mixture to the flour mixture and then gently stir together until just combined. Do not overstir the batter—it is fine for it to be a little lumpy.

3 Divide the muffin batter evenly between the 12 cups in the muffin pan or the paper liners (they should be about two-thirds full). Sprinkle over the remaining pancetta, then sprinkle over the cheese. Transfer to the oven and bake for 20 minutes, or until risen and golden. Remove the muffins from the oven and serve warm, or place them on a wire rack and let cool.

crab & cream cheese muffins

ingredients

MAKES 12

1 tbsp sunflower oil or peanut
    oil, for oiling (if using)
2 cups all-purpose flour
1 1/2 tsp baking powder
1/2 tsp baking soda
1/2 tsp salt
1 large egg
2/3 cup plain yogurt
2/3 cup sour cream
1/4 cup grated cheddar cheese
generous 1/4 cup chopped
    fresh parsley
generous 1/4 cup chopped
    fresh dill

filling

7 oz/200 g canned crabmeat,
    drained
scant 1/2 cup cream cheese
2 tbsp mayonnaise
salt and pepper

method

1 Preheat the oven to 400°F/200°C. Oil a 12-cup muffin pan. Sift the flour, baking powder, baking soda, and salt into a large mixing bowl.

2 In a separate bowl, lightly beat the egg, then pour in the yogurt and sour cream and mix together. Stir in the grated cheese and chopped herbs. Add the sour cream and cheese mixture to the flour mixture, then gently stir together. Do not overstir the batter—it is fine for it to be a little lumpy. Divide the batter evenly between the 12 cups in the muffin pan (they should be about two-thirds full), then transfer to the oven. Bake for 20 minutes, or until risen and golden.

3 Meanwhile, make the filling. Place the crabmeat in a mixing bowl and flake with a fork. Add the cream cheese and mayonnaise and mix together well. Season with salt and pepper to taste. Cover the bowl with plastic wrap and let chill in the refrigerator until ready for use.

4 When the muffins are cooked, remove them from the oven, place on a wire rack, and let cool to room temperature. When they have cooled, cut them in half horizontally. Remove the crabmeat filling from the refrigerator and spread it over the bottom halves of the muffins. Replace the top halves, so that the filling is sandwiched in the middle, and serve.

herb muffins with smoked cheese

ingredients

MAKES 12

1 tbsp sunflower oil or peanut
    oil, for oiling (if using)

2 cups all-purpose flour

2 tsp baking powder

1/2 tsp baking soda

1/4 cup grated smoked hard
    cheese

scant 1 cup finely chopped
    fresh parsley

1 large egg, lightly beaten

1 1/4 cups strained plain yogurt

4 tbsp butter, melted

method

1 Preheat the oven to 400°F/200°C. Oil a 12-cup muffin pan or line it with 12 paper baking liners. Sift the flour, baking powder, and baking soda into a large mixing bowl. Add the smoked cheese and the parsley and mix together well.

2 In a separate bowl, lightly mix the egg, yogurt, and melted butter together. Add the yogurt mixture to the flour mixture and then gently stir together until just combined. Do not overstir the batter—it is fine for it to be a little lumpy.

3 Divide the muffin batter evenly between the 12 cups in the muffin pan or the paper liners (they should be about two-thirds full), then transfer to the oven. Bake for 20 minutes, or until risen and golden. Remove the muffins from the oven and serve warm, or place them on a wire rack and let cool.

sour cream muffins with chives

ingredients

MAKES 12

1 tbsp sunflower oil or peanut
    oil, for oiling (if using)

2 cups all-purpose flour

2 tsp baking powder

1/2 tsp baking soda

1/4 cup grated cheddar cheese

3/4 cup finely snipped fresh
    chives, plus extra
    to garnish

1 large egg, lightly beaten

scant 1 cup sour cream

generous 1/3 cup plain yogurt

4 tbsp butter, melted

method

1 Preheat the oven to 400°F/200°C. Oil a 12-cup muffin pan or line it with 12 paper baking liners. Sift the flour, baking powder, and baking soda into a large mixing bowl. Add the cheese and chives and mix together well.

2 In a separate bowl, lightly mix the egg, sour cream, yogurt, and melted butter together. Add the sour cream mixture to the flour mixture and then gently stir together until just combined. Do not overstir the batter—it is fine for it to be a little lumpy.

3 Divide the muffin batter evenly between the 12 cups in the muffin pan or the paper liners (they should be about two-thirds full). Sprinkle over the remaining snipped chives to garnish and transfer to the oven. Bake for 20 minutes, or until risen and golden. Remove the muffins from the oven and serve warm, or place them on a wire rack and let cool.

parmesan & pine nut muffins

ingredients

MAKES 12

oil or melted butter, for
    greasing (if using)
2 cups all-purpose flour
1 tbsp baking powder
pinch of salt
2 tbsp freshly grated
    Parmesan cheese
1/2 cup pine nuts
2 large eggs
1 cup buttermilk
6 tbsp sunflower oil or melted,
    cooled butter
pepper

topping
4 tsp freshly grated Parmesan
    cheese
1/4 cup pine nuts

method

1 Preheat the oven to 400°F/200°C. Grease a 12-cup muffin pan or line with 12 paper baking liners.

2 To make the topping, mix together the Parmesan cheese and pine nuts and set aside.

3 To make the muffins, sift together the flour, baking powder, salt, and pepper to taste into a large bowl. Stir in the Parmesan cheese and pine nuts.

4 Lightly beat the eggs in a large pitcher or bowl, then beat in the buttermilk and oil. Make a well in the center of the dry ingredients and pour in the beaten liquid ingredients. Stir gently until just combined; do not overmix.

5 Spoon the batter into the prepared muffin pan. Scatter the topping over the muffins. Bake in the preheated oven for about 20 minutes, until well risen, golden brown, and firm to the touch.

6 Let the muffins cool in the pan for 5 minutes, then serve warm.

caramelized onion muffins

ingredients

MAKES 12

oil or melted butter, for
    greasing (if using)
7 tbsp sunflower oil
3 onions, finely chopped
1 tbsp red wine vinegar
2 tsp sugar
2 cups all-purpose flour
1 tbsp baking powder
$\frac{1}{8}$ tsp salt
2 large eggs
1 cup buttermilk
pepper

method

1 Preheat the oven to 400°F/200°C. Grease a 12-cup muffin pan or line with 12 paper baking liners.

2 Heat 2 tablespoons of the oil in a skillet. Add the onions and cook for about 3 minutes, until beginning to soften. Add the vinegar and sugar and cook, stirring occasionally, for an additional 10 minutes, until golden brown. Remove from the heat and let cool.

3 Meanwhile, sift together the flour, baking powder, salt, and pepper to taste into a large bowl. Lightly beat the eggs in a large pitcher or bowl, then beat in the buttermilk and the remaining oil. Make a well in the center of the dry ingredients, pour in the beaten liquid ingredients, and add the onion mixture, reserving 4 tablespoons for the topping. Stir gently until just combined; do not overmix.

4 Spoon the batter into the prepared muffin pan. Sprinkle the reserved onion mixture over the tops of the muffins. Bake in the preheated oven for about 20 minutes, until well risen, golden brown, and firm to the touch.

5 Let the muffins cool in the pan for 5 minutes, then serve warm.

quiche lorraine

ingredients

SERVES 4

9 oz/250 g prepared
   shortcrust pastry
flour, for dusting

filling

1 tbsp butter
1 small onion, finely chopped
4 lean bacon strips, diced
$1/2$ cup grated Gruyère cheese
   or cheddar cheese
2 eggs, beaten
$1^1/4$ cups light cream
pepper

method

1 Roll out the pastry on a lightly floured counter to a circle slightly larger than a 9-inch/23-cm loose-bottom round tart pan, $1^1/4$ inches/3 cm deep. Lift the pastry onto the pan and press it down into the fluted edge, using the back of your finger. Roll the rolling pin over the edge of the pan to trim off the excess. Prick the bottom all over with a fork. Let chill in the refrigerator for at least 10 minutes.

2 Put a baking sheet in the oven and preheat the oven to 400°C/200°C. Place a sheet of parchment paper in the pie shell and fill with dried beans. Place on the baking sheet and bake in the preheated oven for 10 minutes. Remove the paper and beans and bake for an additional 10 minutes.

3 For the filling, melt the butter in a skillet and cook the onion and bacon over medium heat for about 5 minutes, stirring occasionally, until the onion is softened and lightly browned. Spread the mixture evenly in the hot pie shell and sprinkle with half the cheese. Beat the eggs and cream together in a small bowl and season with pepper to taste. Pour into the pie shell and sprinkle with the remaining cheese.

4 Reduce the oven temperature to 375°F/ 190°C. Place the quiche in the oven and bake for 25–30 minutes, or until golden brown and just set. Let cool for 10 minutes before turning out. Serve warm or cold.

triple tomato tart

ingredients

SERVES 6

9 oz/250 g prepared puff
   pastry
3 tbsp sundried tomato paste
9 oz/250 g ripe vine tomatoes,
   sliced
5 1/2 oz/150 g cherry tomatoes,
   cut in half
2 sprigs fresh rosemary
2 tbsp extra virgin olive oil
1 tbsp balsamic vinegar
1 egg yolk
4 1/2 oz/125 g Italian sliced
   salami, chopped
handful thyme sprigs
salt and pepper

method

1 Preheat the oven to 375°F/190°C. Roll out the pastry to form a rectangle 14 inches/36 cm long and 10 inches/25 cm wide and lift onto a heavy-duty baking sheet.

2 Spread the tomato paste over the pastry, leaving a 1 1/4-inch/3-cm margin. Arrange the tomato slices over the tomato paste, sprinkle over the cherry tomato halves, top with the rosemary, and drizzle with a tablespoon of the olive oil and the balsamic vinegar. Brush the edges of the pastry with egg yolk and bake for 10 minutes. Sprinkle over the salami and bake for an additional 10–15 minutes.

3 Remove the tart from the oven and season with salt and pepper. Drizzle with the remaining oil and sprinkle with the thyme.

crab & watercress tart

ingredients

SERVES 6

pie dough

scant 3/4 cup all-purpose flour,
     plus extra for dusting

pinch of salt

6 tbsp cold butter, cut into
     pieces

cold water

filling

10 1/2 oz/300 g prepared white
     and brown crabmeat

1 bunch watercress, washed
     and leaves picked from
     stems

1/4 cup milk

2 large eggs, plus 3 egg yolks

scant 1 cup heavy cream

1/2 tsp ground nutmeg

1/2 bunch fresh chives,
     snipped

2 tbsp finely grated Parmesan
     cheese

salt and pepper

method

1 Lightly grease a 9-inch/23-cm loose-bottom fluted tart pan. Sift the flour and salt into a food processor, add the butter, and process until the mixture resembles fine bread crumbs. Tip into a large bowl and add enough cold water to bring the dough together. Turn out onto a floured counter and roll out the dough 3 1/4 inches/ 8 cm larger than the pan. Carefully lift the dough into the pan and press to fit. Roll the rolling pin over the pan to neaten the edges and trim the excess dough. Fit a piece of parchment paper into the tart shell, fill with dried beans, and let chill in the refrigerator for 30 minutes. Meanwhile, preheat the oven to 375°F/190°C.

2 Remove the tart shell from the refrigerator and bake for 10 minutes in the preheated oven, then remove the beans and paper. Return to the oven for 5 minutes. Remove the pan from the oven and reduce the oven temperature to 325°F/160°C.

3 Arrange the crabmeat and watercress in the tart shell. Whisk the milk, eggs, and egg yolks together in a bowl. Bring the cream to simmering point in a saucepan and pour over the egg mixture, whisking all the time. Season with salt and pepper and nutmeg and stir in the chives. Carefully pour this mixture over the crab and watercress and sprinkle over the Parmesan cheese. Bake for 35–40 minutes, until golden and set. Let stand for 10 minutes before serving.

goat cheese & thyme tart

ingredients

SERVES 6

9 oz/250 g prepared puff
  pastry dough

1 lb 2 oz/500 g goat cheese,
  such as chèvre, sliced

3–4 sprigs fresh thyme, leaves
  picked from stalks

scant 1/3 cup black olives,
  pitted

scant 1/2 cup tinned anchovies
  in olive oil

1 tbsp olive oil

salt and pepper

1 egg yolk

method

1 Roll out the dough into a large circle or rectangle and place on a baking sheet. Preheat the oven to 375°F/190°C.

2 Arrange the cheese slices on the dough, leaving a 1-inch/2.5-cm margin around the edge. Sprinkle over the thyme and olives, and arrange the anchovies over the cheese. Drizzle over the olive oil. Season well and brush the edges of the dough with the egg yolk. Bake in the preheated oven for 20–25 minutes, until the cheese is bubbling and the pastry is browned.

684 bread & savory

spring vegetable tart

ingredients

SERVES 6

pie dough

scant 1³/₄ cups all-purpose
    flour
pinch of salt
generous ¹/₂ cup cold butter,
    cut into pieces
¹/₂ cup grated Parmesan
    cheese
1 egg
cold water

filling

11 oz/300 g selection of baby
    spring vegetables, such as
    carrots, asparagus, peas,
    fava beans, scallions, corn
    cobs, leeks, trimmed and
    peeled, where necessary
generous 1¹/₄ cups heavy
    cream
generous 1 cup grated sharp
    cheddar cheese
2 eggs
3 egg yolks
handful fresh tarragon and
    flat-leaf parsley, chopped
salt and pepper

method

1 Grease a 10-inch/25-cm loose-bottom tart pan. Sift the flour and salt into a food processor, add the butter, and pulse to combine, then tip into a large bowl and add the Parmesan cheese. Mix the egg and water together in a small bowl. Add most of the egg mixture and work into a soft dough, using more egg mixture if needed. Turn out onto a floured counter and roll out the dough 3¹/₄ inches/8 cm larger than the pan. Carefully lift the dough into the pan and press to fit. Roll the rolling pin over the pan to neaten the edges and trim the excess dough. Fit a piece of parchment paper into the tart shell, fill with dried beans, and let chill in the refrigerator for 30 minutes. Meanwhile, preheat the oven to 400°F/200°C.

2 Bake the tart shell for 15 minutes in the preheated oven, then remove the beans and paper and bake for an additional 5 minutes. Remove from the oven and let cool. Reduce the oven temperature to 350°F/180°C.

3 Cut the vegetables into bite-size pieces, and blanch in boiling water. Drain and let cool. Bring the cream to simmering point in a saucepan. Place the cheese, eggs, and egg yolks in a heatproof bowl and pour over the warm cream. Stir to combine, season well, and stir in the herbs. Arrange the vegetables in the tart shell, pour over the cheese filling, and bake for 30–40 minutes. Let cool for 10 minutes before serving.

yellow zucchini tart

ingredients

SERVES 6

pie dough

scant 1³/4 cups all-purpose
    flour, plus extra for dusting
pinch of salt
generous ¹/2 cup cold butter,
    cut into pieces, plus extra
    for greasing
scant ¹/2 cup grated Parmesan
    cheese
1 egg
cold water

filling

2 large yellow zucchini
1 tbsp salt
3¹/2 tbsp unsalted butter
1 bunch scallions, trimmed
    and finely sliced
²/3 cup heavy cream
3 large eggs
1 small bunch fresh chives,
    chopped
salt and white pepper

method

1 Preheat the oven to 400°F/200°C. Grease a 10-inch/25-cm loose-bottom tart pan. Sift the flour and salt into a food processor, add the butter, and pulse to combine, then tip into a large bowl. Add the cheese and mix the egg and water together. Add most of the egg mixture to the flour mixture and work to a soft dough, using more egg mixture if needed. Turn out onto a floured counter and roll out the dough 3¹/4 inches/8 cm larger than the pan. Lift the dough into the pan and press to fit. Fit a piece of parchment paper into the tart shell, fill with dried beans, and let chill for 30 minutes.

2 Bake the tart shell for 15 minutes in the preheated oven, remove the beans and paper, and bake for an additional 5 minutes. Remove from the oven and let cool. Reduce the oven temperature to 350°F/180°C. Meanwhile, grate the zucchini and put in a strainer with 1 tablespoon of salt. Let drain for 20 minutes, then rinse and put in a clean dish towel, squeezing all the moisture from the zucchini.

3 Melt the butter in a wide skillet, sauté the scallions until soft, then add the zucchini and cook over medium heat for 5 minutes, until any liquid has evaporated. Let cool slightly. Whisk the cream and eggs together with the salt and pepper and chives. Spoon the zucchini into the tart shell and pour in the cream mixture, making sure it settles properly, and bake for 30 minutes. Serve hot or cold.

squash, sage & gorgonzola tart

ingredients

SERVES 6

1/2 small butternut squash or
   1 slice pumpkin, weighing
   9 oz/250 g
1 tsp olive oil, for greasing
flour, for dusting
9 oz/250 g prepared
   shortcrust pastry
generous 1 cup heavy cream
6 oz/175 g Gorgonzola cheese
2 eggs, plus 1 egg yolk
6–8 fresh sage leaves
salt and pepper

method

1 Preheat the oven to 375°F/190°. Cut the squash in half and brush the cut side with the oil. Place cut-side up on a baking sheet and bake in the preheated oven for 30–40 minutes, until browned and very soft. Let cool. Remove the seeds and scoop out the flesh into a large bowl, discarding the skin.

2 Lightly grease a 9-inch/23-cm loose-bottom fluted tart pan. Roll out the dough on a floured counter $3^1/_4$ inches/8 cm larger than the pan. Carefully lift the dough into the pan and press to fit. Fit a piece of parchment paper into the tart shell, fill with dried beans, and let chill in the refrigerator for 30 minutes. Meanwhile, preheat the oven to 375°F/190°C.

3 Remove the pastry shell from the refrigerator and bake the tart shell for 10 minutes in the preheated oven, then remove the beans and paper. Return to the oven for 5 minutes.

4 Mash the squash and mix with half the cream, season with salt and pepper, and spread in the pastry shell. Slice the cheese and lay it on top. Whisk the remaining cream with the eggs and egg yolk and pour the mixture into the tart pan, making sure it settles evenly. Arrange the sage leaves in a circle on the surface. Bake for 30–35 minutes and let cool for 10 minutes in the pan before serving.

artichoke & pancetta tartlets

ingredients

MAKES 6

pie dough

generous 3/4 cup all-purpose
flour, plus extra for dusting
pinch of salt
6 tbsp cold butter, cut into
pieces, plus extra for
greasing
cold water

filling

5 tbsp heavy cream
4 tbsp bottled artichoke paste
14 oz/400 g canned artichoke
hearts, drained
12 thin-cut pancetta slices
arugula leaves
1 3/4 oz/50 g Parmesan or
pecorino cheese
2 tbsp olive oil, for drizzling
salt and pepper

method

1 Grease six 3 1/2-inch/9-cm loose-bottom fluted tartlet pans. Sift the flour and salt into a food processor, add the butter, and process until the mixture resembles fine bread crumbs. Tip into a large bowl and add a little cold water to bring the dough together. Turn out onto a floured counter and divide into six equal-size pieces. Roll each piece to fit the pans. Carefully fit each piece of dough into the pan. Cut six pieces of parchment paper, fit a piece into each tartlet shell, fill with dried beans, and let chill in the refrigerator for 30 minutes. Meanwhile, preheat the oven to 400°F/200°C.

2 Bake the tartlet shells in the preheated oven for 10 minutes, then remove the beans and parchment paper.

3 Meanwhile, stir the cream and the artichoke paste together and season well. Divide between the pastry shells, spreading out to cover the bottom of each tartlet. Cut each artichoke heart into three pieces and divide between the tarts, curl two slices of the pancetta into each tart, and bake for 10 minutes. To serve, top each tart with a good amount of arugula, then, using a potato peeler, shave the Parmesan cheese over the tartlets, drizzle with olive oil, and serve at once.

smoked salmon, dill & horseradish tartlets

ingredients

MAKES 6

pie dough

generous 3/4 cup all-purpose
　　flour, plus extra for dusting
pinch of salt
6 tbsp cold butter,
　　cut into pieces, plus extra
　　for greasing
cold water

filling

1/2 cup sour cream
1 tsp creamed horseradish
1/2 tsp lemon juice
1 tsp Spanish capers,
　　chopped
3 egg yolks
7 oz/200 g smoked salmon
　　trimmings
bunch fresh dill, chopped
salt and pepper

method

1 Grease six 3 1/2-inch/9-cm loose-bottom fluted tart pans. Sift the flour and salt into a food processor, add the butter, and process until the mixture resembles fine bread crumbs. Tip the mixture into a large bowl and add a little cold water, just enough to bring the dough together. Turn out onto a floured counter and divide into six equal-size pieces. Roll each piece to fit the tart pans. Carefully fit each piece of dough into a tartlet pan. Roll the rolling pin over the pan to neaten the edges and trim the excess dough. Cut six pieces of parchment paper and fit a piece into each tartlet shell, fill with dried beans, and let chill in the refrigerator for 30 minutes. Meanwhile, preheat the oven to 400°F/200°C.

2 Bake the tartlet shells in the preheated oven for 10 minutes, then remove the beans and parchment paper.

3 Meanwhile, put the sour cream, horseradish, lemon juice, capers, and salt and pepper into a bowl and mix well. Add the egg yolks, the smoked salmon, and the dill and carefully mix again. Divide between the tartlet shells and return to the oven for 10 minutes. Let cool in the pans for 5 minutes before serving.

bleu cheese & walnut tartlets

ingredients

MAKES 12

pie dough

1¹/2 cups all-purpose flour, plus extra for dusting

pinch of celery salt

scant ¹/2 cup cold butter, cut into pieces, plus extra for greasing

¹/4 cup walnut halves, chopped in a food processor

cold water

filling

2 tbsp butter

2 celery stalks, trimmed and finely chopped

1 small leek, trimmed and finely chopped

scant 1 cup heavy cream, plus 2 tbsp extra

7 oz/200 g bleu cheese

3 egg yolks

salt and pepper

chopped fresh parsley, to garnish

method

1 Lightly grease a 3-inch/7.5-cm, 12-hole muffin pan. Sift the flour and celery salt into a food processor, add the butter, and process until the mixture resembles fine bread crumbs. Tip the mixture into a bowl and add the walnuts and a little cold water, just enough to bring the dough together. Turn out onto a floured counter and cut the dough in half. Roll out the first piece and cut out six 3¹/2-inch/9-cm circles. Take each circle and roll out to 4¹/2 inches/ 12 cm diameter and fit into the muffin holes, pressing to fill the holes. Put a piece of parchment paper in each hole, fill with dried beans, then let chill for 30 minutes. Meanwhile, preheat the oven to 400°F/200°C.

2 Bake the tartlets in the preheated oven for 10 minutes, then remove the paper and beans.

3 To make the filling, melt the butter in a skillet, add the celery and leek, and cook for 15 minutes, until softened. Add 2 tablespoons of cream and crumble in the cheese, mix well, and season. Bring the remaining cream to simmering point in a saucepan, then pour onto the egg yolks, stirring all the time. Mix in the cheese mixture and spoon into the tartlet shells. Bake for 10 minutes, then turn the pan around and bake for an additional 5 minutes. Let cool for 5 minutes and sprinkle with parsley.

feta & spinach tartlets

ingredients

MAKES 6

pie dough

generous 3/4 cup all-purpose
    flour, plus extra for dusting
pinch of salt
6 tbsp cold butter, cut into
    pieces, plus extra for
    greasing
1/2 fresh nutmeg, grated
cold water

filling

6 cups baby spinach
2 tbsp butter
2/3 cup heavy cream
3 egg yolks
4 1/2 oz/125 g feta cheese
scant 1/3 cup pine nuts
salt and pepper

method

1 Grease six 3 1/2-inch/9-cm loose-bottom fluted tartlet pans. Sift the flour and salt into a food processor, add the butter, and process until the mixture resembles fine bread crumbs. Tip the mixture into a large bowl and add the nutmeg and enough cold water to bring the dough together. Turn out onto a floured counter and divide into six equal-size pieces. Roll each piece to fit the tartlet pans. Carefully fit each piece of dough in a tartlet pan. Roll over the rolling pin to neaten the edges and trim the excess dough. Cut six pieces of parchment paper and fit a piece into each tart, fill with dried beans, and let chill in the refrigerator for 30 minutes. Meanwhile, preheat the oven to 400°F/200°C.

2 Bake the tart shells in the preheated oven for 10 minutes, then remove the beans and paper.

3 Blanch the spinach in boiling water for just 1 minute, then drain, and press to squeeze all the water out. Chop the spinach. Melt the butter in a skillet, add the spinach, and cook gently to evaporate any remaining liquid. Season well with salt and pepper. Stir in the cream and egg yolks. Crumble the feta and divide between the tartlets, top with the creamed spinach, and bake for 10 minutes. Sprinkle the pine nuts over the tartlets and cook for an additional 5 minutes.

cherry tomato & poppy seed tartlets

ingredients

MAKES 12

pie dough

1 1/2 cups all-purpose flour, plus extra for dusting

pinch of salt

scant 1/2 cup cold butter, cut into pieces, plus extra for greasing

2 tsp poppy seeds

cold water

filling

24 cherry tomatoes

1 tbsp olive oil

2 tbsp unsalted butter

2 tbsp all-purpose flour

generous 1 cup milk

scant 1/2 cup grated sharp cheddar cheese

scant 1/2 cup cream cheese

salt and pepper

12 fresh basil leaves, to garnish

method

1 Lightly grease a 12-hole muffin pan. Sift the flour and salt into a food processor, add the butter, and process until the mixture resembles fine bread crumbs. Tip the mixture into a large bowl and add the poppy seeds and enough cold water to bring the dough together. Turn out onto a floured counter and cut the dough in half. Roll out the first piece and cut out six 3 1/2-inch/9-cm circles. Take each circle and roll out to 4 1/2 inches/12 cm diameter and fit into the muffin holes, pressing to fill the holes. Do the same with the remaining dough. Put a piece of parchment paper in each tartlet shell and fill with dried beans, then let chill for 30 minutes. Meanwhile, preheat the oven to 400°F/200°C.

2 Bake the tartlets in the preheated oven for 10 minutes, then remove the paper and beans. Put the tomatoes in an ovenproof dish, drizzle with the olive oil, and roast for 5 minutes.

3 Melt the butter in a saucepan, stir in the flour, and cook for 5–8 minutes. Gradually add the milk, stirring to combine. Cook for an additional 5 minutes. Season well and stir in the cheeses until well combined. Put 2 tomatoes in each tart shell, spoon in the cheese sauce, then put back into the oven for 15 minutes. Remove from the oven, top each tartlet with a basil leaf, and serve.

eggplant & pesto tartlets

ingredients

MAKES 6

9 oz/250 g prepared puff
    pastry

1 large or 2 small eggplants,
    trimmed and thinly sliced

5 tbsp olive oil

3 buffalo mozzarella cheeses,
    sliced

6 tbsp pesto

1 egg yolk

pepper

method

1 Cut the dough into six, and roll into either circles or rectangles, then place on two baking sheets, three on each. Preheat the oven to 375°F/190°C.

2 Brush the eggplant slices with 2 tablespoons of the oil and cook briefly in a nonstick skillet, in batches, then arrange the slices neatly overlapping on each dough base, leaving a 1-inch/2.5-cm margin around the edges.

3 Lay the mozzarella slices over the eggplant slices and spoon over the pesto. Drizzle with the remaining oil and season with pepper. Brush the edges of the dough with egg yolk and bake in the preheated oven for 15 minutes. Remove from the oven and serve.

potato, fontina & rosemary tart

ingredients

SERVES 4

9 oz/250 g prepared puff
    pastry
all-purpose flour, for dusting
3–4 waxy potatoes
10$^{1}/_{2}$ oz/300 g fontina cheese,
    cut into cubes
1 red onion, thinly sliced
3 large fresh rosemary sprigs
2 tbsp olive oil
1 egg yolk
salt and pepper

method

1 Preheat the oven to 375°F/190°C. Roll out the dough on a lightly floured counter into a circle about 10 inches/25 cm in diameter and put on a baking sheet.

2 Peel the potatoes and slice as thinly as possible so that they are almost transparent—use a mandolin if you have one. Arrange the potato slices in a spiral, overlapping the slices to cover the pastry, leaving a $^{3}/_{4}$-inch/2-cm margin around the edge.

3 Arrange the cheese and onion over the potatoes, sprinkle with the rosemary, and drizzle over the oil. Season to taste with salt and pepper and brush the edges with the egg yolk to glaze.

4 Bake in the preheated oven for 25 minutes, or until the potatoes are tender and the pastry is brown and crisp. Serve hot.

caramelized onion tart

ingredients

SERVES 4–6

7 tbsp unsalted butter

1 lb 5 oz/600 g onions, thinly
    sliced

2 eggs

generous 1/3 cup heavy cream

scant 1 cup grated Gruyère
    cheese

8-inch/20-cm prepared pastry
    shell

7/8 cup coarsely grated
    Parmesan cheese

salt and pepper

method

1 Melt the butter in a heavy-bottom skillet over medium heat. Add the onions and cook, stirring frequently to avoid burning, for 30 minutes, or until well-browned and caramelized. Remove the onions from the skillet and set aside.

2 Preheat the oven to 375°F/190°C. Beat the eggs in a large bowl, stir in the cream, and season with salt and pepper to taste. Add the Gruyère cheese and mix well. Stir in the cooked onions.

3 Pour the egg and onion mixture into the pastry shell and sprinkle with the Parmesan cheese. Place on a baking sheet. Bake in the preheated oven for 15–20 minutes, until the filling has set and begun to brown.

4 Remove from the oven and let rest for at least 10 minutes. The tart can be served hot or at room temperature.

cherry tomato clafoutis

ingredients

SERVES 4–6

vegetable oil, for greasing

14 oz/400 g cherry tomatoes

3 tbsp chopped fresh flat-leaf
   parsley, snipped fresh
   chives, or finely shredded
   fresh basil

1 cup grated Gruyère cheese

generous 1/3 cup all-purpose
   flour

4 large eggs, lightly beaten

3 tbsp sour cream

1 cup milk

salt and pepper

method

1 Preheat the oven to 375°F/190°C. Lightly grease an oval 6-cup ovenproof dish. Arrange the cherry tomatoes in the dish and sprinkle with the herbs and half the cheese.

2 Put the flour in a mixing bowl, then slowly add the eggs, whisking until smooth. Whisk in the sour cream, then slowly whisk in the milk to make a thin, smooth batter. Season to taste with salt and pepper.

3 Gently pour the batter over the tomatoes, then sprinkle the top with the remaining cheese. Bake for 40–45 minutes, or until set and puffy, covering the top with foil if it browns too much before the batter sets. If serving hot, let the clafoutis cool for a few minutes before cutting, or let cool to room temperature.

zucchini & cheese gratin

ingredients

SERVES 4–6

4 tbsp unsalted butter, plus
    extra for greasing
6 zucchini, sliced
2 tbsp chopped fresh tarragon
    or a mixture of mint,
    tarragon, and flat-leaf
    parsley
1³/4 cups grated Gruyère
    cheese or Parmesan
    cheese
¹/2 cup milk
¹/2 cup heavy cream
2 eggs
freshly grated nutmeg
salt and pepper

method

1 Preheat the oven to 350°F/180°C. Grease an ovenproof serving dish and set aside. Melt the butter in a large skillet over medium–high heat. Add the zucchini and sauté for 4–6 minutes, turning the slices over occasionally, until colored on both sides.

2 Remove from the skillet and drain on paper towels, then season with salt and pepper to taste. Spread half the zucchini over the bottom of the dish. Sprinkle with half the herbs and ³/4 cup of the cheese. Repeat these layers once more.

3 Mix the milk, cream, and eggs together and add nutmeg and salt and pepper to taste. Pour this liquid over the zucchini, then sprinkle the top with the remaining cheese.

4 Bake the gratin for 35–45 minutes, or until it is set in the center and golden brown. Remove from the oven and let stand for 5 minutes before serving straight from the dish.

baked eggs with cream, spinach & parmesan

ingredients

SERVES 2

2 tbsp butter, plus extra
    for greasing
scant 3 cups baby spinach
1/2 tsp freshly grated nutmeg
4 small eggs
1/4 cup light cream
2 tbsp freshly grated
    Parmesan cheese
salt and pepper

method

1 Preheat the oven to 325°F/160°C. Lightly grease 2 individual ceramic gratin dishes or similar.

2 Melt the butter in a large skillet over low heat and add the spinach. Cook for 1 minute, stirring with a wooden spoon until the spinach starts to wilt. Season with a little nutmeg, then divide between the prepared dishes.

3 Gently break 2 eggs into each dish. Pour the cream over them, and sprinkle with grated Parmesan, then season to taste with salt and pepper. Bake for 10 minutes, or until the whites of the eggs have set but the yolks remain runny. Serve at once.

celery root, chestnut, spinach & feta filo pies

ingredients

SERVES 4

4 tbsp olive oil

2 garlic cloves, crushed

$1/2$ large or 1 whole small head celery root, cut into short thin sticks

$51/2$ cups baby spinach leaves

scant $1/2$ cup cooked, peeled chestnuts, coarsely chopped

7 oz/200 g feta cheese (drained weight), crumbled

1 egg

2 tbsp pesto sauce

1 tbsp finely chopped fresh parsley

4 sheets filo dough, about 13 x 7 inches/32 x 18 cm each

pepper

green salad, to serve

method

1 Preheat the oven to 375°F/190°C. Heat 1 tablespoon of the oil in a large skillet over medium heat, add the garlic, and cook for 1 minute, stirring continuously. Add the celery root and cook for 5 minutes, until soft and browned. Remove from the skillet and keep warm.

2 Add 1 tablespoon of the remaining oil to the skillet, then add the spinach, cover, and cook for 2–3 minutes, or until the spinach has wilted. Uncover and cook until any liquid has evaporated.

3 Mix the garlic and celery root, spinach, chestnuts, cheese, egg, pesto, parsley, and pepper to taste in a large bowl. Divide the mixture between four individual gratin dishes or put it all into a single medium gratin dish.

4 Brush each sheet of filo with the remaining oil and arrange on top of the mixture. Bake in the preheated oven for 15–20 minutes, or until browned. Serve at once with a green salad.

cheese & tomato pizza

ingredients

SERVES 2

dough

1 1/2 cups all-purpose flour, plus extra for dusting

1 tsp salt

1 tsp active dry yeast

1 tbsp olive oil, plus extra for brushing

6 tbsp lukewarm water

topping

6 tomatoes, thinly sliced

6 oz mozzarella cheese, drained and thinly sliced

2 tbsp shredded fresh basil leaves

2 tbsp olive oil

salt and pepper

method

1 To make the dough, sift the flour and salt into a bowl and stir in the yeast. Make a well in the center and pour in the oil and water. Gradually incorporate the dry ingredients into the liquid, using a wooden spoon or floured hands.

2 Turn out the dough onto a lightly floured counter and knead well for 5 minutes, until smooth and elastic. Return to the clean bowl, cover with lightly oiled plastic wrap, and set aside to rise in a warm place for about 1 hour, or until doubled in size.

3 Turn out the dough onto a lightly floured counter and punch down. Knead briefly, then cut it in half and roll out each piece into a circle about 1/4 inch/5 mm thick. Transfer to a lightly oiled baking sheet and push up the edges with your fingers to form a small rim.

4 For the topping, arrange the tomato and mozzarella cheese slices alternately over the pizza bases. Season with salt and pepper to taste, sprinkle with the basil, and drizzle with the oil.

5 Bake in a preheated oven, 450°F/230°C, for 15–20 minutes, until the crust is crisp and the cheese has melted. Serve immediately.